The Ku Klux Klan in the Southwest

THE
KU KLUX KLAN
in the Southwest

Charles C. Alexander

University of Oklahoma Press
Norman and London

1995

ISBN: 0–8061–2776–7

The paper in this book meets the guidelines for permanence
and durability of the Committee on Production Guidelines
for Book Longevity of the Council on Library Resources,
Inc. ∞

1 2 3 4 5 6 7 8 9 10

Contents

Illustrations

Preface to the Paperback Edition

The Ku Klux Klan in the Southwest originally was published thirty years ago by the University of Kentucky Press, at a very different time in the history of the American people. In 1965 the Cold War, and especially the nuclear arms race with the Soviet Union, still dominated Americans' conceptions of the world. In Indochina we were sinking into a confused conflict that would waste tens of billions of dollars and tens of thousands of American lives. At the same time, a vast, intricately coordinated effort in space exploration was making steady progress toward placing an American on the moon's surface "before this decade is out," as the late President John F. Kennedy had pledged. Unprecedented peacetime prosperity—built upon the surging productivity, savings, and purchasing power triggered by World War II—was reaching its crest, and the majority of Americans shared an affluence and abundance only imagined by previous generations.

President Lyndon B. Johnson, having scored a lopsided election victory the previous November, now exhorted the most liberal Congress in the nation's history to join him in a "war on poverty." By the end of 1965 a bewildering array of new government programs, focused on the presumably attainable objective of banishing unemployment and hunger from the land, would be in place. Yet at the same time, the Johnson administration undertook to defend the "frontiers of freedom" in Europe, Indochina, and elsewhere without raising taxes or otherwise diminishing Americans' glittering living standards. Truly, all things seemed possible in 1965.

The previous year, at President Johnson's urging, Congress had arrayed federal authority squarely against racial discrimination by passing the Civil Rights Act, the most sweeping legislation of its kind in the nation's history. That was followed in 1965 by the Voting Rights Act, which directly involved the Justice Department in the registration and protection of black voters. Those two statutes were Washington's most direct responses to the clamor for basic citizenship guarantees issuing from the American South, where black people still lived under an intricate post-Emancipation system of racial subjugation. The ongoing civil rights movement, utilizing tactics ranging from lawsuits to "sit-ins," marches, and other public demonstrations, was transforming southern race relations. For civil rights activists, both black and white, working for change was often a deadly business.

At the center of a pronounced increase in southern racial violence was a collection of secret societies—all dedicated to the maintenance of white supremacy by whatever means necessary—known collectively as the Ku Klux Klan. The failure of the militant but nonviolent White Citizens Councils to thwart the civil rights movement prompted a substantial number of white southerners to turn to such groups as the United Klans, Knights of the Ku Klux Klan; White Knights of the Ku Klux Klan; Original Klan of the Confederacy; and Gulf Ku Klux Klan. While the different Klan groups publicly disclaimed violent intent, they all secretly countenanced kidnappings, beatings, bombings, and murders. Estimates of Klan membership varied considerably, but by 1965 as many as 35,000–40,000 people (including women in "auxiliary" organizations) may have belonged to the different Klans. The biggest and most ambitious was the United Klans, Knights of the Ku Klux Klan, Inc., headquartered in Tuscaloosa, Alabama, and headed by Imperial Wizard Robert M. "Bobby" Shelton, a Goodrich Rubber Company employee.

In the spring of 1965, in the aftermath of an epochal voters' rights march from Selma to Montgomery, Alabama, and the murder of Viola Liuzzo (a white Detroiter who had taken part in the march), President Johnson publicly warned Klan members to "get out of the Klan now and return to decent society before it is too late."[1] Despite the misgivings of Director J. Edgar Hoover, who feared pro-Communist influences among civil-rights activists, the Federal Bureau of Investigation intensified its efforts against Klan groups. Meanwhile the U.S. House of Representatives Committee on Un-American Activities (HUAC), hitherto known mainly for harassing American Communists, announced that it would look into Klan machinations in the South.

Conducted from October 19 to November 9, 1965, HUAC's investigation centered on Shelton and his United Klans of America. Having fallen into widespread disrepute for its anti-Communist "witch hunts," HUAC now garnered positive media coverage and compiled five volumes of testimony on the structure and operations of Shelton's and other Klans. The substantive consequences of its inquiry, however, were negligible.

Yet for the first time since the Reconstruction period, the apparatus of federal power was arrayed in behalf of the constitutional rights of black Americans and against the historic southern pattern of segregation and disenfranchisement. After 1965, the Klans' and other forms of defiant white supremacy steadily lost ground. By the early 1970s, what historians would come to call the Second Reconstruction—an unrelenting (if century-late) drive to implement full citizenship for black southerners—largely had been realized, although in succeeding decades small numbers of unregenerate white supremacists would continue to organize and

[1]*New York Times*, 27 March 1965, p. 1.

reorganize Klan and Klan-like groups, not only in the South but in widely distanced parts of the United States.

An expansion and elaboration of my master of arts thesis at the University of Texas, *The Ku Klux Klan in the Southwest* was, in its original form, my Ph.D. dissertation. When I first began work on the dissertation in 1961, I really had no idea that by the time it was written, defended before my examining committee, revised, and finally published, the name "Ku Klux Klan" would be prominently featured in national press headlines and on the nightly news broadcasts. As it happened, the publication of *The Ku Klux Klan in the Southwest* was a matter of considerable professional serendipity.

Yet while the publicity given to mid-1960s Klan terrorism in the South drew attention to my work, readers and reviewers soon discovered that it had little direct pertinence to current happenings. As I indicated in my preface, my book was about the Invisible Empire, Knights of the Ku Klux Klan, Inc., which—though founded in 1915 at Atlanta, Georgia, and always headquartered there (until its disbandment in 1944)—had attained its peak size and influence in the post–World War I years *outside* the Deep South states. I designed *The Ku Klux Klan in the Southwest* as a regional study, focusing on the history of the 1920s Klan in Texas, Oklahoma, Louisiana, and Arkansas, four of the strongest and also most violent Klan states. Although I recognized its shared white-supremacy motivations with the post–Civil War and contemporary Klan movements, I was at pains to demonstrate that the post–World War I organization—by far the largest and most powerful of the historic Klans—had projected a more complex and far-reaching appeal.

Several million members nationwide enrolled and subscribed to the creed of the Invisible Empire, Knights of the Ku Klux Klan, Inc. It combined animosity toward black Americans, Roman Catholics, foreign immigrants, and ideological radicals with a militant and frequently violent determination to preserve traditional moral values and standards of behavior and to enforce the new national ban on alcoholic beverages. In varying degrees and in different parts of the country, it featured night-riding vigilantism, political activism, fraternal fellowship, substantial charitable work, and vocal support for what it defined as Protestant Americanism.

As of 1965, scholarly writing on the mighty 1920s Klan—as opposed to a vast body of contemporary commentary—was scarce. Emerson H. Loucks's early study of the Pennsylvania Klan, my study of the Texas Klan, and Arnold S. Rice's sketchy *The Ku Klux Klan in American Politics* were the only extended published works, although two earlier unpublished doctoral dissertations also were available.[2] Then in 1965, at the same time that *The Ku Klux Klan in the Southwest* came out, David M. Chalmers and William Peirce Randel published general histories of the various manifestations of Klanism since Reconstruction, and two years later Kenneth T. Jackson's important examination of the 1920s Klan in several American cities appeared.[3]

For a time, that was about it. In the past two decades, however, scholars have issued a steady outpouring of well-researched and insightful book-length studies, articles in scholarly journals, and unpublished theses and dissertations on the "second Klan" (as the Invisible Empire, Knights of the Ku Klux Klan, Inc., has come to be called). By now nearly

[2]Emerson H. Loucks, *The Ku Klux Klan in Pennsylvania: A Study in Nativism* (Harrisburg, 1936); Charles C. Alexander, *Crusade for Conformity: The Ku Klux Klan in Texas, 1920–1930* (Houston, 1962); Arnold S. Rice, *The Ku Klux Klan in American Politics* (Washington, 1962); Benjamin H. Avin, "The Ku Klux Klan, 1915–1925: A Study in Religious Intolerance" (Ph.D. diss., Georgetown University, 1952); and Norman F. Weaver, "The Knights of the Ku Klux Klan in Wisconsin, Indiana, Ohio, and Michigan" (Ph.D. diss., University of Wisconsin, 1954). Paul M. Angle also had provided an excellent account of the Klan's disruptive history in Williamson County, Illinois, in *Bloody Williamson: A Chapter in American Lawlessness* (New York, 1952).

[3]David M. Chalmers, *Hooded Americanism: The First Century of the Ku Klux Klan* (New York, 1965; reprint, 1981); William Peirce Randel, *The Ku Klux Klan: A Century of Infamy* (London, 1965); and Kenneth T. Jackson, *The Ku Klux Klan in the City* (New York, 1967).

every state where the twenties Klan gained any appreciable
size and significance has undergone close investigation, and a
number of particular localities—from Eugene and LaGrande,
Oregon, and El Paso, Texas, to Athens, Georgia—have been
scrutinized by resourceful scholars. There is even a recently
published Klan encyclopedia that contains thousands of en-
tries on Klan and Klan-related activities since Reconstruction.[4] The generic Ku Klux Klan—whether treated as a
phenomenon persisting over 130 years or as a distinctive
feature of the 1920s—has become one of the most written-
about subjects in our national history.

Readers may wish to make their way through *The Ku Klux
Klan in the Southwest* and then compare it to more recent
studies in the history of the 1920s Klan, some of which utilize
long-hidden membership lists and minutes of local Klan
chapters' meetings—materials of a kind that eluded me in my
own research. Yet I was also able to interview several former
Klan members—men in their sixties when I talked with
them—and thus tap a resource no longer available to students of the Klan. Whatever the strengths or limitations of a
book published thirty years ago, the fact remains that it was
written at a particular time in my own life. If I were to

[4]The principal book-length works treating the 1920s Klan appearing in
recent decades include: Robert Alan Goldberg, *Hooded Empire: The Ku
Klux Klan in Colorado* (Urbana, Ill., 1981); Larry R. Gerlach, *Blazing
Crosses in Zion: The Ku Klux Klan in Utah* (Logan, Utah, 1982); Shaun Lay,
*War, Revolution, and the Ku Klux Klan: A Study of Intolerance in a Border
City* (El Paso, 1985); Wyn Craig Wade, *The Fiery Cross: The Ku Klux Klan in
America* (New York, 1987); William D. Jenkins, *Steel Valley Klan: The Ku
Klux Klan in Ohio's Mahoning Valley* (Kent, Ohio, 1990); Kathleen M. Blee,
Women of the Klan: Racism and Gender in the 1920s (Berkeley, Calif., 1991);
M. William Lutzhold, *Grand Dragon: D. C. Stephenson and the Ku Klux
Klan in Indiana* (West Lafayette, Ind., 1991); Leonard J. Moore, *Citizen
Klansmen: The Ku Klux Klan in Indiana, 1921–1928* (Chapel Hill, N.C., 1991);
Michael and Judy Ann Newton, *The Ku Klux Klan: An Encyclopedia* (New
York, 1991); Shaun Lay, ed., *The Invisible Empire in the West: Toward a New
Appraisal of the Ku Klux Klan of the 1920s* (Urbana, Ill., 1992); and Nancy
MacLean, *Behind the Mask of Chivalry: The Making of the Second Ku Klux
Klan* (New York, 1994). Article-length and unpublished theses and disserta-
tion studies of the 1920s Klan are too numerous to list here.

undertake such a study today, no doubt I would write a markedly different book.

Yet, apart from a few technical corrections and inclusion of illustrations for this paperback edition, I have decided to let *The Ku Klux Klan in the Southwest* remain as it was when published. In that decision, I am reinforced by what the late Richard Hofstadter appended to the reprint edition of his classic *Social Darwinism in American Thought:* "After a period of years a book acquires an independent life, and the author may be so fortunate as to achieve a certain healthy detachment from it, which reconciles him to letting it stand on its own."[5]

As Hofstadter had hoped for himself, I trust that my detachment from *The Ku Klux Klan in the Southwest* is a healthy one. I also trust that students of our country's history again will find this book useful for understanding a remarkably powerful expression of collective anxieties in a period when, it might be argued, the essential contours of American society as we know it today were being formed.

February 1995   CHARLES C. ALEXANDER

[5]Richard Hofstadter, *Social Darwinism in American Thought* (Philadelphia, 1945; reprint, Boston, 1955).

Preface

AT THE MENTION of the words "Ku Klux Klan," most people, including many historians, immediately conceive of a band of sadistic Southerners in white robes and hoods intimidating hapless Negroes. In the popular mind "the Klan" is a fanatical, violent, white supremacy society, dedicated to "keeping the nigger in his place." The average citizen does not realize that historically there are not one but three Klans. The first was the Ku Klux Klan of the Reconstruction period—secret, political, often violent, preoccupied with turning out the Radical Republican state and local governments in the South and with proscribing the recently emancipated Negroes and their white Republican allies. Then there was the "Invisible Empire, Knights of the Ku Klux Klan, Inc."—also secret, frequently violent, and white supremist, but unlike the Reconstruction Klan, ultrapatriotic, nativistic, and moralistic. The formal history of this organization extends from 1915 to 1944. The third Klan is in reality several organizations—the various anti-Negro societies, using the name of the previous Klans, which have appeared from time to time in the southern states since the end of the Second World War.

The modern-day image of the Ku Klux Klan stems largely from the first and third Klans, organizations confined to the southern states and concerned primarily with throttling ambitious Negroes and whatever white sympathizers they might have. It is the middle Klan, however, the secret fraternal order which had its heyday in the 1920s, that is the subject of this study. The Invisible Empire, Knights of the Ku Klux Klan, Inc., was nationwide, spreading into every state in the Union and recruiting perhaps five million Americans to its many-sided cause. The Klan of the twenties was an enemy not only of Negroes but of Catholics, Jews, radicals, immigrants, bootleggers, moral offenders, habitual criminals, modernist theologians, and assorted other types. Its high-flown rituals, exotic nomenclature, and charity work made it, in a narrow sense, like the numerous other adult fraternal orders in America. Yet the Klan differed from the respectable lodges in that not only its ritual but its membership was secret. In most areas where it became strong, the Klan evolved into a political machine which often backed entire slates of candidates and tried to vote its members as a bloc. Finally, it was a giant financial organization which received and disbursed millions of dollars and became one of the most profitable businesses of the prosperity decade.

This study focuses on the career of the Knights of the Ku Klux Klan in Texas, Louisiana, Oklahoma, and Arkansas. I have, rather arbitrarily, termed the area encompassed by these four states "the Southwest," knowing full well that such terminology will probably offend many, and that culturally, Louisiana, Arkansas, and Texas were predominantly southern in the twenties, while Oklahoma bore strong southern influences. I have referred to the four states as the Southwest for purposes of simplicity and brevity and because, since Klan activity in New Mexico and Arizona was negligible, they really did comprise the southwestern part of the Klan's "Invisible Empire," or territory of operations.

For some time I have felt that the chief value of local,

state, and regional history is the opportunity to examine the validity of accepted generalizations about broad, variegated national movements. The Klan of the twenties was such a movement. The theme of this study is that the distinctive quality of the Klan in Texas, Louisiana, Oklahoma, and Arkansas was its motivation, which lay not so much in racism and nativism as in moral authoritarianism. In the first few years of its existence in these four states the Klan was, more than anything else, an instrument for restoring law and order and Victorian morality to the communities, towns, and cities of the region. Its coercive activity and its later preoccupation with political contests make vigilantism and politics the main characteristics of Klan history in the Southwest.

Despite the fact that the Klan enlisted millions of members in the twenties and wielded startling power in all parts of the country, the organization has received comparatively little careful consideration from historians. Outside of a few state and regional studies, scholars have pulled back only a corner of the white sheet covering the Klan. The handful of writers dealing with Texas, Louisiana, Oklahoma, and Arkansas in the twentieth century have either treated the white-clad fraternal order superficially or ignored it completely. This study, by concentrating on four of the strongest Klan states, aims at supplying a part of the complex history of the organization.

The scarcity of scholarship on the Klan, amounting to a hiatus in the historiography of the twenties, is largely a consequence of the secret character of the order and the disrepute into which the Klan has fallen everywhere except among the most fanatical racists in the Deep South. There is almost a complete absence of manuscript materials in the form of Klan correspondence, membership lists, minutes of meetings, or financial records. Consequently, most of the previous work on the Klan has been based largely on daily and weekly newspapers. Such heavy reliance on newspapers also features this narrative of the Klan in the Southwest.

The preparation of this study involved the help of many people, more than I could ever thank adequately. Mrs. James R. Hamilton of Austin, Texas, generously permitted an examination of the papers of her husband, Judge James R. Hamilton, one of the first jurists in the nation actively to oppose the Klan. Two former officials of the Klan in Texas, who now live in Dallas and prefer to remain anonymous, gave valuable personal interviews. V. A. Collins of Livingston, Texas, corresponded with me on the Klan's role in Texas politics. I am obligated to Professor T. Harry Williams, Department of History, Louisiana State University, who confirmed some of my impressions about the Klan's relationship to Huey P. Long in the twenties; Charles Dwyer, interlibrary loan supervisor at the University of Texas; Dr. Dorman Winfrey, former archivist, and the staff of the University of Texas Archives; James Day, archivist of the Library of the State of Texas, and his staff; Mrs. Virginia Gambrell and her associates at the Dallas Historical Society; V. K. Bedsole and the staff of the Department of Archives, Louisiana State University; Dr. A. M. Gibson and Jack Haley of the Division of Manuscripts, University of Oklahoma; Mrs. Louise Cook, newspaper librarian of the Oklahoma Historical Society; and Miss Georgia Clark and Miss Grace Upchurch of the General Library, University of Arkansas. I am also grateful to Professor Robert A. Divine, Department of History, Professor Robert C. Cotner, Department of History, and Professor Howard A. Calkins, Department of Government, all of the University of Texas, for reading the entire manuscript and offering their comments, suggestions, and helpful criticisms; and to Professor Barnes F. Lathrop of the Department of History, University of Texas, for his efforts to secure much-needed microfilms during two critical stages in the project.

My greatest indebtedness is to five people: Professor Joe B. Frantz of the University of Texas History Department, who had no formal connection with this study but who helped in so many ways during the past few years; Professor David D. Van Tassel, also of the Department of History, University of Texas, who supervised the study from beginning to end and whose interest, guidance, and patience have gone far beyond what is required of him; my wife JoAnn, who typed, read, and worried her way through the manuscript; and my parents, Mrs. Pauline Alexander and the late C. C. Alexander, who were the kind of mother and father every son should have, but no son could deserve.

September 1964   CHARLES C. ALEXANDER

Ku Klux Klan Terminology
Used in This Book

THE NOMENCLATURE, ritual, and ceremonial titles used by the Klan, partially copied from the Klan of Reconstruction by William J. Simmons but largely invented by him, were designed to convey a sense of mystery and power. Klan terminology was much more elaborate, alliterative, and weird than that used by other adult fraternal organizations like the Masons or the Knights of Pythias. The following list, consisting only of Klan terms found in the text, represents but a small fraction of the plethora of Klan jargon.

Alien—anyone not a Klansman, and thus a member of the "alien" world outside the "Invisible Empire."

Domain—an organizational unit consisting of a group of states, apparently in existence only during 1921 and 1922.

Elimination primary—a device used especially by Klan leaders in Texas and Arkansas, whereby a poll was taken among Klansmen in the chapters to choose candidates to be backed by the Klan for local, district, and state offices.

Emperor—a title created especially for William J. Simmons after he gave up the Imperial Wizardship to Hiram

W. Evans. After Simmons' departure from the Klan, the title was combined with that of Wizard.

Exalted Cyclops—head of a local Klan chapter, elected by the membership of the chapter and serving a one-year term.

Grand . . .—prefix meaning "of the state Klan organization."

Grand Dragon—the state chief executive appointed by the Imperial Wizard for a term of one year.

Great . . .—prefix meaning "of the district Klan organization."

Great Titan—head of a Province, or district Klan organizational unit, appointed by the Imperial Wizard or the Grand Dragon.

Imperial . . .—prefix denoting the national Klan organization, the headquarters of the order in Atlanta.

Imperial Commander—title held by the chief executive of the Women of the Ku Klux Klan.

Imperial Klazik—national official charged with supervising the affairs of the state Klan organizations.

Imperial Kloncilium—supreme judicial body and executive council of the Klan, with headquarters in Atlanta. The Kloncilium seldom functioned in its judicial capacity.

Imperial Klonvocation—the biennial national convention of the Klan, attended by all national officials, state and district officials, and one delegate from each state and district organization. During the twenties only three publicized Klonvocations were held, in 1922, 1924, and 1926.

Imperial Wizard—supreme ruler of the Klan, in theory an all-powerful chief executive.

Invisible Empire—an amorphous designation meaning, in the narrowest sense, the Klan's administrative structure and territory of operations. The term could also refer to the whole membership of the Klan, the ties between Klansmen, or perhaps the spiritual character of the order. By joining the Klan, one became a "citizen of the Invisible Empire."

Kamelia—the women's organization formed by William J.

Simmons and his allies during their fight with the Evans regime in the spring and summer of 1923. The Kamelia made little headway before opposition by Evans' followers and the new Women of the Ku Klux Klan sanctioned by national headquarters.

King Kleagle—title of the head organizer for the Klan in one state.

Klabee—treasurer at the various organizational levels of the Klan. Known simply as "Klabee" at the local chapter level, but as "Great Klabee," "Grand Klabee," and "Imperial Klabee" at district, state, and national levels, respectively.

Klaliff—vice president at different Klan organizational levels.

Klankraft—all of the practices, concepts, and relationships involved in Klan membership.

Klannishness—the practice of "sticking together" among Klansmen, finding expression especially in economic terms, such as trading with Klan merchants in preference to non-Klansmen.

Klansman-at-Large—a special category of Klan membership set aside by the Imperial Klan for citizens, usually prominent politicians, who wished to join the Klan yet keep their membership secret from their constituents, including the rank-and-file Klansmen.

Klavern—the indoor meeting place of a local Klan, whether owned or rented by the chapter.

Kleagle—a field organizer for the Klan, originally working directly under Edward Y. Clarke and Elizabeth Tyler in the Propagation Department at Atlanta.

Klectoken—the $10 initiation fee paid by a person upon joining the Klan.

Kligrapp—secretary at different Klan organizational levels.

Klokann—the executive committee of a local Klan, comprised of the Exalted Cyclops and the other officers of the chapter.

Klonversation—an exchange of greetings between Klansmen featuring the use of acronyms.

Kloran—the ritual book used in Klan initiations and for the opening and closing of meetings.

Klorero—state convention of delegates from chartered Klans, held annually after the formal establishment of the Realm, or state organization.

Kloxology—a religiously tinged song delivered by Klansmen at the end of a meeting.

Kludd—chaplain at different organizational levels.

Kluxing—a term used primarily by Kleagles to connote their promotional and recruiting activities in an area.

Knights Kamelia—a "second degree of Klankraft" invented by William J. Simmons in 1923 in an abortive effort to lure Klansmen away from Hiram W. Evans' administration. The Knights Kamelia idea was revived by Evans in 1925 as a legitimate second degree for which all Klansmen were eligible.

Knights of the Great Forest—a "third degree of Klankraft" devised by national Klan headquarters in 1928 and supposedly taken by Klansmen when they officially discarded their masks in ceremonies over the nation.

Konklave—any gathering, large or small, of Klansmen, but usually referring to local chapter meetings and initiations.

Naturalization ceremonies—the initiation rites whereby one became a Klansman, a citizen of the Invisible Empire.

Nighthawk—an official whose responsibility was investigating the character of prospective members and the conduct of Klansmen and nonmembers. There was an Imperial Nighthawk, and each local Klan also had such an officer.

Province—an organizational unit composed of a group of counties and headed by a Great Titan. Provinces, analogous to districts, were established simultaneously with the Realm, the state organization.

Realm—the organizational unit within the Klan corresponding to the state. After the chartering of a certain number of local chapters, national headquarters set up a formal state organization.

I.

Brainchild of a Dreamer

IN EARLY DECEMBER of 1915, *The Birth of a Nation*, David Wark Griffith's epochal motion picture, came to Atlanta, Georgia, for the first time. The picture was supposed to be a patriotic portrayal of the division and reunion of the United States during and after the Civil War. It also represented a remarkable advancement in the technological development of motion pictures.[1] But the most conspicuous feature of the film for nostalgic Southerners was its depiction of white-robed Ku Klux Klansmen riding here and there to save the beleaguered South from the evils of Yankee and Negro domination during the Reconstruction period. The film reinforced the romanticized image most Southerners held of the original "Ku Kluxers," and the Georgians sat enthralled through the presentation. When the crowd left the theater after a performance of *The Birth of a Nation*, some Atlantan may have asked his friends if anybody had seen a cross burning on Stone Mountain, outside the city, on Thanksgiving night. What was this he had heard about the Klan being reorganized? Was there anything to the rumor that some Atlanta men were establishing a new Klan?

The rumor was true. On December 4 the state of Georgia granted a charter for a new fraternal order formally named "The Invisible Empire, Knights of the Ku Klux Klan, Inc." The twelve men who signed the petition for the charter described the society as a "patriotic, military, benevolent, ritualistic, social and fraternal order."[2] The instigator of this order was named William Joseph Simmons. On Thanksgiving night he had led a party of friends up Stone Mountain, burned a crude cross, and delivered a grandiloquently phrased lecture on patriotism, white supremacy, and the virtues of racial purity. That ceremony marked the founding of the second Ku Klux Klan, a creation of Simmons' dreamy imagination fated to become the largest and most powerful nativist and vigilante organization in American history.[3]

In 1915 Simmons could look back on a career that was lackluster and a little frustrating. He was born about 1880 in Talladega County, Alabama, the son of a country physician. Simmons was in his early teens when his father died. By that time he was already leading prayer meetings at the community Methodist church. At eighteen he joined the army and served in the Spanish-American War. After his discharge he attended for a time the Southern University

[1] On the technological and social importance of *The Birth of a Nation*, see Everett Carter, "Cultural History Written with Lightning: The Significance of *The Birth of a Nation*," *American Quarterly*, XII (Fall 1960), 347-57.

[2] The charter granted by the state of Georgia to the Klan is reproduced in Winfield Jones, *Knights of the Ku Klux Klan* (New York, 1941), 223-26.

[3] William G. Shepherd, "How I Put Over the Klan," *Collier's*, LXXXII (July 14, 1928), 6-7, 32, 34-35. This article and another by Shepherd were based on interviews with Simmons, and are in many ways more informative than Simmons' testimony before the House Rules Committee. Taken together, they form the basis for much of the material contained in this chapter on the early history of the Klan.

at Birmingham, Alabama, then left school and secured a license as a minister in the Methodist Episcopal Church, South. For several years he was a circuit rider, first in Florida, then in Alabama, but in 1912 he abandoned the ministry in anger after the Methodist Conference of Alabama refused to award him a large church of his own. The ex-preacher now became a fraternal organizer, initially with the Woodmen of the World, and later with other societies. He held the rank of colonel in the Woodmen, and thereafter he referred to himself—and liked others to call him—"Colonel Simmons."

As a professional fraternalist, Simmons earned twenty-three degrees in seven fraternal orders, including the various stages of Freemasonry, the Knights of Pythias, the Odd Fellows, and the Woodmen. He was doing rather well financially when an automobile struck him as he was crossing an Atlanta street. During three months of hospital confinement he outlined on paper something that had been in his mind for years—a plan for a new fraternity to be called the Knights of the Ku Klux Klan. Simmons drew on his knowledge of the idealized Ku Klux Klan of the Reconstruction years, about which he had read voraciously in his childhood, and his own experience in the fraternal world when he sketched his order. He had in mind the appeal the original Klan held for Southerners, who regarded it as the epitome of heroism, the savior of white supremacy and southern womanhood during a period when both were in danger at the hands of carpetbagging Northerners and unruly Negroes. He labeled his brainchild the authentic lineal descendant of the Reconstruction Klan and pledged it as a "living memorial" to the earlier order.

At the same time, as a good lodge man, he realized the drawing power of secrecy, ritual, mystery, and weird nomenclature. Thus, copying and paraphrasing Reconstruction Klan terminology, he dubbed the Klan's territory the "Invisible Empire," over which he ruled as "Imperial Wizard," with subordinates whose titles included "Kligrapp," "Klaliff," "Kludd," "Klabee," and "Nighthawk." He even wrote a ritual book called the "Kloran," wherein, along with numerous other instructions, he specified a "Klonversation" using such acrostic passwords as AYAK ("Are You a Klansman"), AKIA ("A Klansman I am"), and KIGY ("Klansman I Greet You"). Membership in the order was limited to native-born white Protestants, eighteen years old and above.

When "Colonel" Simmons left the hospital, he began a campaign of visiting lodges in Atlanta, talking with the members, and trying to get them interested in his fraternal project. He met with some success, and on October 26 he and thirty-four other men met in the office of his attorney, E. R. Clarkson, to discuss the Knights of the Ku Klux Klan idea more thoroughly. Two of those who came were men who had belonged to the original Klan. John W. Bale, speaker of the house of representatives in the Georgia legislature, called the meeting to order. Simmons talked for an hour and convinced the others that "the idea would grow." He also discussed the problem of the Negroes, who were, according to Simmons, "getting pretty uppity in the South along about that time." The group voted to apply for a state charter. Then on Thanksgiving night they climbed Stone Mountain, carried out the cross-burning ceremony, and "revived" the Klan. After they secured their charter, Simmons and friends began advertising their order through the newspapers and making personal contacts. The advertisements were shrewdly timed to appear simultaneously with the initial Atlanta showings of *The Birth of a Nation,* which gave Simmons some valuable free publicity. As a result, ninety-one new members joined the Klan, each paying $10 as an initiation fee and $6.50 for the cheap white robe the Imperial Wizard sold as the official uniform of the society. Moreover, forty-two new Klansmen signed up for a total of $53,000 worth of Klan life insurance. The insurance feature, a bit of practical economics which did not survive the early years of the Klan, nevertheless revealed that Simmons designed his order at least partly as a moneymaking scheme. For many individuals associated with the Klan in later years, the movement would never be anything else.

On a man-to-man basis Simmons was an effective salesman of the Klan. His personal appearance was impressive, for he stood over six feet tall and weighed around two hundred pounds. His other characteristics included: "A grim, set mouth . . . ; a large nose; eyes of a metallic grayish hue; shaggy, reddish eyebrows; good teeth; a square chin; a spacious forehead; a strong, well-rounded voice and slow deliberation in speaking."[4] But Simmons had little talent for organization and expansion, and he had an unfortunate weakness for being duped by his associates. Before the United States entered the First World War, the Klan had escaped the confines of Georgia and established a few chapters in neighboring Alabama. Jonathan Frost, the Imperial Wizard's most trusted subordinate, then absconded with several thousand dollars frrom Alabama initiation fees, badly crippling the order's finances. The Klan wandered on in obscurity. "There were times during those five early years, before the public knew of the Klan," recalled Simmons, "when I walked the streets with my shoes worn through because I had no money."

During the war Simmons involved the Klan in the national mania for self-appointed spy hunting. He joined the Citizens Bureau of Investigation in Atlanta and proceeded to make "secret service men" of his Klansmen in Georgia and Alabama. He later bragged: "I was in touch in my wartime secret service work with federal judges, federal attorneys, and federal secret service officials and operatives. The Klan secret service reported to me." It was during the war that Simmons changed the Klan, or-

[4] *Ibid.*, 7.

iginally designed as a public order with members wearing lodge buttons, into a secret organization, which it remained for the duration of its existence. Thus the Klan gained the element that made it unique among contemporary fraternal orders—secrecy of membership.[5]

By the end of the war the Klan was fairly well known in Atlanta, Birmingham, and Mobile. For the most part it had left behind its original dual character as a white supremacy society and a memorial to the Reconstruction Klan, and had assumed the mien of a militantly moralistic and patriotic order. It was active in getting rid of prostitutes around military bases, idlers, slackers, and "the laborer who is infested with the I. W. W. spirit."[6] Yet the Klan's membership rolls remained thin; there were only about 5,000 or 6,000 Klansmen scattered through Georgia and Alabama.[7] Simmons realized that he was making little progress on his own and that he must have help if his Invisible Empire were ever to encompass more than a small part of the South. In the summer of 1920 he found two people who possessed the organizing genius his fraternal project required.

In Atlanta there was a two-member advertising and publicity company called the Southern Publicity Association, which had conducted "booster" campaigns for such causes as the Salvation Army, the Anti-Saloon League, and the Red Cross. The owners, managers, and sole employees of the firm were Edward Young Clarke and Mrs. Elizabeth Tyler. Clarke, an unimposing figure in his thirties, with thick black hair and black-rimmed spectacles, had gained quite a reputation in the Atlanta area for his fund-raising abilities. His partner, Mrs. Tyler, was a rotund, bluff

[5] William G. Shepherd, "Ku Klux Koin," *Collier's,* LXXXII (July 21, 1928), 9.

[6] New York *Times,* September 1, 1918, sec. IV, p. 5.

[7] Testimony of William G. Simmons in *The Ku Klux Klan Hearings before the Committee on Rules, House of Representatives,* 67th Congress, 1st Session (1921), 87.

woman who had married at the age of fourteen, been left a widow at fifteen, and had since survived on her own business acumen. Clarke and Mrs. Tyler had heard of Simmons' Klan through her son-in-law, who happened to join the order. At the same time, Simmons had watched the two publicity agents for some months, and he wanted them as salesmen for his stunted secret society. In June of 1920 the three got together and talked about the prospects of the Klan. Clarke and Mrs. Tyler finally signed a contract with Simmons to publicize and propagate the order in exchange for eight dollars of every ten-dollar initiation fee or "klectoken" paid by new Klan members. Of their eight-dollar share the two boosters had to pay all of their expenses, including secretarial and clerical help and the fees they allowed their field agents to keep.[8]

For purposes of administering their publicity campaign and collections they turned the Southern Publicity Association into the "Propagation Department" of the Klan and divided the whole country into what amounted to sales territories—"Domains," or groups of states; "Realms," or states; and "Provinces," or subdivisions of states. They put about 1,100 solicitors, called "Kleagles," into the field, with instructions to play upon whatever prejudices were most acute in the particular areas the Kleagles were working. Simmons must have sighed wistfully when in later years he remembered how "They made things hum all over America."[9]

The organizing Kleagles had plenty of incentive for securing as many new members as quickly as possible. Of the eight-dollar cut of each klectoken which went to

[8] Shepherd, "Ku Klux Koin," 39; New York World, September 22, 1921, p. 2; "For and Against the Klan," Literary Digest, LXX (September 24, 1921), 34. The contract agreed to by Clarke, Mrs. Tyler, and Simmons is reproduced, among other places, in Henry P. Fry, The Modern Ku Klux Klan (Boston, 1922), 38-40, and Ku Klux Klan Hearings, 32.

[9] Shepherd, "Ku Klux Koin," 39.

the Propagation Department, Clarke let the Kleagle have a commission of four dollars. One dollar and fifty cents went to the "Grand Goblin," or Domain administrator; $2.50 went directly to Clarke and Mrs. Tyler; and Simmons received the remaining $2.00.[10]

The application of booster techniques by the two publicity agents brought striking results. In the sixteen-month period from June 1920 to October 1921, the Klan added from 90,000 to 100,000 new members and took in about one-and-a-half million dollars from klectokens and the sale of robes, ritual equipment, and other paraphernalia.[11] By the end of 1921 the secret order had spread throughout the South and Southwest, had crossed the Potomac and Ohio rivers and secured strong footholds in several northern states, and had recruited thousands of Klansmen on the Pacific Coast.

During this initial postwar surge the Klan received three windfalls of publicity which greatly benefited its campaign to get itself before the people. The first related to the burning of gins and cotton bales in the southern states in the fall of 1920. Irate southern farmers, desperate over the collapse of cotton prices, resorted to the old practice of night-riding in an effort to check the sale of cotton until prices advanced. The Klan had no part in this economic warfare, and in fact the property-minded Klansmen sometimes stood guard at gins and warehouses to prevent their destruction. But there was some speculation that the organization might be involved, and letters came into Im-

[10] Fry, *Modern Ku Klux Klan*, 16. Fry was a journalist who joined the Klan in 1921, during its initial expansion, became a Kleagle, and used his experiences in the order as a basis for his book.

[11] Simmons' testimony, *Ku Klux Klan Hearings*, 87; "The 'Invisible Empire' in the Spotlight," *Current Opinion*, LXXI (November 1921), 561. Simmons' commissions during the period totaled about $170,000, while Clarke and Mrs. Tyler showed a net profit of $212,000. Robert L. Duffus, "Salesman of Hate: The Ku Klux Klan," *World's Work*, XLVI (May 1923), 33.

perial headquarters from all parts of the nation seeking information about the Klan, its membership requirements, and its program. Simmons and Clarke eagerly seized the opportunity to advertise the Klan. To the question whether its membership were confined to southern men, Simmons announced: "Any real man, any native-born white American citizen who is not affiliated with any foreign institution and who loves his country and his flag may become a member of the Ku Klux Klan, whether he lives north, south, east or west."[12]

The second windfall came nearly a year later, after the Klan had become a power in the South and Southwest (but only in those areas). The liberal New York *World* undertook to expose the order as an un-American racket, an example of southern backwardness, and generally a malefic influence in American society. From September 6 to 26, 1921, the *World's* well-documented but highly alarmist articles, syndicated in some twenty other newspapers, laid bare the history, ideals, aims, and practices of the new Klan. Opponents of the Klan hailed the articles as the eye opener needed to quash this reactionary movement. Now, thought liberals, reasonable and thinking Americans in the southern and southwestern states would see the Klan for the destructive cancer it really was and abjure it.[13] To their astonishment the *World's* crusade had precisely the opposite effect. The publicity afforded by the exposé introduced the Klan to receptive Americans who had never heard of it, and they were intrigued by the hooded society. When the Kleagles entered the northern and western states, they found thousands of worried citizens who were just as eager to join the Klan as their fellow citizens in the South and Southwest. Some zealots even mailed

[12] New York *Times,* November 1, 1920, p. 27; Shreveport *Journal,* November 20, December 8, 1920.

[13] For an example of this type of naive sentiment, see the editorial in the New York *Times,* September 10, 1921, p. 10.

their applications for membership to Atlanta on sample forms printed in the newspapers to illustrate the *World's* articles.[14]

The furor raised by the newspaper publicity and letters from constituents soon prodded members of Congress to action, and the Rules Committee of the House of Representatives began a series of hearings on the Klan. The result: more publicity, and more new Klansmen. Simmons, Clarke, and other Klan officials appeared before the committee to refute the testimony of the *World's* investigators and to enlarge on the image of the Klan as a nonviolent, nondivisive defender of the American way, a simple brotherhood of patriotic, native-born Protestants. After several days of leading questions propounded by the Congressmen and extended paeans offered by Simmons, the committee suddenly ended its inquiry without making any recommendations.[15] The silence of the solons seemed to place their stamp of approval on the secret fraternity. "Things began to happen as soon as I got back to my little office in Atlanta," Simmons remembered. "Calls began pouring in from lodge organizers and others all over America for the right to organize Klans."[16] The Kleagles now reported enlistments at a rate of 5,000 a day. The profits of the Propagation Department jumped to an estimated $40,000 per month.[17]

Now the Klan could travel on its momentum, and the

[14] Tulsa *Tribune*, March 6, 1922; Thomas E. Dabney, *One Hundred Great Years: The Story of the Times-Picayune from Its Founding to 1940* (Baton Rouge, 1944), 417. The New Orleans *Times-Picayune* was one of the newspapers carrying the syndicated articles. Other dailies in the southwestern states running the feature were the Dallas *Morning News* and the Oklahoma City *Daily Oklahoman*.

[15] *Ku Klux Klan Hearings*, 67-185; New York *Times*, October 2, 4, 8, 11-15, 18, 1921.

[16] Shepherd, "Ku Klux Koin," 38.

[17] "For and Against the Klan," 34; Stanley Frost, "When the Klan Rides: The Giant Clears for Action," *Outlook*, CXXXV (December 26, 1923), 717.

Atlanta leadership could relax a little and watch the application forms pile up and initiation fees flow into the Imperial Treasury. Clarke, Mrs. Tyler, and their money-hungry Kleagles, with assists from night-riding cotton farmers, the hostile New York *World,* and Congress, had done an effective job of selling the Klan, or "kluxing," as the Kleagles came to call their recruiting. The success of Clarke and his well-fed cohort was so phenomenal that the early critics of the Klan, led by the *World,* tended to explain the dismayingly rapid expansion of the movement in terms of the evil genius of the two publicity agents coupled with the stupidity of the people they lured into the order. To these hostile observers the Klan was just not supposed to be. It was wholly alien to the democratic ideal, an intruder in American life. In the third decade of the twentieth century, in a nation that had just fought a war to make the world safe for democracy and was now resuming its inexorable advance toward the good society, how could this "un-American monstrosity" happen?[18]

The explanation for the Klan's resurgence lay in a reality of which many liberals were ignorant—the character of major elements of American society in the years after the First World War.[19] All the tensions of a society becoming

[18] John Moffat Mecklin, *The Ku Klux Klan: A Study of the American Mind* (New York, 1924), 236. See also Clarke A. Chambers, "The Religion of Progress in Twentieth Century America," *Journal of the History of Ideas,* XIX (April 1958), 197-224.

[19] Much has been written in an attempt to explain the remarkable growth of the Klan; a substantial part of it is of dubious value. Among the best items are: Benjamin H. Avin, "The Ku Klux Klan, 1915-1925: A Study in Religious Intolerance" (unpublished Ph.D. dissertation, Georgetown University, 1952); John Higham, *Strangers in the Land: Patterns of American Nativism, 1860-1925* (New Brunswick, N.J., 1955), 234-99; Mecklin, *Ku Klux Klan;* Frank Tannenbaum, *Darker Phases of the South* (New York, 1924), ch. I; Frank Bohn, "The Ku Klux Klan Interpreted," *American Journal of Sociology,* XXX (January 1925), 385-407; Guy B. Johnson, "A Sociological Interpretation of the New Ku Klux Movement," *Social Forces,* I (May 1923), 440-45; Norman F. Weaver, "The Knights of the Ku

more and more complex and undergoing sweeping trans-
formation converged to produce the spectacular growth
of the Klan. During the war the American people had been
subjected to the first systematic, nationwide propaganda
campaign in the history of the Republic. From both official
and unofficial sources poured a torrent of material having
the objective of teaching Americans to hate—specifically
to hate Germans but, more broadly, everything that did not
conform to a formalized conception of "100 percent Americanism."[20] In the fall of 1918, just as the indoctrination
process was reaching its peak, as patriotic feeling was
mounting to frenzy, the war came abruptly to an end.
Americans who had stored up an enormous volume of
superpatriotic zeal now no longer had an official enemy on
whom to concentrate this fervor. In the months after the
Armistice, as the Versailles Conference deteriorated into
a cynical display of national interest, as labor strife, soaring
prices, and the continued scarcity of consumer goods
plagued the economy—in short, as it became apparent
that the war had brought nothing like the hoped-for
millennium—disillusionment and a vague feeling of betrayal settled over the country.

Embittered by the confusion of urbanization and industrialization, caught in a society that was changing rapidly
and radically, where nothing seemed permanent anymore,
Americans fell victim to a sort of national choler. They
acquiesced as the United States Senate repudiated the
Treaty of Versailles and Woodrow Wilson's League of
Nations. They listened approvingly when Warren Gamaliel

Klux Klan in Wisconsin, Indiana, Ohio, and Michigan" (unpublished Ph.D. dissertation, University of Wisconsin, 1954), ch. II;
and Robert L. Duffus, "Ancestry and End of the Ku Klux Klan,"
World's Work, XLVI (September 1923), 527-36.

[20] On the wartime propaganda effort in this country, see J. R.
Mock and Cedric Larson, *Words That Won the War* (New York,
1939), and George Creel, *How We Advertised America* (New York,
1920).

Harding and the Republican party told them that the country needed "not nostrums but normalcy . . . not submergence in internationality but sustainment in triumphant nationality," and they elected Harding by a lopsided margin in 1920.[21] They sought new outlets for their pent-up animosities, and they found them by creating new enemies. The wartime messianic spirit and the drive for conformity became postwar hysteria. The year 1919 saw fearful Americans, spurred by the spectacle of bloody chaos in Bolshevik Russia, engage in a nationwide hunt for ubiquitous Communists, anarchists, and nihilists. Even moderate Socialists and labor unionists were branded as "radicals." This was the "Red Scare," out of which came the Sacco-Vanzetti case; the doubtfully constitutional raids carried out by agents of A. Mitchell Palmer, Wilson's attorney general, and by state and local authorities; and wholesale deportations of supposed revolutionaries.[22] The anti-Red paroxysm subsided even more quickly than it had arisen, but in the fall of 1920 a sharp economic depression caused citizens to continue the frantic search for scapegoats, for something or someone to blame for the ills of modern America.

Historically the Negro had served well as a scapegoat. The year 1919 was one of lynchings and savage race riots in such diverse places as Chicago and Elaine, Arkansas. Eighty people were lynched during the year, the largest number in a decade. Seventy-four of these victims of rope justice were Negroes.[23] White people, North and South, were uneasy about warnings that a "new Negro," filled with ambitions for social and economic equality, was coming home from the war. Southerners feared any "big ideas" the

[21] Wesley M. Bagby, *The Road to Normalcy: The Presidential Campaign and Election of 1920* (Baltimore, 1962).

[22] The standard account of the Red Scare, marred by some serious errors regarding the Klan's relationship to the phenomenon, is Robert Murray, *Red Scare* (Minneapolis, 1955).

[23] New York *World, World Almanac and Encyclopedia* (1923), 352.

blacks might have, while Northerners worried about the tremendous migration of Negroes northward beginning during the war and continuing into the postwar years.[24] Yet most Negroes proved to be not so ambitious after all, and in the postwar period the few who tried to climb upward soon fell back before the legal and extralegal defenses of the American caste system.

A far more menacing specter was the Church of Rome and its temporal monarch, the Pope. In 1920 Roman Catholics made up 36 percent of the American religious population; and many Protestants were convinced that the papacy was closer than ever to establishing dominance in the United States. The tense postwar period produced the last great outburst of anti-Catholic sentiment in this country. Twice before, in the Know-Nothing movement of the 1840s and 1850s and in the American Protective Association of the 1890s, hostility toward Catholics had erupted into organized opposition to the real and imagined aims of the Roman Church.[25]

In the decade before the First World War, enmity toward Catholics abated considerably in most parts of the nation, although in the South the embers of anti-Romanism were kept smoldering by such figures as the onetime Georgia Populist crusader Tom Watson, who tied Catholics, Jews, and Negroes together in one xenophobic bundle, and Sidney J. Catts of Florida, who rode up and down the peninsula warning of a popish plot to take over the United States. Watson eventually went to the United States

[24] See Rollin Hartt, "The New Negro," *Independent*, CV (January 15, 1921), 59-60, and John Hope Franklin, *From Slavery to Freedom: A History of American Negroes* (2d ed., New York, 1956), 444-78.

[25] On Know-Nothingism, see Ray Allen Billington, *The Protestant Crusade, 1800-1860* (New York, 1938), and William D. Overdyke, *The Know-Nothing Party in the South* (Baton Rouge, 1950). On the American Protective Association, see John Humphrey Desmond, *The A.P.A. Movement* (Washington, 1912), and Donald L. Kinzer, *An Episode in Anti-Catholicism: The American Protective Association* (Seattle, 1964).

Senate, where he continued to rant against minority groups, while Catts served a term as governor of his state.[26] Both were around after the war to see their passions become respected sentiments throughout the nation. And the principal agent lending respectability to the Watson and Catts brand of hate was the Klan.

The postwar years also saw an acceleration of the drive to restrict foreign immigration, a movement that had been gaining momentum since the 1890s, when the preponderance of immigration to the United States began to shift from western and northern Europe and the British Isles to the southern and eastern parts of the Continent. The fact that most representatives of the so-called "new immigration" were poverty stricken by the time they reached this country was one count against them. The presence of a few radicals among them, like Nicola Sacco and Bartolomeo Vanzetti, was another. But probably of more importance in building support for restrictionism and keeping it aroused was the growth of racial nativist thinking, fostered by the pseudoscientific pontifications of a generation of self-styled historians and anthropologists, the new intellectual racists. Most citizens never read the published theories of such writers as the New England politician Henry Cabot Lodge or the Park Avenue lawyer Madison Grant.[27] Nevertheless, the doctrine that some kinds of white people, notably Italians, Greeks, and Slavs, were racially inferior to other white people, notably Scandanavians and Anglo-Saxons, found its way into congressional hearings on immigration restriction bills, the popu-

26 C. Vann Woodward, *Tom Watson: Agrarian Radical* (New York, 1938); Higham, *Strangers in the Land*, 292.

27 See Barbara M. Solomon, *Ancestors and Immigrants: A Changing New England Tradition* (Cambridge, Mass., 1956), and Charles C. Alexander, "Prophet of American Racism: Madison Grant and the Nordic Myth," *Phylon*, XXIII (Spring 1962), 73-90. The best treatment of the growth of intellectual racism beginning in the late nineteenth century is Thomas F. Gossett, *Race: The History of an Idea in America* (Dallas, 1963), 310-69.

lar press, and ultimately into the thinking of millions of Americans who liked to consider themselves "Nordic" or "Teutonic." Thus the Klan propagandists denounced the "cross-breeding hordes" from southern and eastern Europe who continued to swarm into the country, asserted that only the "real whites" could attain the standards of American citizenship, and called on the racially pure Caucasians to keep the nation free of "mongrelizing taints."[28]

Some of the "new immigrants" were Jews from Poland, Russia, or elsewhere, and they ran into a nativist crossfire. Anti-Semitism, endemic in virtually every Christian country, appears to have been relatively weak in the United States until the late nineteenth century.[29] Probably the most famous single anti-Semitic episode in American history occurred in 1915 at the state prison farm at Milledgeville, Georgia, where Leo Frank, wrongly convicted of raping a young girl, was lynched by a large mob. Tom Watson and his vitriolic weekly newspaper had a major part in whipping up lynch feeling in the Frank case.[30] In the years after the war, hatred of Jews, even of those whose family lines reached far back into the American past, mounted steadily. The Klan chose the Jewish population as one of its principal targets and profited substantially from general animosity toward Jewish Americans. Yet during the twenties not even the efforts of the Klan could provoke an epidemic of anti-Semitism equal to that which swept Western society, and most spectacularly Nazi Germany, in the succeeding decade.

The white, native-born Protestant American, as a member of the religious and racial majority, was usually incapable of doubting his "native" institutions. The blame

---

[28] *Papers Read at the Meeting of Grand Dragons, Knights of the Ku Klux Klan* (Asheville, N.C., 1923), 132-33; Hiram W. Evans, *The Menace of Modern Immigration* (Dallas, 1923), 20.

[29] John Higham, "Anti-Semitism in the Gilded Age: A Reinterpretation," *Mississippi Valley Historical Review*, XLIII (March 1957), 559-78.

[30] Woodward, *Tom Watson*, 435-49.

for the maladies of his world must rest elsewhere. And so he looked to "alien influences"—Roman Catholics who supposedly challenged Protestant hegemony and the separation of church and state, "unassimilable" Catholic, Eastern Orthodox, and Jewish immigrants crowding onto American shores, Negroes seeking more equitable treatment, American Jews who kept living costs up while wages went down, and numerous other elements of frustration before which he felt helpless. Then the Klan entered his community and offered him a way to fight back.

People of southern ancestry, wherever they might live in the United States, had before them a clear precedent for fighting back—the original Klan of Reconstruction. In establishing his new Klan back in 1915, Simmons had shrewdly associated it with the earlier secret society. The overwhelming majority of people reared in the romantic traditions of the South believed that the Reconstruction Klan had sprung into being over the former Confederate States as a desperate response to the abuses of carpetbagger, scalawag, and Negro dominance. Operating with discipline and effectiveness, it was supposed to have helped defeat the Yankee scheme for social revolution. They ignored its atrocities, its degeneracy, and the fact that it actually had achieved very little. It was, according to the popular view, "the fulcrum on which the lever worked that freed the Confederate people, and tore from the hands of the fanatics the fruit they expected to gather."[31]

[31] W. C. Wood, "The Ku Klux Klan," *Quarterly of the Texas Historical Association,* IX (April 1906), 262-68. On the Reconstruction Klan, see also Stanley Horn, *The Invisible Empire* (New York, 1939); J. C. Lester and D. L. Wilson, *The Ku Klux Klan: Its Origin, Growth, and Disbandment* (New York, 1905); William Garrott Brown, *The Lower South in American History* (New York, 1902), 191-225; Fred Deming, *The Organization and Political Influence of the Ku Klux Klan* (Des Moines, 1910); John A. Carpenter, "Atrocities in the Reconstruction Period," *Journal of Negro History,* XLVII (October 1962), 234-47; and Herbert Shapiro, "The Ku Klux Klan during Reconstruction: The South Carolina Episode," *ibid.,* XLIX (January 1964), 34-55.

In this study Louisiana, Arkansas, Texas, and Oklahoma, partly for convenience, are referred to as the Southwest. Yet in their attitudes in the twenties, citizens in Louisiana, Arkansas, Texas, and even Oklahoma were predominantly southern. For them the new Klan's purported tie with the old Klan was just as magnetic as it was to Americans of southern background elsewhere. The first Klan was, and the later Klan came to be, the embodiment of what W. J. Cash has called the Southerner's "savage ideal" of repression and intolerance.[32] The showings and reshowings of *The Birth of a Nation*—beginning in 1915 and continuing into the twenties, until theaters in practically every town had run the film—helped to perpetuate the tradition of direct action, not only for Southerners, but for Americans throughout the country.[33]

In reality, racism, secrecy, and violence were the only features the two Klans had in common. For by amalgamating longstanding distrust of Catholics and hatred of Negroes with anti-Semitism, fear of radicals, and the Anglo-Saxon superiority complex, the Klan, as promoted by Clarke and Mrs. Tyler, went beyond Know-Nothingism, the American Protective Association, the Reconstruction Klan, and every other instrument of prejudice in American history. The Klan offered a target for every frustration. And people from every stratum of society found their way into the secret order. To assume that only riffraff and fanatics joined the Klan is to reveal a basic lack of understanding of the movement. Excluding nonwhites and non-Protestants, the membership of the order was remarkably cross-sectional. Bankers, businessmen, salesmen, physicians, lawyers, ministers, and even university professors donned their white robes and hoods alongside

[32] W. J. Cash, *The Mind of the South* (New York, 1941).

[33] Also helping to revive and spread the heroic conception of the early Klan were Thomas B. Dixon's novels of Reconstruction, especially *The Clansman* and *The Leopard's Spots*, published in the early years of this century but still selling well in the postwar period.

mechanics, farmers, and day laborers. The Klan had something for them all. But as John Moffatt Mecklin early observed, "The strength of the Klan lies in that large, well-meaning but more or less ignorant and unthinking middle class, whose inflexible loyalty has preserved with uncritical fidelity the tradition of the original American stock."[34]

Anti-Catholicism, white supremacy, hatred of Jews, anti-radicalism, opposition to foreign immigration—these were the salients of Klan ideology.[35] These were the biases continually harped on in the literature of the order and stressed by Kleagles and Klan lecturers in every area. All of these appeals attracted members. Even so, there was another side of the Klan, having less historical basis, but fully as important as the formal antagonisms of the order. This earthier component of the Klan's makeup, emphasizing not the ethnic or religious but the *moral* status quo, found expression in a quest for "law and order" and a drive to maintain crumbling Victorian standards of personal conduct. Herein, it seems, lay the most powerful stimulus for the prodigious growth of the Klan in Texas, Louisiana, Oklahoma, and Arkansas. There, more than anywhere else, the Klan transcended the limits of a nativist and racist organization and became a device for the ruthless dictation of community morals and ethics.

[34] Mecklin, *Ku Klux Klan*, 103.

[35] The most concise and comprehensive exposition of Klan ideals is to be found in the writings of Hiram Wesley Evans, who became Imperial Wizard of the order late in 1922. See the following items, all published under his name: *The Public School Problem in America* (Atlanta, 1924); "The Klan: Defender of Americanism," *Forum*, LXXIV (December 1925), 801-14; "The Klan's Fight for Americanism," *North American Review*, CCXXIII(March 1926), 33-63; "For New Marriage Laws," *Forum*, LXXVII (May 1927), 730-39; "The Catholic Question as Viewed by the Ku Klux Klan," *Current History*, XXVI (July 1927), 563-68; and "Ballots Behind the Ku Klux Klan," *World's Work*, LV (January 1928), 243-52.

2.

"A Passion for Reform"

DURING THE 1920s many writers tried to explain the phenomenon of the Klan movement. Most of them, like H. L. Mencken and his staff on the *American Mercury*, remained in their eastern offices and penned caustic prose about grown men in white robes and hoods burning crosses on hillsides and trying to scare their neighbors. Others ventured into the hinterlands, to places like Birmingham, Tulsa, Dallas, Indianapolis, Denver, or even Augusta, Maine, to observe the Klan in action. They were the interpreters who came closest to fathoming "the mind of the Klan." Stanley Frost, a journalist who had followed Klan activities in the Southwest, wrote that the "fundamental and unifying idea [behind the Klan] is nothing more abnormal than a passion for reform. . . . With the Klan this very common trait has an intensity, a directness and a concept of personal duty to do something, such as are seldom found. . . . Reform of some sort has been the moving spirit of the Klan."[1]

"A passion for reform" underlay the varied actions of the Klan in the Southwest, from kidnapings and beatings to politics and cross burnings. This emotion, more than any other, accounts for the fact that during the early years of Klan power the southwestern states were troubled by more episodes of hooded violence than any other part of the nation. To the Klan, reform meant preserving or restoring the status quo—at the national level, the separation of church and state, the primacy of Fundamentalist Protestantism, white supremacy, a capitalist economic system, dominance of the native-born whites in American society. There was also in the Klan a definite strain of moral bigotry. Especially in the Southwest this zeal found expression in direct, often violent, attempts to force conformity. Hence the southwestern Klansman's conception of reform encompassed efforts to preserve premarital chastity, marital fidelity, and respect for parental authority; to compel obedience of state and national prohibition laws; to fight the postwar crime wave; and to rid state and local governments of dishonest politicians. Klan reform in the Southwest centered on personal conduct rather than on institutional change, on "law and order" rather than on social amelioration. And to the Klansman, law and order meant "not overscrupulous observance of the forms of justice, but making the law-breakers quit or get out; not squeamishness about the legal rights of defendants, but unceremonious and drastic 'cleaning' of the community."[2]

Frost, again thinking mainly of the Southwest, estimated that not more than 10 percent of the people who joined the Klan did so because they were attracted by the "national aims" of the order.[3] It is quite true that Klan lecturers, editorialists, and pamphleteers flooded the south-

[1] Stanley Frost, *The Challenge of the Klan* (Indianapolis, 1924), 159-60.
[2] Edward T. Devine, "The Klan in Texas," *Survey*, XLVIII (April 1, 1922), 10-11.
[3] Frost, *Challenge of the Klan,* 173.

western states with attacks on Catholics, Jews, Negroes, immigrants, and radicals, just as they did in other sections of the country. The various weekly newspapers sponsored by the Klan in the southwestern states published scurrilous editorials on the imminence of popish plots to take over America, and alleged ex-nuns toured from city to city exposing the cruelties of convent life. Klan propagandists harangued about anarchist conspiracies, the "indigestible" character of "Dagos," "Wops," and "Kikes," Jewish dominance of the nation's economic life, and the need to "keep this a white man's country."[4] The usual Klan line was not neglected in promoting the order in the Southwest. In a general way this propaganda doubtless met approval. Yet the preponderance of evidence indicates that the ideology of the Klan, the tenets of the order, held a secondary appeal for most of the Texans, Oklahomans, Arkansans, or Louisianians who entered the Invisible Empire.

The "Negro problem," for example, seemed to give surprisingly little impetus to Klan expansion in the Southwest, considering the popular present-day image of the Klan. In Oklahoma, of a total population of 2,028,283 in 1920, there were only 149,408 Negroes, a percentage of 7.4. In Louis-

---

[4] For plain, often crude, but honest expressions of Klan ideals, the best sources are the many weekly Klan newspapers, which printed mainly editorials and speeches by lecturers of the order, plus some Klan news items. The Atlanta *Searchlight* and the *Fiery Cross* (various state editions) were officially sanctioned by national headquarters. Enjoying wider circulation in Texas were the Dallas *Texas 100 Per Cent American,* Houston *Colonel Mayfield's Weekly,* Fort Worth *American Citizen,* Elgin *Pure Democracy,* and Tyler *American.* In Louisiana, Klan weeklies were the Merryville *Protestant Standard,* Columbia *Caldwell* [Parish] *Watchman,* and Winnfield *Sergeant Dalton's Weekly.* In Arkansas there was the Little Rock *Arkansas Traveller;* in Oklahoma, the Muskogee *Oklahoma Herald,* Tulsa *Oklahoma Patriot,* and Oklahoma City *Fiery Cross.* Of these various weeklies the writer has seen files of *Colonel Mayfield's Weekly, American Citizen, Texas 100 Per Cent American, Pure Democracy, Caldwell Watchman, Fiery Cross* (Oklahoma edition), and *Searchlight.*

iana there were in 1920 many more Negroes, 700,257 of a total population of 1,798,509, but as a result of Negro migration north during the war, the percentage had declined from 43.1 to 38.9 in the decade 1910-1920. A similar decline in the percentage of the Negro population had occurred in Texas and Arkansas. In Texas, with a population of 4,663,228 in 1920, there were 741,694 Negroes, 15.9 percent, whereas in 1910 the percentage of Negroes had been 17.7. Arkansas in 1920 had a population of 1,752,204, of which 472,220 were Negroes. Here the percentage of Negroes was 27.0; in 1910 it had been 28.1.[5]

The actions of the Klan in these four states indicated a strikingly small amount of hostility toward Negroes. A traveler through the Southwest in 1922 wrote that "the Ku Klux movement hereabouts is not conspicuously anti-Negro. The . . . Negroes with whom I have had an opportunity to talk are not greatly disturbed by it so far as the security of their own people is concerned. They say, as others do, that it is mainly an anti-bootlegging and anti-home-breaking organization."[6] Klansmen in Oklahoma and Louisiana rarely made physical assaults on Negroes. A significant number of acts of Klan violence against Negroes occurred only in Arkansas and Texas, and most of these incidents took place in the first few months after the order entered the two states. In the early twenties, fear of the more aggressive Negro the war was supposed to have produced subsided as he either accepted his old place or moved north. The most sensational examples of masked terrorism in the Southwest—the murder of two Klan haters in north Louisiana, the brutal beating of an adulterous man and woman in Texas, the flogging, tarring, and feathering of a defeated candidate for the state legislature in Okla-

[5] U. S. Bureau of the Census, *Fourteenth Census of the United States* (1920), III (*Composition and Characteristics of the Population*), 812, 388, 984, 86.

[6] Edward T. Devine, "More About the Klan," *Survey*, XLVIII (April 8, 1922), 42.

homa—these offenses, and the great majority of others, involved only white people.

Concern over the foreign-born and immigrant element of the population does not appear to have been intense in the Southwest. In 1920, foreign-born whites made up 2.0 percent of the population in Oklahoma, 0.8 percent in Arkansas, 2.5 percent in Louisiana, and 7.7 percent in Texas.[7] What few foreigners there were in the four states lived mainly in the larger cities, especially New Orleans and San Antonio. In one corner of Texas, the Rio Grande Valley, worry over the growing number of Mexican laborers who entered the state during the fruit-picking season and stayed probably contributed to the establishment of local Klans, or chapter units, in a string of towns along the river.[8] Evidence of this anti-Mexican feeling was scarce farther north.

As in other parts of the nation, fear of bomb-carrying Bolsheviks, anarchists, and radical labor organizers (they were all the same to most Americans) was present in the Southwest during the war. In Tulsa, one night in November 1917, a mob calling itself the "Knights of Liberty" whipped, tarred and feathered, and drove from the city seventeen agents of the Industrial Workers of the World who had attempted to organize laborers in the Oklahoma oilfields.[9] This act presaged the kind of terrorism that would

[7] *Fourteenth Census*, III, 812, 86, 388, 984.

[8] Along the Rio Grande there were local Klans in Brownsville, Harlingen, Mercedes, Edinburgh, McAllen, and Laredo. On the problem of Mexican migrants, see, for example, U. S. Bureau of the Census, *Immigrants and Their Children, 1920*, by Niles Carpenter (Washington, 1927), 52-53, 128-29; John H. Burma, *Spanish-Speaking Groups in the United States* (Durham, N.C., 1954), ch. II; Pauline R. Kibbe, *Latin Americans in Texas* (Albuquerque, 1946); Manuel Gamio, *Mexican Immigration to the United States* (Chicago, 1960).

[9] American Civil Liberties Union, *The "Knights of Liberty" Mob and the I.W.W. Prisoners at Tulsa, Okla.* (New York, February 1918), pamphlet on microfilm in Division of Manuscripts, University of Oklahoma Library, Norman.

mark the Klan's career in the state. Antiradicalism carried over after the war, but by the time the Klan entered the Southwest, late in 1920, most of it had disappeared. Lack of large-scale industrial enterprise besides the railroad, oil, and lumbering industries militated against unionist activity in the Southwest. The Klan always frowned on attempts by unions to organize semiskilled or unskilled laborers, but the writer has come across only two instances of direct conflict between southwestern Klansmen and union organizers, one in Arkansas and one in Louisiana.[10]

Although anti-Catholicism and anti-Semitism were important in the kluxing of the Southwest, these prejudices were not as prominent in that region as in the East or Midwest. One way to measure Klan motivation is by looking at Klan actions. And in the four states under consideration there was comparatively little of the type of quiet but vicious activity against Catholic and Jewish citizens carried on by Klansmen in such states as Indiana, Ohio, Pennsylvania, or New Jersey. Southwestern Klansmen did not openly boycott Jewish and Catholic merchants, attempt to fire Catholics and Jews from public school faculties, or burn crosses before convents or synagogues. Not even in Louisiana, where about half of the population—most of them of French ancestry—belonged to the Roman Catholic faith, did the Klan center its attention on the religious question. Most of the Klan's strength in Louisiana was concentrated in the Protestant northern part of the state. There, as in Arkansas, Texas, and Oklahoma, moral and political reform were the primary objectives of Klansmen.

In Texas the editor of a pro-Klan newspaper minimized Catholic influence in state politics and estimated the num-

[10] These incidents occurred at El Dorado, Arkansas, and Shreveport. See Little Rock *Arkansas Gazette*, February 5, 1922; New Orleans *Times-Picayune*, January 15, 16, 1922; Shreveport *Journal*, January 14, 1922.

ber of Catholic voters at only 65,000.[11] As late as 1926 a newspaper correspondent said that there were about 40,000 Catholic voters in Oklahoma and that the supporters of a gubernatorial candidate who was a Klansman were expecting their man to draw some Catholic votes.[12] Yet Klansmen in the Southwest were no more trustful of Catholics than their hooded fellows in other areas. Anytime a member of the Roman Church announced for public office in any state, he was certain to confront the unified opposition of the Klan.

There is little evidence of overt antipathy on the part of the Klan toward Jews in Texas, Arkansas, Louisiana, or Oklahoma. The Imperial Klan made much of the "unblendable" character of the Jews, but outside of such eastern states as New York or New Jersey, anti-Semitism seems to have only moderate appeal during the 1920s, whereas the next decade would see an intensification of hostility toward Jews throughout the Western world. In the Southwest, as everywhere else, Klansmen grumbled about the alleged ruthlessness of Jewish businessmen and the racial and religious cohesiveness of the Jewish people. But their resentment had little effect on the social standing or economic well-being of prominent Jewish families like the Florsheims and the Kahns in Shreveport, the Dreyfusses in Little Rock, the Steinhagens and the Gordons in Beaumont, or the Rosenfields in Dallas. In Monroe, Louisiana, one of the strongest Klan towns in the Southwest, the Klan twice refused to campaign openly against Mayor Arnold Bernstein.[13]

Thus nativist sentiment, an ethnic and religious reaction against foreign ideals and institutions, appears to have played a secondary role in the Invisible Empire's spread over Texas, Louisiana, Oklahoma, and Arkansas. Judging

[11] Houston *Colonel Mayfield's Weekly*, November 24, 1923.
[12] Tulsa *Tribune*, June 5, 1926.
[13] Shreveport *Journal*, February 20, April 11, 1923.

from the evidence at hand, the Klan's growth in the Southwest stemmed mainly from a desire to protect and defend the native American's own conception of what was right and wrong—not so much from "alien" influences, as from such homegrown evils as the rise of the city, the advent of the bootlegger, and a general postwar letdown in private and public morals. Paradoxically, while the Klansman called himself "progressive," the goals he had in mind were conservative, even reactionary. The Klan became the ideal of progressivism for hundreds of thousands of middle-class white Protestant Southwesterners, just as trust regulation, the secret ballot, initiative, and referendum, and prohibition of liquor drinking were the progressive archetypes of the prewar era. Postwar disillusionment largely stifled genuine reformism in the twenties, a decade when liberal thought centered on prohibition repeal and modernist theology, neither of which had much direct connection with social amelioration. To a great extent, rural-minded America found its outlet in the Klan. This was especially true in the Southwest, where progress became reaction, progressivism became proscription.[14]

The rural-mindedness which lay at the bottom of the Klan movement throughout the nation featured not an isolated provincialism, but a sharp conflict between rural values and the changing mores of a society undergoing rapid industrialization and concentration. There was no section of the country where the process of urbanization and industrialization was more acute than the Southwest. While the urban population of the nation as a whole increased by 28.8 percent from 1910 to 1920, the number of urban dwellers in Arkansas increased 43.3 percent; Oklahoma, 68.5 percent; and Texas, 61.2 percent. The increase

[14] For a more thorough exposition of the idea that prohibitionism and the Klan represented a degradation of progressivism, see Richard Hofstadter, *The Age of Reform: From Bryan to F.D.R.* (New York, Vintage ed., 1960), 282-97. This writer is not prepared to accept Hofstadter's views completely.

of the urban population of Louisiana was only 26.5 percent, but 34.9 percent of the people in the state lived in urban centers in 1920, whereas 30.0 percent of the population was nonrural in 1910. All of the southwestern states were predominantly rural in 1920—83.4 percent in Arkansas, 65.1 in Louisiana, 73.4 in Oklahoma, and 67.6 in Texas. But in 1910 the percentages of rural dwellers had been 87.1 for Arkansas, 70.0 for Louisiana, 80.7 for Oklahoma, and 75.9 for Texas.[15]

Almost all the cities of the Southwest displayed conspicuous growth in the decade 1910 to 1920. In Arkansas the population of the Little Rock—North Little Rock complex increased from 57,079 to 79,190 during the ten-year period. Oil and gas discoveries in north Louisiana swelled the size of Shreveport from 28,015 to 43,874 inhabitants; while oil and a general population influx into Oklahoma brought a growth from 64,205 to 91,295 in Oklahoma City, 4,176 to 17,430 in Okmulgee, and 18,182 to 72,075 in Tulsa. Among Texas cities the population of Dallas jumped from 92,104 to 158,976; Fort Worth, from 73,312 to 106,482; Houston, from 78,800 to 138,276; and San Antonio, from 76,614 to 161,379. Other cities experiencing rapid growth were Alexandria and Baton Rouge in Louisiana; Muskogee and Ardmore in Oklahoma; and Austin, El Paso, Beaumont, and Wichita Falls in Texas.[16] The Klan was powerful in every one of the above-mentioned cities. Only San Antonio and Baton Rouge, together with cosmopolitan New Orleans, escaped partial or complete control by the Klan. Dallas probably had more Klansmen per capita than any other city in the nation, about 13,000 in 1924.[17]

[15] William F. Rossiter, *Increase of Population in the United States, 1910-1920* (Washington, 1922), 75; *Fourteenth Census*, I (*Population 1920: Number and Distribution of Inhabitants*), 150, 159, 169, 172.

[16] *Fourteenth Census*, I, 181-82, 226-27, 280-82, 303-307.

[17] This is the figure given in 1926 by former Grand Dragon Z. E. Marvin of the Realm of Texas in New York *Times*, February 21, 1926, sec. VIII, p. 1.

Thus there is a correlation between the rapid growth of southwestern cities and the presence of prosperous Klan chapters. Urban centers were comprised of diverse aggregations of individuals, transplanted into a strange environment and removed from the influence of stern public opinion and family counsel of the rural community. An increase of crime, the erosion of traditional morality, and some degree of social deterioration usually accompanied the boom of a new city. Many respectable, middle-class city dwellers in the Southwest, who found themselves living in an urban environment but seeking to preserve the values of their rural upbringing, saw in the Klan a method to bring "law and order" to the cities.[18]

As in other postwar periods, the years after the First World War saw a marked increase in crime of all types. In many areas local law enforcement officials seemed unable or unwilling to halt criminal activity. Police officials in Houston and Dallas reported that thefts were so numerous that accurate records could not be kept.[19] "Murder, theft, robbery, and hold-ups are hourly occurrences that fill the daily press," declared Pat Morris Neff, the governor of Texas. "The spirit of lawlessness has become alarming. Our loose method of dealing with violators of the law is in a large degree responsible for the conditions that today confront us."[20] Neff, asserting that the issue was "clearly drawn . . . between law and lawlessness, between virtue and vice, between social order and open violence, between law-abiding citizens and insolent violators of the law," pro-

[18] Several historians have assumed that the Klan thrived in the small towns throughout the country but not usually in the cities. See Hofstadter, *Age of Reform*, 293; William E. Leuchtenburg, *The Perils of Prosperity, 1914-1932* (Chicago History of American Civilization; Chicago, 1958), 209; and Arthur M. Schlesinger, Jr., *The Crisis of the Old Order, 1919-1933* (The Age of Roosevelt; Boston, 1957), 98, 99. This assumption is not valid for Klan history in any part of the country except the northeastern United States.

[19] Galveston *Daily News*, December 21, 1920.

[20] 37th Texas Legislature, Regular Session, *House Journal*, 316.

claimed "Law and Order Sunday" in Texas.[21] Governor
Thomas C. McRae of Arkansas cited the crime wave sweeping over his state and issued a similar proclamation.[22]
"Lawlessness in Tulsa MUST STOP," fulminated the Tulsa
Tribune. "If you have not enough police Mr. Mayor make a
loud noise that sounds like HELP and demand that the
citizens give you help. . . . Our jails are sieves and at times
our courts appear to be jokes. But the jokes are getting
too common and too costly."[23] And when an editorialist in
Louisiana asked "why it is that moonshiners and bootleggers in our district are not being handled," the Little
Rock *Arkansas Gazette* answered: "We could put down the
crime wave by enforcing the law rigidly and by eliminating those senseless delays that are so valuable to criminals.
. . . These days, in too many cases, there is neither severity
nor certainty."[24]

Probably the most frequent kind of law violation occurring in the postwar period was the illicit manufacture
and sale of alcoholic beverages—"moonshining" and "bootlegging." Liquor had never been legal in Oklahoma, its
constitution drawn up before its admission to statehood
in 1907 containing a prohibition article. Arkansas voted
"bone dry" in 1916, and Texas followed with statewide
prohibition during the war. The Eighteenth Amendment
and the national Volstead Act in 1919 dried up Louisiana,
although prohibition had come to most of the northern
part of the state some years earlier through the device of
local option. Widespread abridgment of the prohibition
statutes, or rather widespread public concern over such
abridgment, came only after the war. In 1920, having
created a legal structure for prohibition, dry advocates

[21] Dallas *Morning News,* February 18, 1921.
[22] Little Rock *Arkansas Gazette,* January 19, 1921.
[23] Tulsa *Tribune,* June 2, 1920.
[24] Shreveport *Journal,* January 2, 1921; Little Rock *Arkansas
Gazette,* April 12, 1922.

found themselves without the legal means to enforce the antiliquor laws.[25]

Bootlegging was especially prevalent in the oil boom areas, where burgeoning wealth and population brought the usual social parasites—prostitutes, procurers, gamblers, saloonkeepers. In El Dorado, center of the southern Arkansas oil strike of 1920, in Haynesville in the north Louisiana oil and gasfields, in Tulsa, Muskogee, and Okmulgee in the eastern Oklahoma field, and in various boom areas of Texas, vice was rampant. One account from El Dorado revealed that "thousands of 'wild women'" were in the town and that "at least a dozen hotel operators are raking in blood money hand over fist, carrying on and abetting the illegitimate and damnable traffic." Another observer of conditions in El Dorado wrote: "Gambling has been run wide open in several places. . . . Booze has been sold right over the bar, and every known kind of vice has been going full sway. . . . All night long . . . women can be seen on the downtown streets with men in a drunken condition."[26]

Moral laxity may have been worse in the oil towns, but many worried Southwesterners living in towns that were far from an oil well believed that they also were in the midst of moral chaos. The rural-minded American, schooled in a stern tradition of Victorian prudishness, observed

[25] On the relationship of progressivism to the prewar prohibitionist crusade, see James H. Timberlake, *Prohibition and the Progressive Movement, 1900-1920* (Cambridge, Mass., 1963). Adequate surveys of prohibition in the twenties are Herbert Asbury, *The Great Illusion: An Informal History of Prohibition* (Garden City, N. Y., 1950); Andrew Sinclair, *Prohibition: The Era of Excess* (Boston, 1962); and Charles Merz, *The Dry Decade* (New York, 1931).

[26] El Dorado *Daily Tribune,* quoted in Shreveport *Journal,* June 16, September 24, 1921. The writer's father, the late C. C. Alexander, as a young man worked as a roughneck in the southern Arkansas oilfields. He often related to the writer his recollections of open vice conditions in the towns of El Dorado, Norphlet, and Smackover.

"petting parties," "joy rides," "loose dancing," and other indiscretions indulged in by "flaming youth," and announced that "modernism" was not for him. He needed some bulwark against the new social tides rising in the postwar years, and he found it in the Klan. He listened receptively when Klan propagandists told him that the order "stands pre-eminently against night auto-riding and roadside parking," "the salacious literature and the modern dress," the "jazz dance," and "the seducer of girls or the rape fiend."[27]

Local public officials were the ones the Southwesterner most frequently blamed for the breakdown in law enforcement and morals. In 1920 an epidemic of dissatisfaction with local officeholders, particularly mayors, judges, sheriffs, and police chiefs and commissioners, hit Oklahoma. "Things are pretty damned rotten in Tulsa and Tulsa County," exploded the crusading *Tribune.* "They have been kept rotten year in and year out by a band of low-down politicians whose one aim has been to protect the outlaws."[28] In the April city elections, Tulsa Democrats bolted the "rotten" Democratic machine and elected a completely Republican city administration, which promised reform.[29] But only a few weeks after the new administration was inaugurated, the crime wave accelerated and the bombardment of criticism resumed. In Oklahoma City, Ardmore, Okmulgee, and other places, there was similar unrest over the increase of "hi-jackings," as robberies were called in the Southwest; prohibition violations; open prostitution; gambling; and drunkenness.[30]

When the Kleagles entered the communities, towns, and cities of the Southwest, they found indignant citizens who

27 Houston *Colonel Mayfield's Weekly,* November 21, December 3, 1921, January 7, 1922; Tyler *American,* May 26, 1922.

28 Tulsa *Tribune,* July 27, 1920.

29 Tulsa *Daily World,* April 6, 1920.

30 Tulsa *Tribune,* October 13, 1920, August 24, 1921; Oklahoma City *Daily Oklahoman,* April 15, 1920.

were searching for a solution to the disordered conditions that surrounded them. The Klan offered a solution: Here was a fraternal order whose membership was secret, whose national officials did not seem to care what the local chapters did, and which looked like the perfect instrument for extralegal cleanup operations. In charging his grand jury to investigate the Klan, a Texas judge pictured the Klansman as one who "picks up a newspaper and sees where there has been a miscarriage of justice, then broods over this iniquity, turns one hundred percent American, sends $16.50 to Georgia, buckles on a pistol, covers his face with a mask, dresses in a long, white robe, leaves his family, and goes out into the darkness and disturbs another man's family by trying to stop crime waves with a bucket of tar and feathers."[31]

In the four states of the Southwest the Klan benefited from the deep strain of violence running through the history of the region. Here there existed "a tradition of restlessness, of impatience with restraint, of aggressive action," which over the years had taken the form of lynchings, the formation of vigilante bodies, and family feuds.[32] The original Klan or similar night-riding groups roamed Arkansas, Louisiana, and Texas during the Reconstruction years. Oklahoma had been the Indian Territory, a giant reservation, until 1889, when it was opened to white settlement with a mad race for land from the Kansas and Texas borders. Only thirteen years old as a state in 1920, it was blessed with abundant natural resources and a thirst for progress, but plagued by inadequate law enforcement and intolerance of slow justice.

The white Protestant citizen of the Southwest had many anxieties. His fears for the safety of his property, the chas-

[31] Judge James R. Hamilton, Charge to the Travis County Grand Jury, October 2, 1921, James R. Hamilton Papers, in the possession of Mrs. Hamilton, Austin.
[32] H. J. Haskell, "Martial Law in Oklahoma," *Outlook*, CXXXV (September 26, 1923), 133.

tity of his daughter, the honor of his wife, and the peace of his community were supplemented by concern over foreign immigration, the Catholic hierarchy, insolent Negroes, greedy Jews, and Bolsheviks. And so he turned to the Klan. When all the calamities he had feared did not occur, he credited the Klan with the salvation of the nation in general and his community in particular. In October of 1921, during the investigation of the Klan by the Rules Committee of the United States House of Representatives, a Muskogee, Oklahoma, Klansman defended the order in a letter to his Congressman, a member of the committee. His letter vividly expressed the conditions and feelings that inspired the Klan's growth in the Southwest:

"In the oil towns filled with the bad and 'no counts' of men and females and where no school girl is safe from this rough and tumble bootleg element, one 'visit' [from Klan regulators] and the town is almost a 'Sunday-School class.'

"I could mention three or four towns I have been in and personally took the trouble to see if good had come out of this 'new way' of dealing with this bad and tough element. . . . I find that the very best Americans in all these towns speak out in its favor. . . .

"I have not seen a case . . . that all the leading good people of the town have not said, 'It's a good thing, push it along.' It moves out the gangster, bootlegger, chock [beer] shop, fast and loose females, and the man who abuses and neglects his wife and children. It certainly was born of a great necessity in this oil country. . . . The delay in our laws is a great protection to the criminal class, and the people, taxed to the limit, are taking this method to put a stop to this cost on the town and country."[33]

In the fall of 1920, people in Texas, Arkansas, Oklahoma, and Louisiana were ready to adapt the Klan to their own

[33] *The Ku Klux Klan. Hearings before the Committee on Rules, House of Representatives,* 67th Congress, 1st Session (1921), 6.

needs and use it as a shortcut to political and moral reno-
vation, to the reestablishment of law and order. The Southwest was ready for the Klan; this truth the order's Kleagles
would gleefully discover when they undertook the kluxing
of Texas, the first state of Klan prominence.

3.

The Klan Moves into the Southwest

ONE DAY in late September 1920, Klansman Z. R. Upchurch stepped from a train at the Southern Pacific depot in Houston. Upchurch was the chief agent for Edward Y. Clarke and Mrs. Elizabeth Tyler in the Propagation Department of the Klan's Atlanta headquarters, where he was considered one of the order's top Kleagles. Upchurch had a twofold purpose in coming to Texas: to represent the Klan at the annual reunion of the United Confederate Veterans, to be held in Houston October 6 to 9; and to survey prospects for making Texas part of the Invisible Empire, ruled over nominally by Imperial Wizard William J. Simmons but now actually administered by Imperial Kleagle Clarke. At this time the Klan had chapters operating only in Georgia, Alabama, Mississippi, and Tennessee.[1] Georgia was the one state where the Klan had attracted much attention; everywhere else the organization remained small and obscure.

Upchurch traveled over Houston, making contacts and

talking to men about the Klan. Almost all of those he contacted signed applications for membership in the masked fraternity. By the first week in October, Upchurch had signed up about a hundred Houstonians, the number ordinarily required for the establishment of a local Klan. The Kleagle from Atlanta wired Clarke of his success, suggesting that the Confederate Veterans' Reunion might be an ideal occasion for the installation of the first chapter in Texas. Clarke replied that he and Simmons would come to Houston to preside personally at the creation of the new Klan.[2]

On Thursday, October 9, the Confederate Veterans staged their grand parade through the main streets of Houston. The heroes of the Lost Cause walked, hobbled, and rode at the head of the procession, followed by carloads of dignitaries. One of the automobiles carried Imperial Wizard Simmons, his red hair blowing in the autumn wind and his pince-nez eyeglasses perched properly on his nose. Probably few of the thousands who watched the parade recognized Simmons or understood what he was doing in the procession, although they could not help seeing the banners reading "Knights of the Ku Klux Klan, Atlanta, Georgia," plastered on the sides of his vehicle. But the onlookers clearly realized the meaning of the line of marchers and horsemen in Klan garb appearing farther back in the train. Some of the white-robed and hooded marchers carried banners bearing the messages "We were

[1] Testimony of Z. R. Upchurch in *Knights of the Ku Klux Klan, Inc.* v. *George B. Kimbro, Jr.* (No. 105180) (61st District Court, Harris County, Texas), reported in Houston *Post-Dispatch*, March 24, 1925. This case was a civil action in which the Klan brought suit against former Grand Goblin and Kleagle Kimbro for $25,000 in funds owed to the Klan. Kimbro filed cross action of $250,000 for libel and $50,000 in unpaid salary and commissions. The amounts eventually awarded by the court to the two parties virtually canceled each other out. The transcript of this trial, like many other state court records, is in shorthand; thus testimony as printed in the newspapers was used.

[2] *Ibid.*

here yesterday, 1866," "We are here today, 1920," and "We will be here forever."[3]

That night, in a field lighted with flaming crosses near Bellaire, a suburb of Houston, the candidates for citizenship in the Invisible Empire went through the Klan's "naturalization ceremonies" and became full-fledged Klansmen. Simmons, Clarke, Upchurch, and other Klan officials were on hand to participate in the rites and to administer the necessary oaths. Immediately after the ceremonies the new Klansmen held their first meeting. They chose "Sam Houston Klan No. 1" as the name of the first chapter to be established in Texas and in the four states of the Southwest.[4]

Before he left Houston, Upchurch appointed George B. Kimbro, a former deputy sheriff and presently part owner of an ice cream factory, Kleagle for Texas. Kimbro had full authority to conduct organization work in the state. He rented an office in Room 427 of the First National Bank Building in Houston and, with a staff of about twenty Kleagles, began kluxing operations.[5] Kimbro's Kleagles quickly moved into several southeast Texas towns, securing the requisite one hundred membership applications and granting provisional charters. The permanent charters usually came from Imperial headquarters a few days later.

The kluxing of Texas followed no particular pattern. It seems that local Klans were established in towns and cities as the Kleagles reached them or as the inhabitants contacted Kimbro's Houston office and requested that an organizer be sent. Thus the second Klan to be chartered was in the little oil town of Humble, north of Houston,

[3] This description of the Confederate Veterans' parade is taken from Houston *Post*, October 10, 1920, and Galveston *Daily News*, same date.

[4] Upchurch testimony, *Ku Klux Klan* v. *Kimbro*, in Houston *Post-Dispatch*, March 24, 1925.

[5] Fourth New York *World* article on Klan, printed in New Orleans *Times-Picayune*, September 9, 1921.

while to the southeast, Goose Creek Klan No. 4 was organized. The Beaumont Klan was the seventh to be chartered, the Wharton County Klan the eighth. Galveston Klan No. 36 came into being at an initiation in the island city on November 18, an indication of the rapid, and at the same time aimless, spread of the Klan over southeast Texas.[6] The San Antonio Klan, having the charter number 31, was organized in early November. But the Kleagles did not solicit members and organize Klans in most of the other cities in Texas until the first months of 1921. The Dallas Klan was No. 66; Wichita Falls, No. 78; Austin, No. 81; El Paso, No. 100; and Fort Worth, No. 101. Amarillo, the largest city in the Texas Panhandle, did not have a local Klan until the fall of 1921, a year after the Klan began organizing Texas.[7] In the meantime the order had spread up and down the Gulf Coast of the state, into the piney woods of east Texas, the blacklands of the northern part of the state, and the prairies of the central portion, and over that vast area between the hundredth meridian and the Pecos River known as West Texas.

Representatives of the Klan arrived in Louisiana about the same time that Upchurch came to Houston, perhaps slightly later. As far as is known, no Texans belonged to the Klan before the establishment of the Houston chapter. But there were at least two Klansmen in Louisiana before the Klan began organization work in the state. L. P. Butler of Shreveport and A. B. Booth of New Orleans joined the order back in 1917. At that time Imperial Wizard Simmons termed them charter members of "Klan No. 0, Realm of Louisiana," meaning that there were then no chapters in the state.[8]

W. V. Eaton was the Kleagle for Louisiana. Sometime

[6] Galveston *Daily News,* November 19, 1920.

[7] Dallas *Morning News,* November 17, 1921; San Antonio *Express,* December 10, 1921.

[8] Shreveport *Journal,* November 24, 1920.

in late 1920, probably in October, he set up propagation headquarters in Room 414 of the Canal Commercial Bank Building in New Orleans. His staff was small, probably fewer than ten Kleagles. The first chapter installed in Louisiana was "Old Hickory Klan No. 1" of New Orleans. The New Orleans Klansmen rented Shalimar Grotto Hall, 1125 Dauphine Street, at forty dollars a month for their meetings. The vice chairman of the hall, a member of the lower house of the state legislature and a prominent Mason, was Thomas F. DePaoli. Despite his name, DePaoli was a Protestant, and he would become one of the top Klan officials in Louisiana.[9]

In mid-November 1920 a Shreveport newspaper reported in an obscure corner of one of its issues: "Definite announcement was made today that plans are now being made for organizing in Shreveport a branch of the Knights of the Ku Klux Klan." A Kleagle from Eaton's New Orleans office was in town to confer with "prominent citizens . . . interested in the movement."[10] A week or so later a Klan unit was installed in Shreveport, and in the last days of the month a Kleagle visited Baton Rouge, the state capital, to sign up new Klansmen and grant a provisional charter.

The Louisiana Kleagles appear to have had more system in their organizing campaign than Kimbro's agents had in Texas. The expansion of the Klan in Louisiana has the mark of a rather well planned kluxing operation. Whereas in Texas, Klan organization work followed no real pattern except one of expansion in all directions from Houston, in Louisiana the Kleagles first entered and organized the cities of the state, regardless of how far they had to travel from New Orleans. The Klan in Shreveport was the second to be chartered. The Baton Rouge Klan was No. 3; Monroe

[9] Fourth New York *World* article, printed in New Orleans *Times-Picayune*, September 9, 1921. See also the *Times-Picayune*, September 30, 1921.
[10] Shreveport *Journal*, November 14, 1920.

Klan, No. 4; Lake Charles Klan, No. 7; Alexandria Klan, No. 12. From the cities the Klan spread into the towns and villages of northern and central Louisiana. Chapters were established in most of the parish seats of south Louisiana, but the heavily Catholic, antiprohibitionist population in that region of ricegrowers, sugar planters, and fur trappers always stifled the Protestant, and dry, Klan.

The Klan attracted little attention during its first three or four months in Texas and Louisiana. In February of 1921, however, the Texas Klan emerged with a vengeance, initiating a campaign of violent moral and social reform. On February 4 Kimbro, the head Kleagle for Texas, led a party of hooded Klansmen who whipped, tarred, and feathered a Houston lawyer named B. I. Hobbs because Hobbs had the "wrong kind" of clients—mostly Negroes and habitual lawbreakers. The Hobbs incident precipitated a wave of Klan brutality in Texas that would continue for the next two and a half years. The spring and summer of 1921 saw masked regulators take the law into their own hands on fifty-two occasions to punish moral transgressors, bootleggers, and others whose conduct was in some way objectionable to the Klan. In Dallas a band of local Knights, probably led by Exalted Cyclops Hiram W. Evans, dragged Negro bellhop Alex Johnson from the Adolphus Hotel and branded the initials "K.K.K." across his forehead with acid. Klansmen in Fort Worth gave a local gambler coats of tar and feathers on two separate occasions. At Tenaha, in the pine forests of east Texas, Klansmen tarred and feathered a woman accused of bigamy and clipped her hair.[11]

[11] Testimony of George B. Kimbro in *Ku Klux Klan* v. *Kimbro*, in Houston *Post-Dispatch*, March 19, 1925; testimony of Erwin J. Clark in *Senator from Texas. Hearings before a Subcommittee of the Committee on Privileges and Elections, United States Senate*, 68th Congress, 1st and 2d Sessions (1924), 117-18; Dallas *Morning News*, July 18, 1921. For a survey of the Klan's career in Texas, see Charles C. Alexander, *Crusade for Conformity: The Ku Klux Klan in Texas, 1920-1930* (Houston, 1962).

Outside Beaumont masked Puritans flogged, tarred, and feathered J. S. Paul, a local physician suspected of performing abortions on two women, and then whipped a Deweyville citizen who sent one of the women to Dr. Paul. After the two assaults, Beaumont Klansmen published a letter under the official Klan seal in a local newspaper. The Klansmen admitted punishing Paul and R. F. Scott, the other man. "The eyes of the unknown had seen and observed the wrong to be redressed," proclaimed the hooded Knights. "Dr. Paul stood convicted before God and man. . . . The law of the Klan is JUSTICE. . . . The lash was laid on his back and the tar and feathers applied to his body."[12]

As often as not, an act of violence or the dispatch of a threatening note heralded the entrance of the Klan into a Texas community. On other occasions the Klansmen posted warning signs around town or paraded at night with all the street lights turned out, the only illumination furnished by a fiery cross or torches carried by the white-robed marchers. Frequently the parading Klansmen carried banners of admonition making clear their reasons for organizing. Typical messages painted on the banners were: "One hundred percent Americanism," "Booze must and shall go," "Bring in the stills or we will come after them," "Love thy neighbor as thyself, but leave his wife alone," "Crap shooters beware," and "Wife beaters beware."[13]

In contrast with the violent debut of the Klan in Texas society, the order was quiescent in Louisiana during the early months of 1921. The Klan made its first public appearance in Louisiana the night of April 9, 1921, when about three hundred Klansmen paraded in single file through the streets of Shreveport. The next month several

[12] *Senator from Texas Hearings*, 683-86; quotation from thirteenth New York *World* article, printed in New Orleans *Time-Picayune*, September 18, 1921.
[13] See Fort Worth *Star-Telegram*, July 8, 16, 18, 24, 1921; Galveston *Daily News*, May 9, 1921; Houston *Post*, August 4, 1921.

members of Old Hickory Klan No. 1 of New Orleans entered the Carrollton Presbyterian Church and gave a lecture on Klan principles to the congregation.[14] The Klan had been organizing in Louisiana for more than six months before Klansmen in the state were implicated in an act of violence. On May 25, 1921, Shreveport police abruptly released wifebeater and vagrant Jack Morgan. A few minutes later he was seized by hooded men, taken to a point on the Mooringsport road, stripped naked, and coated with tar and feathers. The next day Morgan, having doused himself with gasoline to remove the tar and feathers, donned some borrowed clothes and left Shreveport for parts unknown. Two months later Shreveport Klan No. 2 published a full-page advertisement in the local afternoon newspaper offering a $500 reward for "persons guilty of acts of violence or of sending or posting anonymous communications bearing the name or initials of the Ku Klux Klan."[15]

Oklahoma did not become a factor in the Klan's history until early 1921. In February, word came from Imperial headquarters in Atlanta that Simmons and associates, acting on "numerous requests" for the extension of the Klan to the Sooner State, had dispatched an "imperial officer" to survey prospects in Oklahoma.[16] The Imperial officer was probably Clarke himself, who sometimes personally took charge of a major kluxing campaign. The head Kleagle for Oklahoma (by now this official was called "King Kleagle") was George C. McCarron. McCarron's home was Houston, where he had served on the original staff of Kleagle Kimbro in late 1920. He had been promoted and sent north to conduct Kleagling activities in Oklahoma. McCarron's state headquarters were in Room 503 of the Baltimore Building in Oklahoma City, where

---

[14] Shreveport *Journal*, April 11, 1921; Thomas E. Dabney, *One Hundred Great Years: The Story of the Times-Picayune from Its Founding to 1940* (Baton Rouge, 1944), 415.

[15] Shreveport *Journal*, May 26, 27, July 27, 1921.

[16] Tulsa *Tribune*, May 26, 1921.

he started work with about twelve Kleagles on his staff.[17]

McCarron's agents did their work even more covertly than Kleagles in other states. Like Louisiana, and unlike Texas, the kluxing of Oklahoma followed a pattern of organizing the cities first, then moving on to the county seats, towns, and villages. By the spring of 1921, thriving chapters were quietly furthering Americanism and morality in Oklahoma City, Tulsa, Muskogee, Lawton, and Enid. Yet the Klan remained undercover, despite persistent rumors of its existence in the state. In May the Tulsa *Tribune* must have felt the Klan near when it commented: "Tulsa has had a pretty exhibit of the sort of thing that brings such as the Ku-Klux into a town. [Its] purpose . . . might be as much to put the fear of God into the hearts of derelict officials as the fear of death into the hearts of the criminal."[18] A few days later, May 31 and June 1, a savage race riot broke out in Tulsa. For more than twenty-four hours armed mobs roamed through the Negro district of the city, burning, pillaging, and fighting gun battles with armed Negroes.[19] There is not a particle of evidence to connect the Klan with the riot, but it is likely that the brief, devastating race war gave some spur to the Klan's growth in Tulsa.

The first reported appearance of the Klan in Oklahoma came the night of July 6, when fifteen or twenty men wearing the white hoods of the Klan walked into a cafe in Muskogee and, at gunpoint, abducted a dishwasher named Billy Ware. Grabbing a nearby newspaperman and taking

[17] Fourth New York *World* article, printed in New Orleans *Times-Picayune*, September 9, 1921.

[18] Tulsa *Tribune*, May 26, 1921.

[19] Tulsa *Daily World*, June 1, 2, 3, 1921; Tulsa *Tribune* same dates. Governor J. B. A. Robertson had his attorney general institute ouster proceedings against Police Chief Gustafson of Tulsa for negligence during the race riot. On July 22 a Tulsa jury found him guilty and suspended him from office. For an assessment of blame for the riot, see Gaston Litton, *A History of Oklahoma at the Golden Anniversary of Statehood* (4 vols., New York, 1957), I, 552-53.

him along, the maskers drove out of town. They stopped in a clump of woods and whipped Ware until he confessed to kidnaping a teenage boy because the boy could identify him as a burglar. The newspaperman reported the incident to the Muskogee police, who did nothing. In a thinly veiled reference to the Klan the police disclosed that Ware's assailants were "members of a secret organization which has figured in similar affairs throughout the southwest."[20]

In mid-July a band of hooded men seized Walter Billings, a theater owner, near the Rock Island depot in Enid, spirited him out of town, accused him of wifebeating and philandering, and administered a severe horsewhipping. Later that month Mayor John C. Walton of Oklahoma City ordered his police chief to conduct an investigation of a "secret night-riding organization" which had been holding meetings at the state fairgrounds. A few nights later Oklahoma City law officers came upon a meeting of several hundred Klansmen on the outskirts of the city. Federal officials in the capital city said that 1,000 to 2,500 citizens belonged to Oklahoma City Klan No. 1. And August saw the first sign of the Klan's presence in Tulsa, when the Reverend Caleb R. Ridley, the Imperial Kludd (chaplain) from Atlanta and a popular Klan lecturer, addressed a crowd in Convention Hall on the principles of the Klan. Wash E. Hudson, who one day would be the Klan leader in the state senate, introduced the Klan lecturer.[21]

By the summer of 1921 the Klan was well established in Texas, Louisiana, and Oklahoma, although it had attracted an appreciable amount of public attention only in Texas. In that state the hooded fraternity undertook a campaign of systematic terrorism, aimed mostly at boot-

[20] Tulsa *Tribune,* July 7, 1921.
[21] *Ibid.,* July 13, August 11, 1921; Oklahoma City *Daily Oklahoman,* July 19, 23, 1921.

leggers, moral offenders, gamblers, and wifebeaters. The
order's campaign of violence brought stirrings of opposition from various quarters. In the Texas house of representatives, Wright C. Patman introduced a resolution at-
tacking the Klan, which the jittery solons tabled indefinitely by a vote of 69 to 54. District judges in San Antonio,
Austin, Beaumont, and other cities charged their grand
juries to investigate the epidemic of masked assaults, but
no indictments would be returned until 1923. Mayor Oscar
F. Holcombe of Houston, who had joined the Klan and then
quickly resigned, imported a half dozen peace officers from
West Texas to protect Bayou City citizens from hooded
regulators operating without fear of the city police department.[22] Throughout the state, city and county law officers were hurrying to join the Klan, some of them impressed by the secret society's claims as an aid to law enforcement, others fearful of the growing power of the Klan
in their communities and counties.

For the most part the Klan's expansion over Louisiana
and Oklahoma went unnoticed. In September, C. L. Chap-
puis of Acadia Parish introduced a bill in the Louisiana
house of representatives making it unlawful for anyone in
the state to belong to an organization whose membership
rolls were not open for public inspection. Jules Dreyfous
of Iberia Parish submitted a bill to prohibit any group of
persons from appearing masked except at Mardi Gras.
During hearings on the bills before a house committee,
Representative Thomas F. DePaoli of New Orleans defended the Klan and claimed that "some of the best citizens in New Orleans" belonged to the order. Both of the

[22] 37th Texas Legislature, *House Journal*, 1st Called Session, 51,
73-74; San Antonio *Express*, August 21, 1921; Fort Worth *Star-
Telegram*, November 8, 1921; Judge James R. Hamilton, Charge
to the Travis County Grand Jury, October 2, 1921, James R. Hamilton Papers, in the possession of Mrs. Hamilton, Austin; testimony of
Oscar F. Holcombe in *Ku Klux Klan* v. *Kimbro,* in Houston *Post-
Dispatch,* March 25, 1925.

47

bills were reported from committee without action, and their sponsors withdrew them.[23]

The next month, at DeQuincy, near the Sabine River in Calcasieu Parish, the local Klan introduced itself by posting signs warning disorderly boys and negligent parents; threatening "professional loafers, whiskey dealers, and law violators"; and promising help for "Negroes who conduct themselves as they should."[24] The Klan nevertheless grew slowly in Louisiana, perhaps because the state's deplorable road system made travel and communication difficult and because about half the population, the Catholic "Cajuns" in southern Louisiana, were bitterly hostile to the order.

The Klan moved rapidly over Oklahoma, but there, as in Louisiana, the organization was tardy about coming into the open. In the late summer of 1921, when investigators for the New York *World* were using Klan activities in Texas as evidence for their charges of Klan violence to be published in the fall, the order had still not made a formal public appearance in Oklahoma. To be sure, there were signs of Klan doings here and there—the tarring and feathering of a mailclerk by masked men at El Reno, near Oklahoma City; the dispatch of notes signed by the Klan warning a judge, a deputy sheriff, and a constable at Slick, an oil town in Creek County, to cease their collaboration with bootleggers; the gift of twenty dollars to a destitute widow by Klansmen at Ada.[25] But the initiation of a class of about three hundred by Tulsa Klan No. 2 on the last night in August marked the first time that "aliens" witnessed Klan activity in Oklahoma.[26] Thenceforth, throughout Sep-

---

[23] Louisiana General Assembly, *House Journal*, First Extra Session (1921), 35, 41, 42, 49, 505; New Orleans *Times-Picayune*, September 30, 1921.

[24] New Orleans *Times-Picayune*, October 5, 1921.

[25] Oklahoma City *Daily Oklahoman*, August 12, 1921; Tulsa *Tribune*, August 28, 29, 1921.

[26] Tulsa *Tribune*, September 1, 1921.

tember and the autumn months, reports came from all parts of the state of silent parades by white-robed figures, mysterious initiations or "naturalization ceremonies" in pastures and on hillsides outside towns, and the direct, often violent, efforts of Klansmen to effect law enforcement and morality in their communities.

An especially popular method Oklahoma Knights used to announce their presence featured a lone Klansmen on horseback galloping furiously down the main street of a town, a burning cross held high and signs like "Beware bootleggers, hijackers and gamblers" and "Decent people have no fear" attached to the sides of the horse. The Klansmen would also form their automobiles into a line and ride in their white robes and hoods through a town. At other times they marched, carrying banners warning undesirables to leave the community.[27] Frequently the hooded Knights used more forceful means to let "aliens" know they were at hand. In Tulsa, twenty masked men brought along a newspaperman when they whipped suspected car thief and hijacker J. E. Frazier. Afterward the leader of the regulators told the group: "We will now return home, conscious that we have done our duty in ridding Tulsa of one criminal—may the others fare likewise." County Attorney John Seaver, when asked about the Frazier whipping, replied that there would be no inquiry into the affair. Frazier probably got what he deserved, said Seaver, and, besides, an investigation would only bring criticism to the investigators.[28] Such an attitude amounted to an open invitation for the Klan's extralegal marauding. During the next four months masked bands whipped twelve persons in various parts of Tulsa County.

After it moved into an Oklahoma community, the Klan

[27] See, for example, Oklahoma City *Daily Oklahoman*, September 12, 21, 1921; Tulsa *Tribune*, September 2, 15, 24, 1921; New York *Times*, September 22, 1921, p. 3.
[28] Tulsa *Tribune*, September 3, 4, 1921.

lost little time making its influence felt. A minister at Ponca City, in the northern part of the state, expressed feelings common to many in Oklahoma when he told his congregation: "There is certainly a great opportunity in Ponca City for the Ku Klux Klan to do its work. Law violators here know every one of the police officers and it is almost impossible to get evidence against them." Klansmen got their own evidence, not only on criminals, but on negligent law officers as well. Irate citizens at Bristow, Creek County, probably inspired by the Klan's presence, chose a law and order committee and made plans for cleaning the town of bootleggers, prostitutes, gamblers, and hijackers. At Sapulpa, near Tulsa, a jury convicted the local police chief of allowing liquor and prostitution in the town and removed him from office. In Okmulgee a superior court jury found the sheriff guilty of official misconduct and permanently relieved him of his duties, prompting the county attorney to assure his constituents: "So far I am for the activity of the Klan in Okmulgee County." And late in the year Tulsa Klan No. 2, claiming a membership of 3,200, sent Sheriff William D. McCullough a note demanding law enforcement in Tulsa County and threatening ouster proceedings against the harassed sheriff if he failed to curb lawbreaking.[29]

During this early period, opposition to the Klan on the part of "respectable" elements in Oklahoma was virtually nonexistent. In Louisiana the order encountered stiff resistance from the citizenry and from most public officials in the parishes and towns of south Louisiana. In New Orleans, the largest southern or southwestern city in 1920, with a population close to 400,000, the size of the membership of Old Hickory Klan No. 1 probably never approached that of Klan No. 2 of Shreveport, a city less than one-ninth as large as New Orleans. A considerable amount of

[29] *Ibid.*, October 11, September 25, October 14, November 13, 17, 1921; Tulsa *Daily World,* December 22, 1921.

antipathy existed toward the Klan in Texas, where the order grew at a mercurial rate. In charging their grand juries, judges over the state excoriated the white-sheeted society; the Texas Chamber of Commerce went on record against the Klan; and a few holdover progressives, like the former lieutenant governor and attorney general Martin M. Crane of Dallas and United States Senator Charles A. Culberson, attacked the divisive character of the order. Even an occasional law officer spoke out against the Klan. John W. Saye, the sheriff of Young County, denied the need for the organization in his county and warned Klansmen not to go outside the law.[30] Another sheriff, Bob Buchanan of McLennan County, where Waco Klan No. 33 thrived, tried to stop a Klan parade at Lorena, a village south of Waco. His actions precipitated a gun and knife fight in which several people were wounded and one man stabbed to death. For his troubles Sheriff Buchanan received a bullet in his leg and a sweeping rebuke from the McLennan County grand jury.[31]

The riot at Lorena, which brought nationwide publicity to the sleepy central Texas village, was not the only time that enemies of the Klan met violence with violence. In December a band of about 150 robed and hooded Klansmen met at night near the southern Oklahoma town of Wilson, in Carter County, to plot a raid on the home of suspected bootlegger Joe Carroll. A short time later nine of the self-appointed liquor raiders tried to force their way into Carroll's house and met a volley of gunfire from Carroll and from his neghbors in the house next door. The Klansmen returned the fire, and a gun battle of several minutes' duration followed. When the Klansmen retired, Carroll was dead inside his house, and one of their own

[30] Dallas *Morning News,* October 16, 1921; Fort Worth *Star-Telegram,* December 30, 1921.

[31] Fort Worth *Star-Telegram,* October 3, 4, 5, 1921; Waco *Times-Herald,* November 5, 1921.

number, John Smith, lay dead before the crude shack. A few hours later law officers found the lifeless body of C. G. Simms in a blood-spattered Klan robe and hood outside Wilson.[32]

Governor James B. A. Robertson sent his attorney general to conduct a preliminary hearing and gather evidence for the state. The hearing disclosed the full story of the riot, and eleven citizens of Carter County, all confessed Klansmen, were indicted by the grand jury. A year passed before the first of the defendants, Jeff Smith, came to trial. The jury deliberated thirty-six hours on Smith's guilt, finally reporting its failure to agree on a verdict. At a second trial, held in late February 1923, Smith was acquitted, whereupon the county attorney admitted that he had exhausted all his evidence in the Smith trial and dropped charges against the remaining ten defendants.[33]

By late 1921 Texas had become the most notorious state of the Invisible Empire, Oklahoma Klansmen were making headlines with their vigilante raids, and the Klan was firmly implanted in Louisiana. But no one had yet seen a white-robed figure or a flaming cross in Arkansas. Klan organizers had come into Arkansas in the summer. In September, King Kleagle A. E. Brown sat behind a desk in a room at the Marion Hotel in Little Rock. There were no chartered Klans in the state at that time, and the only field Kleagle on Brown's staff was his brother, L. J. Brown.[34] The Klan's progress in Arkansas was slow, a condition probably resulting from the poor system of roads and communications, which virtually isolated parts of the state, and the state's overwhelmingly rural and semirural character. In the early twenties, Arkansas was essentially a rural and small town state; the only cities of any size were Little Rock and Fort

[32] Oklahoma City *Daily Oklahoman*, December 18, 21, 23, 1921.

[33] *Ibid.*, December 24, 27, 1921; Tulsa *Tribune*, January 29, 31, February 1, 4, 26, 28, March 1, 1923.

[34] Fourth New York *World* article, printed in New Orleans *Times-Picayune*, September 9, 1921.

Smith. The Browns recruited enough native-born white Protestants for the installation of a chapter in Little Rock, with local attorney and former Republican political leader James A. Comer as Exalted Cyclops. But Prescott, not Little Rock, was the scene of the Klan's first public act in Arkansas. In mid-December the Prescott Klan gave fifty-four dollars to the Christmas fund of the local newspaper.[35]

The Christmas season saw the Klan come into the open in different parts of Arkansas. The debuts of most local Klans did not feature masked assaults or torchlit parades, but acts of charity like donations to the poor at Christmas, about the only time of the year when communities remembered their destitute citizens. During December, Klansmen appeared at Gurdon, Hot Springs, Malvern, Russellville, and Little Rock.[36]

The Christmas season over, Arkansas Klansmen turned to the main order of business—cleaning up their communities. In Texarkana, the stateline town whose Klan chapter both Texans and Arkansans supported, masked regulators whipped a young Negro for "fooling about a white woman." In El Dorado a crowd led by a local Klansman ordered out of town an attorney for eleven members of the Industrial Workers of the World. Three men wearing Klan hoods flogged a Little Rock poolhall operator, warned him to sell his establishment and stop associating with Negroes, and advised him to support his wife properly. In Hope, Klansmen beat up a local bootlegger, told him to clothe his children and put them in school, and dumped him from an automobile on a downtown street. Early in February a mass meeting of El Dorado citizens brought into existence the "Law Enforcement League" to combat prostitution and other forms of vice in the oil-rich southern Arkansas town. The chairman of the League said that he was a member

[35] Little Rock *Arkansas Gazette*, December 14, 1921.
[36] *Ibid.*, December 17, 21, 22, 25, 26, 1921.

of Little Rock Klan No. 1 and that the chapter would furnish whatever men and money were needed to enforce the law in Union County. And the first public "naturalization ceremonies" in Arkansas occurred a few days later, when members of Klan No. 1, aided by Knights from Benton, Hot Springs, Morrilton, Clarksville, Conway, Malvern, and other towns, initiated about 650 "aliens." A newspaperman reported that the class included "state, county and city officials, preachers, lawyers, doctors, merchants, laborers. . . . There were men who have barely reached their majority, and there were men whose hair is snowy white." The initiation supposedly brought the Klan's active membership to three thousand in Pulaski County.[37]

By the spring of 1922 the Klan was moving at a startling pace in almost every part of the nation. The order had already entered Indiana and Ohio, where it would reach its numerical peak in later years. In Oklahoma about 70,000 men had joined the Klan; in Texas, according to Clarke, between 75,000 and 90,000.[38] About 25,000 Klansmen for Arkansas and about 30,000 for Louisiana seem to be reasonable guesses of Klan membership at that time. When people thought of the Klan as a night-riding and terrorist organization, they thought mainly of the deeds of the order in the southwestern states. They perhaps conceived of an incident such as took place in Alexandria, Louisiana, where nine robed Klansmen, revolvers buckled around their waists, walked into a hotel lobby and warned the manager to leave town or suffer the consequences. Or perhaps they had read of the Methodist preacher in DeRidder, Louisiana, accused of wife desertion and business dishonesty,

[37] *Ibid.*, January 9, February 5, 7, 11, 1922; Shreveport *Journal*, February 6, 9, 1922.

[38] The estimate for Oklahoma is from Tulsa *Tribune*, March 6, 1922. Edward Y. Clarke gave the estimate for Texas in an interview with a newspaper reporter, in Dallas *Morning News*, January 23, 1922.

who was abducted at his office by white-robed men, tarred and feathered, and then thrown from a car in front of the town drugstore.[39]

These and numerous other episodes of brutality, insult, and intimidation colored the Klan's early career in the Southwest. The Houston *Chronicle* asserted in the late summer of 1921 that "Texas Klansmen have beaten and blackened more people in the last six months than all the other states combined."[40] By the next spring, Klansmen in Oklahoma, Louisiana, and Arkansas had also done their part toward making the name of the Klan synonymous with terror.

But the order's violent crusade to bring "law and order" and moral orthodoxy to the Southwest had just begun. During the next few years, perhaps a half million Southwesterners would pay their initiation fees, buy their robes, and become hooded Knights of the Invisible Empire. This total included a good portion of the "substantial" people in the communities of the Southwest. It was the responsibility of these supposedly respectable and law-abiding citizens to see that law enforcement remained in the hands of the duly constituted authorities, not with bands of masked terrorists. Yet all too often the "better element" acquiesced as the more fanatical Klan members took it upon themselves to define right conduct and punish transgressors.

[39] Bouanchaud Campaign Committee, *The Ku Klux Klan in Alexandria and Rapides Parish* (pamphlet), Louisiana Collection, Louisiana State University Library, Baton Rouge; New Orleans *Times-Picayune*, February 26, 1922.

[40] Houston *Chronicle*, quoted in "For and Against the Klan," *Literary Digest*, LXX (September 24, 1921), 39.

4.

The Klan's Drive for Law and Order

IN THE SUMMER of 1922 a wave of Klan terrorism was sweeping Oklahoma. "Alfalfa Bill" Murray, the crusty "Sage of Tishimingo," surveyed conditions in the state from the vantage point of a temporarily retired politician and concluded: "It is a sad commentary that just now the hope of good morals and restraint against criminality is found in a body of men whose organized method is not sanctioned by law."[1] Although Murray did not care for the Klan, his comment carries a sentiment shared not only by his fellow Oklahomans, but by numerous other Americans in the 1920s. Alarmed and exasperated by a rapidly changing social order and the rising crime rate, many citizens, especially in the Southwest, found in the Klan "the hope of good morals and restraint against criminality." They saw thieves, bootleggers, gamblers, and other sinners going unpunished by law enforcement officials and the courts; and they turned to the Klan with the hope of bringing retribution to the wrongdoers, by one way or another. And if sometimes they went outside the law, what of it? Wasn't it better to horsewhip a hoodlum everybody knew was guilty than to bring him into court and see him set free?

Because of such thinking, a considerable amount of social approval attached to the Klan's night-riding forays in Louisiana, Arkansas, Oklahoma, and Texas. The sense of helplessness felt by people in the Southwest, together with a tradition of violence and vigilantism, goes a long way toward explaining why, for the most part, the Klan escaped public chastisement for its terrorist campaign. As an Oklahoma judge remarked after the Klan had nearly ceased its vigilante pursuits in all the southwestern states: "In actual results, the thing [Klan coercion] worked pretty well. I don't defend it, of course, but from what I've seen I should say that the night-riders averaged nearer justice than the courts do."[2]

Yet the Klan's continual abrogation of due process of law alienated large numbers of citizens. In the Southwest and in every part of the country there were people who might offer no objection to the Klan's nativism and racism, but who could not accept the order's arrogation to itself of the function of moral arbiter. Even some Klansmen were disgusted by the Klan's habit of prying into other people's affairs, and occasionally they spoke out against masked vigilantism or left the Invisible Empire. As one traveled from south to north in Klandom, the number of Knights who had no stomach for violence increased. In the northern and eastern states, Klansmen rarely indulged in physical coercion, although they frequently resorted to nonviolent

[1] William H. Murray to Campbell Russell, July 20, 1922, Campbell Russell Collection, Division of Manuscripts, University of Oklahoma Library, Norman.

[2] Quoted in Stanley Frost, "Night Riding Reformers: The Regeneration of Oklahoma," *Outlook*, CXXXV (November 14, 1923), 439.

coercive techniques—threats, boycotts, cross burnings.[3] In the South and Southwest, however, the majority of Klan members, while they may never have done any night-riding themselves, made little protest when "the boys," their fellow Klansmen, set out to punish evildoers.

The Klan's official attitude toward acts of violence was almost always to deny that the order was involved.[4] William J. Simmons established the formal "Klan line" on this subject when he appeared before the Rules Committee of the United States House of Representatives, which investigated the Klan in the fall of 1921. There Simmons maintained that he knew of no instances of Klan lawlessness, but if there were indeed any such cases, he could assure the committee that the charters of the guilty Klans would be revoked. But really, asked Simmons, how could the Klan be guilty of lawless acts when one of the tenets of the order was assistance of the authorities in law enforcement?[5] The founder of the Klan could have answered his own question by admitting that to many Klansmen "assisting" law enforcement meant going outside the law, doing things the duly constituted authorities could not legally do.

The policy of denying the existence of Klan night-riding, followed by the Simmons-Clarke regime in the immediate postwar years, was perpetuated by Hiram W. Evans and the "insurgent" group which won control of the Klan in November 1922. Time after time, when someone was whipped, tarred and feathered, run out of town, or otherwise mistreated, Klan leaders disclaimed any responsibil-

[3] See, for example, Emerson H. Loucks, *The Ku Klux Klan in Pennsylvania: A Study in Nativism* (Harrisburg, 1936), ch. III, IV.

[4] A notable exception to this policy was the Beaumont, Texas, Klan's public acknowledgment of responsibility for assaulting Dr. J. S. Paul and R. F. Scott in 1921. See above, p. 42.

[5] *The Ku Klux Klan. Hearings before the Committee on Rules, House of Representatives*, 67th Congress, 1st Session (1921), 67-185.

ity and charged the incident up to lawless elements outside the order. On some occasions Klan chapters offered sizable rewards for the arrest and conviction of persons misbehaving under the guise of the Klan.[6]

There was at least a particle of truth in the Klan's portrayal of itself as victimized by unruly parties trying to discredit the organization. Anyone could put on a mask and go prowling about the community, or send a threatening note signed "K. K. K." There were doubtless some crimes committed in the name of the Klan for which the order bore no direct responsibility. This was especially true in the northern states, where Klansmen usually refrained from violent activity. Even so, in this writer's opinion the whole idea of non-Klan violence in the southern and southwestern states has been greatly exaggerated, most frequently, of course, by the Klansmen themselves. It seems that responsibility for a large majority of the vigilante forays in the Southwest rested heavily—and justly —on the secret fraternity. If people outside the order were to blame for the myriad of masked attacks occurring in the early twenties, then why could not the Klan, with its reputation for helping to apprehend criminals, working in conjunction with law officers who were members of the organization, bring the culprits to justice? The obvious answer is that the local chapters were naturally reluctant to punish their own members.

The epidemic of hooded attacks which followed the entrance of the Klan into each of the southwestern states continued during 1922 and 1923, long after the order had established itself in the region. The great bulk of these personal indignities was directed against white people. There were a few examples of Klan brutality involving Negroes, but the infrequency of assaults on colored citizens

[6] See Dallas *Morning News*, March 22, 1922; Fort Worth *Star-Telegram*, July 11, 1922; Shreveport *Journal*, July 27, 1921.

only reinforces the contention that anti-Negroism was not of primary importance to the Klan's growth in the Southwest. Coercion of Negroes was socially accepted procedure in Texas, Arkansas, Louisiana, and Oklahoma; yet southwestern Klansmen spent most of their time proscribing the conduct of errant whites.

Probably the preponderance of Klan vigilante acts featured a handful of Klansmen acting precipitately and without the sanction of local officers of the order. One or two Klansmen might see some person misbehaving in the community, perhaps a man who beat his wife and children. Thereupon the Knights would get a few brothers together, don their robes and hoods or some other disguise, climb into a Model-T Ford, and sally forth to right the wrong that had been done.[7]

Some local Klans, usually the larger ones, went about the task of purifying society much more elaborately and systematically. One of the officers of a chapter was the Nighthawk, or investigator, whose only function was supposed to be inquiring into candidates' suitability for admission to membership, but whose duties frequently included spying on the morals of the community.[8] Sometimes the "Klokann," the Exalted Cyclops' executive committee, served as the instigator of regulatory activities. The Klokann of Waco Klan No. 33, in Texas, supervised an elaborate spy system and meted out punishment to evildoers. A former official of the Waco Klan recalled: "If we had a report about a man's immoral conduct we would select one of his neighbors, some one who knew him well, and we would authorize this party to watch him from day to day and

[7] After reading accounts of about two hundred acts of hooded violence occurring in the Southwest in the years 1921-1924, this writer is forced to conclude that most of these deeds involved a few Klansmen acting independently of their leaders.

[8] *Constitution and Laws of the Knights of the Ku Klux Klan* (Atlanta, 1921), art. xviii, sec. 12.

night to night and render reports. . . . If we wanted telephone conversations, why we got them; or anything else
of that nature."[9]

In Oklahoma, where the volume of Klan violence was
probably greater than in any other state, the order's terrorist campaign was especially well organized. Oklahoma
City Klan No. 1 had a "whipping squad" comprised of
eighteen Klansmen appointed by Exalted Cyclops Grant
Landon. The squad, which the members of Klan No. 1
called the "Sanhedrin" after the ancient Hebrew council,
was "to take care of . . . these little matters in our neigh-
borhoods."[10] Shawnee Klan No. 8 had not one whipping
squad, but five, with a local Klansman and captain in the
Oklahoma national guard serving as the overall head of the
chapter's vigilante program. But the Exalted Cyclops of
Klan No. 8, Dr. J. A. Walker, always gave his permission
before any punishment was inflicted on wayward towns-
people.[11]

Louisiana Klansmen often gave their chapter whipping
bands names like "Vigilance Committee," "Citizens Committee," or "Law Enforcement League." Such groups operated under the supervision of the chapter executive
board, the Klokann. At the close of a meeting, or "Klon-
klave," the Exalted Cyclops announced that a meeting
of the Klokann and the Vigilance Committee would follow. The Exalted Cyclops or some other officer presided
at this meeting. Each member of the Vigilance Committee
reported any misdeeds he had discovered in the com-

[9] Testimony of Erwin J. Clark in *Senator from Texas. Hearings before a Subcommittee of the Committee on Privileges and Elections,
United States Senate,* 68th Congress, 1st and 2nd Sessions (1924),
125, 128-29.

[10] Testimony of Dr. A. A. Maupin before the military court in
Oklahoma City, reported in Oklahoma City *Daily Oklahoman,* September 21, 1923.

[11] Howard A. Tucker, *Governor Walton's Ku Klux Klan War* (Oklahoma City, 1923), 41-43. See also Tulsa *Tribune,* September 14, 1923.

munity and made recommendations on how the wrong-doers should be handled. The presiding officer then appointed several Klansmen to attend to a particular individual and specified the type of punishment to be administered. No member of a punishment squad was to reveal the names of his fellow regulators, not even to other Klansmen, on fear of banishment from the Klan. If the Klokann feared that the victim would recognize his assailants, the council might call in Klansmen from a neighboring Klan to perform the vigilante work.[12]

There were a few occasions when the Klan used what might be termed "front" organizations to carry out its cleanup operations in towns and areas. During the early part of 1922, Klan organizers moved into the Ozark Mountain region of northern Arkansas. In kluxing the towns of the Ozark counties the Kleagles profited from the resentment many conservative people in the area felt against the striking workers on the Missouri and North Arkansas railroad line. The strike, which began in the summer of 1921, lasted throughout 1922 and into the next year. Strong Klans were organized in Harrison, Heber Springs, Marshall, and other towns in the Ozarks. Hostility between union members and nonunion citizens grew steadily as the strike crippled the economic life of the towns along the M. & N.A., and as the workers, becoming increasingly desperate, began blowing up railroad trestles and sabotaging locomotive engines.[13] The nonunion element, many of them Klansmen, countered by forming "Citizens' Committees" in various towns. There is evidence that the local Klans served as nuclei for the committees, although the

[12] These facts were disclosed by "a former federal agent who is a former Klansman," reported in New Orleans *Times-Picayune*, January 10, 1923.

[13] The issues of Little Rock *Arkansas Gazette* and Fort Smith *Southwest American* for the autumn months of 1922 are full of accounts of the strikers' sabotage activities.

citizens' groups unquestionably included scores of individuals who did not belong to the order.

A citizens' organization calling itself the "Committee of 1,000" went into action at Harrison on January 16, 1923, and at Eureka Springs, Heber Springs, and elsewhere the next day. At Harrison a band of men wearing black masks lynched a striker named E. C. Gregor and flogged a businessman and strike sympathizer, George W. O'Neal. A "Citizens' Court" of twelve members, wholly extralegal, assumed authority in Harrison and began quizzing strikers brought before the kangaroo court by armed vigilantes. The Citizens' Court listed a member from each of twelve towns along the M. & N.A.—Harrison, Leslie, Marshall, St. Joe, Everton, Alpena, Green Forest, Berryville, Eureka Springs, Western Grove, Jasper, and Heber Springs. The regular courts, under the dominance of the Committee of 1,000 and the Citizens' Court, quickly sentenced two strikers to prison. The Citizens' Court also forced the city council at Harrison to resign and decreed the expulsion of strikers and their families from Boone, Carroll, Marion, and Searcy counties. Soon every place of business in the M. & N.A. towns displayed a placard proclaiming that the proprietor was "100 Per Cent for the Railroad."[14]

The Arkansas legislature appointed a joint committee to investigate the disturbances in Harrison and the other towns. Hundreds of witnesses, union and nonunion, appeared before the legislative committee, which held sessions at both Little Rock and Harrison. One member of the Citizens' Committee of Heber Springs testified that the organization had several squads led by captains to take whatever measures were necessary to curb the strikers' activities. He also said that there was an "inner organization" which "knew about what was going to happen, something similar in character to the Ku Klux Klan; an

[14] Fort Smith *Southwest American,* January 17-21, 1923; Little Rock *Arkansas Gazette,* same dates.

organization which seemed to function but which nobody knew anything about."[15] The legislative investigating committee listened to weeks of testimony but was unable to establish a definite connection between the Citizens' Committee and the lynching of Gregor, or to identify the individuals responsible for the violence in the railroad towns. In its report to Governor Thomas C. McRae, submitted more than four months after the breaking of the strike, the investigating committee made no recommendations for action and refused to assess blame for the antiunion disturbances.[16]

Episodes of Klan violence transpiring in the four states of the Southwest are too numerous and too repetitious in character for all to be mentioned. Examples of assaults carried out by hooded night-riders in Texas included the tarring and feathering of D. L. Matthews of Beaumont on two separate occasions; the flogging and expulsion from San Augustine County, in east Texas, of jitney driver Charles Sisson; the whipping of B. F. Clark, a constable at Mineral Wells, Palo Pinto County; the vicious beating of a man and woman accused of adultery in the oilfields outside Goose Creek, southeast of Houston; the lashing of storeclerk Ray Daniels at Marshall, a thriving east Texas market town. Each of these cases involved some alleged moral offense or violation of the prohibition laws by the victim.[17] Only one of these episodes, the attack on the man and woman near Houston, brought indictments from a grand jury, and in that case twelve admitted members of Goose Creek Klan No. 8 got off with fines of $100 each. "It cost Goose Creek just $1200 to clean up," exulted the editor of a pro-Klan weekly newspaper. "It cost the boys

[15] Fort Smith *Southwest American*, February 2, 1923.
[16] Little Rock *Arkansas Gazette*, April 29, 1923.
[17] San Antonio *Express*, January 12, 22, 1922; Fort Worth *Star-Telegram*, July 8, 11, 1922; Denison *Herald*, March 2, 1922; Austin *Statesman*, January 13, 17, May 6, 1923; Dallas *Morning News*, July 6, 26, 1923.

down there $1200 to transform a rough and tumble oil camp into a progressive and God-fearing community of industrious toilers. . . . The Ku Klux Klan has made a new and different town of Goose Creek."[18]

Examples of Klan truculence were not nearly as numerous in Arkansas as in the other southwestern states, perhaps because the Klan got a late start in the Wonder State and, outside of Little Rock, grew slowly. Yet Arkansas Klansmen committed their share of physical attacks on sinners. Early in 1922 the Nashville Klan sent Joel Harris, an old man, and Walter H. Gibbs, his young friend and protector, warning notes about keeping Negro women. When two carloads of vigilantes clad in overalls and gunnysack masks tried to kidnap the two men, Gibbs fired at the assailants from inside his and Harris' house. The maskers riddled the house with buckshot, killing Gibbs, and then seized Harris and beat him with a plank. The sheriff of Ward County conducted a brief inquiry and announced that he was destitute of clues.[19] In July of the next year a mob of 75 to 100 men, some of them wearing regular Klan garb, others in black robes and hoods, entered the bunkhouse of the El Dorado Natural Gas and Petroleum Company, seized rigworker Eddie Foreman, and whipped him severely for making advances to a Klansman's wife. Sheriff Hancock of Union County arrested five men for the attack on Foreman and charged them with night-riding, a felony in Arkansas. But the grand jury failed to return indictments, and the five accused floggers went free.[20]

Hooded moralists were especially active in Oklahoma, so

[18] Houston *Colonel Mayfield's Weekly,* July 28, 1923.
[19] Little Rock *Arkansas Gazette,* March 21, 22, 1922.
[20] *Ibid.,* July 7, 8, 20, 1923; New Orleans *Times-Picayune,* same dates. The official Klan regalia of course consisted of white robes and hoods, but it appears that some Klan chapters also had black robes and hoods, which the Klansmen wore during their night-riding work.

much so that a power-hungry governor, attempting to cover up the ineptness and corruption of his administration, could use the Oklahoma Klan's penchant for violence as an excuse for putting the entire state under martial law. The account of John C. Walton's war with the Klan during the summer and fall of 1923, culminating in his removal from the governorship, properly belongs in a political context, and consequently that story is reserved for a later chapter. But the testimony given before the military courts established in different parts of the state provided some startling revelations of the Klan's night-riding career in Oklahoma.[21]

National guardsmen, sometimes working with county authorities, arrested about forty men in Tulsa, Oklahoma, Creek, Wagoner, Pottawatomie, and other counties during the course of military rule in Oklahoma. Hundreds of witnesses testified before the military courts, many of them victims of assaults by masked bands. Most of the deeds of violence disclosed under the martial law regime occurred during 1922. There was, for example, the case of Edward S. Merriman, an Oklahoma City cabdriver abducted from a restaurant the night of March 7, 1922, by two men posing as law officers. The two men threw Merriman into an automobile and drove to a spot outside town, where about eight carloads of white-robed men accused him of immorality with a young woman in Oklahoma City, whipped him with a rope, and told him to leave town. Merriman returned to Oklahoma City after a month's absence and gave the names of eighteen men he believed were among his attackers to the county attorney's office.

[21] Unfortunately the writer was unable to locate transcripts of the hearings before the various military courts. Adjutant General Roy W. Kenny of the state of Oklahoma informed the writer (January 11, 1962) that the records were not in his office and he had no idea where they might be. The governor's office made public some of the testimony through the newspapers at the time of the hearings. Howard A. Tucker, a confidant of Governor Walton, also had access to the testimony for the preparation of his polemical history of Walton's fight on the Klan, cited in n. 11 above.

The authorities did nothing. A few days later his employer threatened to fire him if he did not withdraw his charges, but he refused. A former member of Oklahoma City Klan No. 1, Dr. A. A. Maupin, swore that N. Clay Jewett, the Grand Dragon of the Realm of Oklahoma, told him regarding the Merriman affair: "I am the man who led that one, I led that party, and I know what I was doing. I am the fellow who held the whip and put it on his back and made him confess." The military court charged Jewett with whipping Merriman and had him arrested. But the Grand Dragon soon established an alibi, and the military authorities dropped their charges.[22]

John K. Smitherman, a prominent Tulsa Negro, testified that about 2 A.M. on March 10, 1922, three masked men forced him from his home, beat him with a pistol butt when he struggled with them, and shoved him into an automobile. He was driven to a hillside near Tulsa, where he faced twelve men, eight masked by handkerchiefs, four unmasked. Smitherman said he was handcuffed around a tree and accused of registering Negroes to vote in the Democratic primaries and of being discourteous to a Tulsa white woman. A little man spat in his face; the maskers then lashed him with a blacksnake whip. After the whipping, the little man cut off Smitherman's ear with a pocketknife and tried to make the Negro eat the ear, all the time beating him with the butt end of the whip. The regulators finally left Smitherman with a warning to get out of the state, but he remained in Tulsa.[23]

During the summer of 1922, at the little southeastern Oklahoma town of Broken Bow in McCurtain County, a group of robed and hooded Klansmen kidnaped a middle-

[22] Tucker, *Governor Walton's Klan War*, 22-24; Dr. A. A. Maupin's testimony before the Oklahoma City military court, reported in Oklahoma City *Daily Oklahoman*, September 21, 1923. See also *Daily Oklahoman*, September 22, 23, October 11, 1923.

[23] Tucker, *Governor Walton's Klan War*, 28-32; Tulsa *Tribune*, September 24, 1923.

aged married couple, Joe and Annie Pike, from their home. The Klansmen accused the Pikes of brewing Choctaw beer, an intoxicating beverage made from an Indian recipe, and flogged them both. At the time Mrs. Pike wore only a nightgown. The Pikes related the story to officials in Governor Walton's office, adding that they had gone to the county authorities several times but had never received any serious attention.[24]

In Tulsa County alone, military authorities filed charges of night-riding and assault against thirty-one citizens, all of whom eventually admitted membership in the Klan. Four of the defendants confessed to participating in flogging parties and promised to aid the state's investigations in exchange for light prison sentences. Only one of the convicted Klansmen, Constable William Finley of Broken Arrow, ever served any time in the state penitentiary at McAlester; and he soon was pardoned by Martin E. Trapp, who became governor after the Oklahoma legislature impeached and ousted Walton. The other three Klansmen remained in Tulsa until the spring of 1924, when the state, now under the Trapp administration, vacated their sentences and discharged them. Later they were fined twenty-five dollars apiece in court of common pleas for assault and battery. In July the attorney general's office dropped charges against twenty-seven Tulsa County citizens implicated in twelve flogging episodes dating from November 28, 1921, to July 25, 1923.[25]

Walton found that martial law was not the answer to Klan violence. The imposition of military rule on Oklahoma accomplished very little except to speed Walton's ouster. The failure of the military courts and the attorney general's office to get wholesale convictions, despite abundant testimony from victims, demonstrated that arrests and

[24] Tucker, *Governor Walton's Klan War*, 36-38.
[25] Tulsa *Tribune*, August 24, 26, 27, November 4, 1923, February 29, March 30, June 13, July 19, 1924.

charges were of small benefit in the face of hostility from local civil authorities and citizens. But Walton could have learned this fact from the governor of Louisiana, who experienced similar frustration earlier in 1923 in his attempts to secure the convictions of Klansmen in the notorious Mer Rouge murder case.

Easily the most famous instance of Klan terrorism, and one of the best known murder cases of the 1920s, the Mer Rouge affair provides an illustration of the Klan's ability to move into an area and nourish longstanding jealousies and animosities between communities and citizens.[26] For twenty-five years a bitter rivalry had existed in Morehouse Parish, in northeastern Louisiana, between the towns of Bastrop and Mer Rouge. Bastrop, the parish seat, was a grimy town of about 3,000 people, dominated by the Baptist church and fiercely proud of the pulpmill and carbon plant located nearby. Mer Rouge, by contrast, was only a village, more easygoing than Bastrop, less "progressive," less puritanical. The Klan came to Morehouse Parish late in 1921. It quickly enlisted most of the adult males of Bastrop and the other towns in the parish—except Mer Rouge, the majority of whose inhabitants held the Klan in contempt. So the Klan became one more element in the bitterness between the people of the two Louisiana towns.[27]

In the spring of 1922 the membership of Morehouse Klan No. 34, with the acquiescence of Sheriff Fred Carpenter and his deputies, all Klansmen, instituted a vigorous drive for moral reform in the parish. Led by Exalted

[26] The contemporary coverage of the Mer Rouge cases in the newspapers and magazines was quite extensive. For periodical material dealing with the episode, see Robert L. Duffus, "Salesman of Hate: The Ku Klux Klan," *World's Work*, XLVI (May 1923), 31-38; Leonard L. Cline, "In Darkest Louisiana," *Nation*, CXVI (March 15, 1923), 292-93; "Murders of Mer Rouge," *Literary Digest*, LXXVI (January 13, 1923), 10-12; "Mer Rouge Murders Unpunished," *ibid.* (March 31, 1923), 10-11.

[27] This summary of the background for the murders is from Cline, "In Darkest Louisiana," *passim.*

Cyclops J. K. Skipwith, an irascible Civil War veteran in his seventies, Morehouse Klansmen broke into the homes of suspected bootleggers, ran a teenage girl out of town for immorality, and threatened to swoop down "100 strong" to wipe out liquor-making and concubinage in Mer Rouge. The Klan haters of Mer Rouge cursed the Klan and dared Skipwith and his raiders to invade the village. Among the most vocal opponents of the Klan were old J. L. Daniel, a wealthy Mer Rouge planter; his son F. Watt Daniel, a graduate of Louisiana State University; and Watt Daniel's friend Thomas F. Richards, a garage mechanic.[28]

Early in August 1922, Dr. B. M. McKoin of Mer Rouge, leader of the Morehouse Klan's whipping squad, returned from a professional night call with a bullet hole in the front seat of his automobile. McKoin said someone had fired on him from ambush. The Klansmen in Bastrop and the rest of the parish were convinced that Watt Daniel and Richards, who had threatened to kill the physician, were the ones who fired the shot. Wearing black robes and hoods, their raiding attire, the Klansmen kidnaped Richards in broad daylight from the Bastrop garage where he worked and quizzed him about his threats on McKoin's life. When Richards remained silent, the Klansmen released him unharmed. A few days later Watt Daniel stumbled upon a moonlight meeting of Klansmen in a wooded area near Mer Rouge. "Old Skip" or "Captain" Skipwith, as the aged Cyclops was called, and other Klansmen held guns on Daniel while they warned him to behave and stop talking about the Klan.[29]

On August 24 the people of Morehouse Parish gathered

[28] *Ibid.*

[29] The facts included in this discussion of the kidnapings came from the testimony given by various witnesses before the open hearing held in Bastrop during January of 1923. Dozens of newspapers over the nation carried the wire releases on the murders, but for firsthand coverage of the testimony during the open hearing, the writer has relied on the issues for January 6 to 26, 1923, of New York *Times,* New Orleans *Times-Picayune,* and Shreveport *Journal.*

in Bastrop for a "good roads" bond rally, picnic, and base-
ball game. After the festivities a train of about fifty automobiles started the seven-mile drive back to Mer Rouge.
About halfway between the two towns a score or more of
black-robed and hooded men stopped the procession and
began walking down the line of cars, peering closely into
each vehicle. At gunpoint they forced Watt Daniel, Richards, J. L. Daniel, W. C. Andrews, and C. C. "Tot" Davenport from their cars and ordered the drivers of the other
vehicles to proceed to Mer Rouge. That was the last time
Watt Daniel and Richards were seen alive. Late that night,
Andrews and J. L. Daniel wandered onto the Collinston
road, their backs lacerated by leather straps. Davenport
appeared in Mer Rouge uninjured. Still later in the night
a family sleeping in their car near Lake Lafourche, south
of Bastrop, saw an automobile and a runabout truck filled
with black-hooded men speeding toward the lake. Two
blindfolded men sat in the bed of the truck. About forty-
five minutes later the car and truck reappeared, but this
time minus the two blindfolded men. In Bastrop, Skipwith ordered a telephone operator to terminate service between the parish seat and Mer Rouge; after she refused, the
telephone lines were cut.

The Morehouse Parish grand jury met in September. In
all likelihood a majority of its members were Klansmen.
At any rate, the grand jury conducted a hurried investigation of the disappearance of Watt Daniel and Richards
and the flogging of the elder Daniel and Andrews. Its report did not even mention the incident, although the
grand jurors noted, ironically, that "there was a marked
decrease in crime in Morehouse Parish since the last grand
jury was in session."[30]

Open warfare impended between the Klansmen in Bastrop and the anti-Klan faction in Mer Rouge. Mrs. Richards and a group of Mer Rouge citizens appealed to

[30] New Orleans *Times-Picayune,* September 9, 1922.

Governor John M. Parker, who answered: "Neither mob violence nor the Ku Klux Klan shall run this state." Parker reopened the case and offered a reward of $500 for the arrest and conviction of the kidnapers. "Old Skip" wrote a public letter to Parker condemning the reopening of the case and accusing the governor of "aligning yourself with a lot of midnight assassins and open law violators in Morehouse Parish."[31] In November, Parker and Attorney General Adolph V. Coco journeyed to Washington to ask President Harding and Attorney General Harry M. Daugherty for a few Department of Justice investigators to help the state's inquiry into the kidnapings. This brought cries of federal interference and denunciations of the governor from Representative James B. Aswell, in whose district Morehouse Parish was located, and other Louisiana public officials.[32] But Parker, now determined to crush the Klan, pressed his attack on the secret organization. He denounced the hooded order before various groups over the state. In return the Klan slammed the mustachioed governor as a political opportunist and charged him with working for the Democratic vice-presidential nomination in 1924. Baton Rouge Klansmen decorated the lawn of the governor's mansion with placards shaped like gravestones advertising a Klan initiation, and tied Parker's Airedale puppy to a tree.[33]

On December 19 Governor Parker declared Morehouse Parish under martial law. A Louisiana national guard detachment took positions around the courthouse at Bastrop, in Mer Rouge, and at Lakes Lafourche and Cooper, where divers began a search for the bodies of Daniel and Richards. Newspaper correspondents from over the nation swarmed into Bastrop, packing the town's lodging places

[31] *Ibid.*, September 10, 12, 1922.
[32] For material on Congressman Aswell's tilt with Parker, see James B. Aswell and Family Papers, scrapbook #15, pp. 131-39, Department of Archives, Louisiana State University, Baton Rouge.
[33] New Orleans *Times-Picayune*, November 29, 1922.

and exhausting its restaurant facilities. The local telegraph operator worked around the clock to send their pungent dispatches to newspapers in every part of the country. Three days after the declaration of martial law, a mysterious dynamite explosion in Lake Lafourche brought two badly decomposed bodies to the surface. Parker immediately dispatched Attorney General Coco, Assistant Attorney General T. Semmes Walmsley, and two New Orleans pathologists to examine the bodies and begin preparation of a case for the state. The pathologists identified one of the bodies as Watt Daniel by a belt buckle bearing the initials "F. W. D."; the other was identified as Richards because of the presence of patches of shirt material Richards wore the day he disappeared.[34]

Federal agents, cooperating with the state officials, arrested T. Jeff Burnett, a Bastrop Klansman, as one of the black-robed kidnapers. They also arrested McKoin, now in Baltimore doing postgraduate medical study, and brought him back to Bastrop.[35] Parker, Coco, and their subordinates arranged an "open hearing" to aid the investigation of the kidnapings and murders. Such a hearing made it possible for any citizen to come forward and testify about anything he had seen, heard, or suspected in connection with the crime. The attorney general's office, assuming that District Attorney David I. Garrett and his staff in Morehouse Parish were under the dominance of the Klan, now relied for the establishment of its case solely on evidence secured by the federal operatives or disclosed in the hearing.

During the open hearing, the grand jury investigation that followed, and the whole course of the Mer Rouge cases, the state contended that the bodies found in the lake were those of Watt Daniel and Richards; that they had been

[34] New York *Times,* December 20, 1922, p. 1, December 21, p. 6, December 23, p. 12; New Orleans *Times-Picayune,* same dates.

[35] New York *Times,* December 26, 1922, pp. 1, 3, December 27, pp. 1-2, January 4, 1923, p. 21.

murdered and thrown in the lake by a band of about seventy-five Klansmen from Morehouse, Franklin, Richland, and West Carroll parishes in Louisiana and two Arkansas counties; and that the killings were part of a systematic reign of terror carried out by the Klan in north Louisiana. The official Klan version of the affair, reiterated by local Klansmen and national officials, was that Watt Daniel and Richards were whipped by unknown parties, but not by Klansmen; that they simply ran away after the whippings and were still alive; and that the bodies in Lake Lafourche were cadavers from a medical school "planted" by the state.

The state called more than fifty witnesses during the open hearing, which lasted from January 5 to 25, 1923. Klansmen, ex-Klansmen, and anti-Klanners testified, some willingly, some reluctantly. The state established almost conclusively that members of Morehouse Klan No. 34 were among those responsible for the kidnaping and beating of J. L. and Watt Daniel, Richards, Andrews, and Davenport. But Coco and his aides were unable to prove that Klansmen actually murdered Watt Daniel and Richards and disposed of their bodies, or to show what Klansmen were involved in the beatings and killings. After the open hearing, the state took its findings before a new grand jury which, after listening to testimony from 125 witnesses, refused to return indictments because of "insufficient" evidence. "It is needless to say that I am highly elated," commented Skipwith, the venerable Cyclops, before he embarked on a speaking tour to tell Klansmen in other states about the "frameup" in Morehouse. "The state has done its duty and I hope it is satisfied and will let the matter rest."[36]

But the state would not let the matter rest. In April, Attorney General Coco had District Attorney Garrett file thirty-one bills of information against eighteen Morehouse

[36] New Orleans *Times-Picayune,* March 16, 1923.

Klansmen for conspiracy to kidnap, assault with deadly weapons, unlawfully carrying firearms, and other offenses, all misdemeanors. All of the charges pertained to offenses committed before the disappearance of Daniel and Richards. Among those named in the bills were Skipwith, his son Oliver, McKoin, and T. Jeff Burnett. Shortly before the misdemeanor trials were heard in district court in Bastrop, the two pathologists who had identified the bodies in Lake Lafourche as Watt Daniel and Richards made a disclosure that threw a shadow over the state's entire case. The pathologists said that the bodies could not have been in the lake three months, as the state contended, and that they were there not more than forty-eight hours. Yet the state had ignored this piece of information during the open hearing and the grand jury investigation. In May of 1924, just before Parker vacated the governorship, the head of the Louisiana Department of Health wrote the governor that national guardsmen had prevented the parish coroner from examining the decomposed bodies and that the coroner had never signed a death certificate.[37] It appears that the state's conduct during the inquiries in Morehouse was questionable in at least some respects.

Parker's and Coco's continued prosecution of the Klansmen on misdemeanor charges ultimately came to have the appearance of political spite. In November 1923 District Judge Fred Odum found Skipwith, Benton Pratt, Marvin Pickett, and W. G. McIntosh guilty of "carrying firearms on the premises of another" while raiding a bootlegger, and fined them ten dollars each plus court costs. Before the judge could pass any more sentences, William C. Barnette of Shreveport, counsel for the Klan in Louisiana, demanded that Odum withdraw from the case because of his prejudice against the defendants. When the judge refused, Barnette filed notice of appeal to the state supreme

[37] *Ibid.*, April 19, October 31, 1923; Shreveport *Journal*, May 21, 1924.

court. That was the last of the state's prosecutions. The supreme court refused to uphold Barnette's appeal, but the rest of the Morehouse cases were postponed until February of 1924, when the state dismissed its charges.[38] In such an obscure fashion the great Mer Rouge murder cases came quietly to an end. They remain on the list of unsolved crimes of the state of Louisiana.

Thus far the discussion of the Klan's drive for law and order has featured the order's direct and violent efforts. Yet there was more to the Klan's vigilantism than physical coercion. The white-robed reformers also used nonviolent methods to effect law enforcement and morality, and such activities could be fully as annoying and offensive, if not as physically painful, as the corporal attacks. One objective of the Klan's parades and cross burnings was to "put the fear of God" into whiskey makers and other evildoers. Local Klans frequently sent threatening notes bearing their official seals to errant citizens; regulatory "visits" might or might not follow the notes.[39] If the Klansmen were dissatisfied with the status of law enforcement in their communities and counties, they often adopted resolutions in which they demanded better performance from their public officials. Harrisonburg, Louisiana, Klan No. 75, for example, cited the lawless condition of Catahoula Parish, where "the criminal and law-violating element . . . openly defies the Law, resist [sic] and threatens the life of the Sheriff and his deputies, holds the Law in contempt, openly and above board boasts of the fact that they handle the Judge, and that the District Attorney is easy." The resolution called on "all good citizens of this Parish whether you are Klans-

[38] Shreveport *Journal*, November 22, 24, December 6, 1923.
[39] For examples of threatening letters sent by Texas Klansmen, see Klan No. 27, Knights of the Ku Klux Klan of Edna to Sherell Carville, September 7, 1921, photographic copy, Oscar B. Colquitt Papers, University of Texas Archives, Austin; Ku Klux Klan to Judge James R. Hamilton, March 31, 1922, James R. Hamilton Papers, in possession of Mrs. Hamilton, Austin.

men or not to cooperate with us in seeing that the Law is enforced."[40]

Members of Denison Klan No. 113 in Texas donned their white robes and hoods to frighten amorous couples parking on the roads outside the town.[41] Houston Klansmen made a practice of tapping telephone wires over the city, intercepting messages at the telegraph offices, and maintaining spies in the city postoffice. "Klan spies would go out in a car with a listening set and tap the wire up the pole near the house they'd want to listen in on," related an ex-member of the Houston Klan.[42] The Klan continually admonished bootleggers to "bring in the stills" and halt their illegal business, and there were a number of occasions when Klansmen "captured" stills and deposited them in the middle of town. The Klan was always quite proud of these "citizens arrests" of liquor-making apparatus. Local chapters readily acknowledged their responsibility for such acts and received credit from law officers.[43]

Sometimes the Klan undertook veritable wars on bootleggers. Although these purification drives were supposed to be nonviolent, frequently they did not remain so. In November of 1922 two hundred members of the "Cleanup Committee" of Ouachita and Union counties in southern Arkansas, wearing the white robes and hoods of the Klan and representing the "better element" in the area, moved through the oilfields around Smackover, burning gambling dens, prostitute houses, and saloons. At one point twenty-five vice operators fought a gun battle with the vigilantes.

[40] Printed in *Caldwell* [Parish, La.] *Watchman*, July 13, 1923.

[41] Houston *Colonel Mayfield's Weekly*, August 4, 1923.

[42] Testimony of Fred A. Bryan and L. E. Ogilvie in *Knights of the Ku Klux Klan, Inc.* v. *George B. Kimbro, Jr.* (No. 105180) (61st District Court, Harris County, Texas), reported in Houston *Post-Dispatch*, March 25, 1925.

[43] See, for example, Atlanta *Searchlight*, March 18, 1922; Houston *Colonel Mayfield's Weekly*, April 21, 1923; Little Rock *Arkansas Gazette*, April 17, 1922; Fort Smith *Southwest American*, November 4, 1922.

One anti-Klanner was shot down as he tried to escape the Klansmen, and about a dozen other people were flogged, tarred, and feathered. Sheriff Ed Harper of Ouachita County finally arrived after the rioting had ended. He estimated that the white-clad regulators drove about two thousand "undesirables" from the oilfields.[44]

The Klan's preoccupation with morality and crime in the Southwest led Klansmen to enter local politics in an effort to control the law enforcement machinery in towns and counties. Practically every city in the Southwest came under the dominance of the Klan, as well as numerous smaller communities and hundreds of county governments. But the Klan did not stop with electing sheriffs, mayors, and prosecuting attorneys; it sought control of jury commissions, judges, and even the juries themselves. Lee Cazort, the Klan's candidate for governor of Arkansas in the 1924 campaign, bragged about the order's law enforcement program in his hometown and county. "In Johnson County," Cazort told the crowds, "we had a mighty crew of bootleggers and innumerable liquor dispensaries which were debauching the youth of Lamar and of the county. I joined the Klan and with others sat on juries and backed up the prosecuting attorney and circuit judge until we cleaned up Lamar and Johnson County."[45]

The Klan secured control of grand and trial juries for one purpose—to indict and convict. Except for Klansmen charged with night-riding, law violators in Klan-dominated communities could ordinarily expect convictions and hard sentences from biased juries and stern judges. By the spring of 1925 the Klan was on the decline in most areas of the Southwest, but Lake Charles, Louisiana, in the western part of the state, was one town where the Invisible Empire remained supreme. That spring two bootleggers, Byron and

---

[44] Shreveport *Journal,* November 29, 30, 1922; Little Rock *Arkansas Gazette,* same dates.
[45] Little Rock *Arkansas Gazette,* July 4, 1924.

Robert Dunn, were arrested, tried, and convicted for the murder of Deputy Sheriff Sam E. Duhon of Calcasieu Parish. The Dunns received death sentences from District Judge Jerry Cline. Attorneys for the two condemned men appealed to the state supreme court, which in 1926 upheld the decision handed down in the district court.[46]

The Dunns applied for writs of habeas corpus before state district court in Baton Rouge, the state board of pardons, federal district court in Monroe, and the United States Supreme Court, and for stays of execution before Governor Oramel H. Simpson. In all of their appeals and petitions the Dunns maintained that the court in Lake Charles that convicted them was controlled by the Klan and that as a consequence they did not receive a fair trial and were denied due process of law. Specifically they charged that District Judge Cline, Sheriff J. Horace Lyons, and Court Clerk E. Claude House were charter members of Lake Charles Klan No. 7, and that several Klansmen lied about their membership in the organization to get on the jury, including a relative of Duhon, the victim. They also charged that wealthy businessman and Klansman William K. Gray sat beside the judge with a pistol in his pocket; that Paul D. Perkins, a former state official of the Klan, made hand signals to the jury throughout the trial; and that the Klan threatened two witnesses until they refused to testify in the defendants' behalf.[47] In 1928, after the Supreme Court had denied the Dunns' second appeal, Governor Simpson commuted Robert Dunn's sentence to life imprisonment. Byron Dunn died on the gallows, long after the organization that had helped to convict him had ceased to be an important factor in Louisiana society.[48]

The Klan worked through the legal processes to impose

[46] State v. Dunn et al., 109 So. 56.

[47] New Orleans Times-Picayune, June 20-24, 1927; Dunn v. Louisiana 273 U.S. 656.

[48] Dunn v. Lyons, 276 U.S. 622; Shreveport Journal, January 27, 1928.

its ideas of morality and law and order, as long as it had any strength in an area. But after 1923 the order virtually ceased to use "direct action" methods—threats, intimidations, beatings, unauthorized liquor raids. The main reason for the decline of vigilantism was the Klan's increasing entanglement in politics, not only in the Southwest, but throughout the nation.

The Klan's entry into politics resulted largely from the machinations of one man—Hiram Wesley Evans, former Exalted Cyclops of Dallas Klan No. 66. Evans, like Simmons, was a native of Alabama, where he was born in 1881 in the town of Ashland. He came to Texas before the war and set up a profitable dental practice in Dallas. He was a charter member of the Dallas Klan and its first Exalted Cyclops. Lacking eloquence, but possessing an attractive frankness and a great deal of determination, the stout Evans became a "Great Titan," or district leader, when the Realm of Texas was organized early in 1922. In the spring of that year, Simmons appointed Evans Imperial Kligrapp (national secretary), from which office the Dallasite could exert great power. At Evans' instigation the Klan jumped into state and local primaries and elections in various parts of the country, but especially in the southwestern states. The new emphasis on politics brought a deemphasis of the Klan's terrorist activities.[49]

In November of 1922, at the first Imperial Klonvocation, or national convention, of the Klan, Evans won election to the Imperial Wizardship, thereby seizing control of the order from the Simmons-Clarke faction.[50] Evans quickly moved to strengthen the order's political potential by changing several aspects of Klan practice. He realized that the Simmons-Clarke policy of paying little attention to

[49] Biographical material on Evans from Stanley Frost, *The Challenge of the Klan* (Indianapolis, 1924); Winfield Jones, *Knights of the Ku Klux Klan* (New York, 1941), 246.

[50] See William G. Shepherd, "Fiery Double Cross," *Collier's*, LXXXII (July 28, 1928), 8-9, 47, 48-49.

local Klan doings, as long as the chapters remitted the proper amount of money to Atlanta, made possible the terrorist operations for which the order had become notorious. He also realized that vigilantism weakened the Klan's political force by creating opposition which would not form otherwise. Hence the new Imperial Wizard instituted several "reforms" in an effort to erase the common conception of Klansmen riding through the night to punish wrongdoers. Under the Evans regime an attempt was made, at least ostensibly, to rid the order of lawless elements, and national headquarters denounced any chapter that engaged in violence. Evans decreed that robes and hoods could be taken from the local meeting place, the Klavern, only for use at official Klan functions like parades, initiations, or church visitations. The Klan sent nine Imperial investigators to Morehouse Parish, Louisiana, during the open hearing on the Watt Daniel and Richards murders, theoretically to see if the state's allegations were true. If the Klan sleuths found anything, they never made public their findings.[51]

The new Klan policy of discouraging violence was based strictly on political ambitions and a desire to improve the organization's public relations; it did not mean that Imperial Wizard Evans and his associates at Atlanta were any more humanitarian than their predecessors. While Exalted Cyclops in Dallas, back in April of 1921, Evans allegedly had led a party of Klansmen in the kidnaping and acid-branding of Negro bellhop and suspected panderer Alex Johnson.[52]

Evans' edicts controlling use of regalia and his policy of eliminating vigilantism in favor of political action did eventually bring a halt to Klan terrorism, at least in the

[51] Arnold S. Rice, *The Ku Klux Klan in American Politics* (Washington, 1962), 10-11; Stanley Frost, "When the Klan Rules: The Giant Clears for Action," *Outlook*, CXXXV (December 26, 1923), 717-18; New York *Times*, October 31, 1923, p. 19.

[52] Clark testimony, *Senator from Texas Hearings*, 117-18.

states of the Southwest. The spring and summer of 1923 saw a brief renewal of masked violence in Texas and Oklahoma. In Texas, Lieutenant Governor T. W. Davidson sent Texas Rangers to various parts of the state to help the county authorities apprehend the floggers.[53] In Oklahoma the outbreak of night-riding brought the entire state under martial law. But by late 1923 the truculent phase of the Klan's career in Texas and Oklahoma, and in Arkansas and Louisiana as well, had about ended.

The Mer Rouge revelations, the disclosures before the Oklahoma military courts, and the publicity given to other instances of Klan coercion probably contributed to growing opposition to the Klan in some areas. In the fall of 1923, in Texas, a Klansman was convicted and sentenced to two years in prison for flogging a traveling salesman in Williamson County. In Amarillo another Klansman received a two-year sentence for "whitecapping," threatening a person while disguised, although the conviction was later reversed in criminal appeals court.[54] In the spring of 1924 two Klansmen at Altus, Oklahoma, were convicted of assaulting a man on the highway outside town a year earlier. They received two-year sentences, which the criminal court of appeals upheld.[55] But it was mainly the Klan's attempts to achieve its objectives politically that brought an end to two and a half years of night-riding.

What can be said of the Klan's reign of repression? Stanley Frost, from his observations in Oklahoma, credited the Klan with working for public morality, with carrying out an effective drive against crime, and with organizing public opinion behind law enforcement.[56] Yet Frost is

[53] Dallas *Morning News*, August 19, September 9, December 12, 1923.
[54] *Ibid.*, April 15, September 25, October 10, 11, 1923; *Murray Jackson* v. *State*, 103 Texas Crim. Rep. 318; *T. W. Stanford* v. *State*, 99 Texas Crim. Rep. 111.
[55] *Perkins et al.* v. *State*, 250 Pac. 544.
[56] Frost, "Night Riding Reformers," 438.

about the only spokesman one can find outside the Klan who believed the violent activities of the order had any truly commendable effect.

In the mid-1920s newspaper editors still pointed with alarm to the mounting crime rate, while young men and women still went for nocturnal automobile rides and parked on the roadside. Drunken husbands still beat their wives and deserted their families. Bootleggers still corrupted public officials and operated without hindrance throughout the nation. After nearly three years of organized terrorism and meddling in other people's affairs, the Klan had accomplished little in the way of moral and social reform.

The major effect of the Klan's brutal efforts at community uplift was adverse—the alienation of thousands of people who shared the outlook of the Klansmen on matters of morals, race, and religion. Although the Klan may have "cleaned up" a few places, although it tried to match its deeds of violence with a highly organized program of philanthrophy, and although it later discarded force for political action, thoughtful persons must have seen the incongruity of hooded zealots, intent on law enforcement, taking the law into their own hands. And even many Klansmen could not help realizing that such actions in the name of law and order only incited others to lawlessness.

5.

Gestures of Peace

NOEL P. GIST, a student of American fraternalism, has offered as many as twelve categories for modern secret societies. Although Gist classified the Klan as a "patriotic" society, the sheeted fraternity might also fit into at least four other divisions for secret organizations—"benevolent and philanthropic," "insurance," "religious," and "convivial."[1] Initially in the southern and southwestern states the Klan was a vigilante organization, an instrument of masked terrorism that threatened and punished people suspected of "objectionable" behavior. For most of its leaders under the Simmons-Clarke regime the Klan was also a moneymaking scheme, and the opportunity for financial gain remained a strong attraction for the men who supposedly "reformed" the organization under Evans. In practically every state where it was very strong the Klan evolved into a political machine at both local and state levels.

As a rule, the Klan's vigilantism, its political machinations, and its practice of hiding behind a mask were the features that inspired the most opposition among people who might share the order's ideological framework. On

the other hand, the average white Protestant did not mind
the Klan's posturing as a militant wing of American Protestantism. He ordinarily did not care if the local Knights
paraded, held their mysterious and entertaining public initiations, or carried on the other activities of an adult fraternal order. If members of the local Klan gave money to
widows or the town's poor at Christmas, this was accepted
as a sincere manifestation of the benevolent spirit; the
Klan's charitable ventures seemed particularly admirable
in a period of parsimony in public affairs. Whatever else
there was objectionable about the Klan, people in the
Southwest and in the rest of the nation generally found little
fault in the religious, charitable, and fraternal phases of its
career. Indeed, these aspects sometimes seemed to excuse
the numerous acts of violence and terrorism.

A fervent religiosity pervaded almost every facet of the
Klan movement. "I've attended a lot of church gatherings
and conventions," remarked a Pennsylvania Exalted Cyclops who went to the Klan's 1924 national convention, "but
I never attended one where the revival spirit was as pronounced as it was at the Klan Klonvocation."[2] And this
revival spirit was evident in practically everything the
Klansmen did. The crusading zeal most hooded Knights
possessed largely accounts for their devotion to the Klan
and their fierce loyalty in the face of corruption, ineptness,
and cynicism on the part of many of their leaders.

Religious symbolism was sprinkled throughout Klan
thought and practice. The Klan's initiation ritual, oath of
allegiance, and numerous official documents of the order
bristled with such phrases as "the tenets of the Christian
religion," "the law of Christ," "my witness, Almighty God,"
and "God being my helper." One of the officers of a local

[1] Noel P. Gist, *Secret Societies: A Cultural Study of Fraternalism in
the United States* (University of Missouri Studies, XV, October 1,
1940), 24.

[2] Quoted in Emerson H. Loucks, *The Ku Klux Klan in Pennsylvania: A Study in Nativism* (Harrisburg, 1936), 120.

Klan was the "Kludd," or chaplain, who ended each meeting with a benediction in which he reminded the brethren that "the living Christ is a Klansman's criterion of character."[3] The Klansmen then gathered before their altar, an essential piece of furniture in every Klavern, and sang a hymn called the "Kloxology" or some traditional Protestant hymn. Among hymns the Klansmen especially liked were "Blest Be the Tie That Binds," "When I Survey the Wondrous Cross," "The Old Rugged Cross," and "Onward, Christian Soldiers," the last piece becoming something of an unofficial anthem of the order.

When the Klan claimed to be the defender of "Protestant Americanism," it meant the Fundamentalist variety of Protestantism. To Klansmen, Modernist theology was nearly as inimical to the American way as Roman Catholicism. The Klan championed the "oldtime religion," although it would be a mistake to impute any official connection to the Klan and Fundamentalist movements of the twenties.[4] The white-robed movement and the Fundamentalist crusade, taking form in attempts to eradicate Darwinian science from the public schools, stemmed from the same fearful reaction to change in the South and Southwest. But Biblical literalism was a basic assumption for an overwhelming majority of people in the two regions, and perhaps for citizens in the midwestern states. Most of the white Protestants who for one reason or another fought the Klan shared the order's notions concerning the divine character of the Scriptures.

In 1923 the Oklahoma house of representatives, with Klansmen comprising a substantial portion of its membership, passed a bill to provide free textbooks for children in the public schools of the state. The bill carried an

---

[3] *Kloran* (Klan ritual book), 2, quoted *ibid.,* 118.
[4] See Robert M. Miller, "A Note on the Relationship between the Protestant Churches and the Ku Klux Klan," *Journal of Southern History,* XXII (August 1956), 257-66; Norman F. Furniss, *The Fundamentalist Controversy, 1918-1931* (New Haven, 1954), 37-38.

amendment denying the textbooks to elementary and secondary schools that taught Darwin's theory of biological evolution. The state senate accepted the bill with the Fundamentalist amendment, and the measure became law. Two years later a legislature more concerned with economy than theology repealed the free textbook law, and thus the antievolution amendment. The same year that the Oklahoma solons acted against Modernism, several pro-Klan members of the Texas house of representatives introduced a bill to prohibit the teaching of evolution in the public schools. The bill passed the house but died in the senate. In 1929, long after the Klan had fallen apart in Texas, the state legislature passed a resolution urging the state textbook commission not to accept textbooks in which the Darwinian theory was taught. The Klan was no longer a factor in Louisiana politics and government in 1926, when the state house of representatives passed an antievolution bill which the senate killed by voting to postpone indefinitely. The next year a bill to prohibit the presentation of evolution to the state's children passed the Arkansas house of representatives, but as in Louisiana, the state senators voted to postpone its consideration indefinitely. In 1928, however, the people of Arkansas by referendum vote enacted an antievolution law.[5]

Hence, four of the six attempts Fundamentalists made in the southwestern legislatures to prohibit teaching of the Darwinian theory came after the Klan had passed its peak in the region. Klansmen and ex-Klansmen unquestionably

[5] Oklahoma City *Daily Oklahoman*, February 22, March 21, 1923; 38th Texas Legislature, *House Journal*, Regular Session, 49, 163, 185, 655, 1165, 1313, 1459; *ibid, Senate Journal*, 1064-66; 41st Texas Legislature, *House Journal*, 2d Called Session, 31, 112, 115, 217, 362-63, 487-88; New Orleans *Times-Picayune*, June 16, 22, 23, 1926; Louisiana General Assembly, *House Journal*, 3d Regular Session (1926), 167, 190, 575, 700, 762; *ibid., Senate Journal*, 597; 46th Arkansas General Assembly, *House Journal*, Regular Session, 68, 78, 277.

supported these later legislative drives for theological orthodoxy, but they were joined by thousands of non-Klan Southwesterners. And the best the Klan as an organization could
do was to help attach an ephemeral Fundamentalist amendment to a free textbook law.

Throughout the nation, thousands of Protestant ministers
(one Klan lecturer estimated the number at 40,000) took
citizenship in the Invisible Empire.[6] Others, while not joining the Klan, looked kindly on the order and encouraged
the male members of their flocks to join. While it was on
the rise in the Southwest, the Klan made constant overtures
to the Fundamentalist ministers. These overtures included
posing as the preserver of the conservative moral code, making war on bootleggers, contributing money to impover-
ished preachers and their churches, and exhorting Klansmen to be "one hundred percent Christian" and "go to
church every Sunday; give your support and encouragement to your ministers; send your children to Sunday
school."[7]

The most familiar device Klansmen used to demonstrate
their devotion to Protestantism was the church visitation,
which served remarkably well to publicize the order's religiosity. A rather popular procedure followed by southwestern Klansmen when they called on a church featured
an unannounced appearance by Knights in full regalia,
including hood visors worn down. Klansmen would enter
a church abruptly, march down the aisle to the pulpit, in-
terrupt the minister in the midst of the service, give him
an envelope, usually full of money, and march from the
building to their waiting automobiles. Or perhaps one of
the Klansmen would use the occasion to deliver a short talk
to the surprised congregation on the principles of the Klan.

[6] The figure is one given by the Reverend John H. Moore, a Klan
lecturer, in a speech in Little Rock, reported in Little Rock *Arkansas
Gazette*, July 11, 1923.

[7] Atlanta *Searchlight*, December 1, 1923.

The donation the minister found when he opened the envelope was usually large enough to compensate for whatever irritation he felt at the interruption of his service.[8]

The Klan pictured itself as the great unifying force in a divided American Protestantism, the essence of a solid front against the Roman Catholic menace. Within some churches and congregations, however, the Klan frequently became a source of trouble. In the Baptist churches at Denison and Austin in Texas and at Tullas, near Monroe, Louisiana, wrestling bouts and fist fights broke out when Klansmen entered the places of worship and encountered the ire of anti-Klan church members. An Apostolic congregation at DeQuincy, Louisiana, forced its minister to resign when he refused to return a donation given him by Klansmen.[9] In 1924 a newspaper correspondent reported from Winn Parish in Louisiana: "Efforts are being made to bring . . . a more harmonious state . . . among the churches. Feeling concerning the Klan has been so intense for more than a year that many of the churches have been divided in their congregations and very little work has been done along religious lines."[10] And a former member of the Klan at Corsicana, Texas, told how the local chapter brought pressure on the ministers of the town to join the order. The Presbyterian pastor refused, whereupon the leaders of his church, all Klansmen, advised him to resign. When the congregation voted on the matter, "All that voted

[8] For accounts of Klan church visitations, see, for example, Little Rock *Arkansas Gazette*, March 6, 7, 1922; Tulsa *Tribune*, March 20, 1922; Shreveport *Journal*, May 29, July 11, 1922; New Orleans *Times-Picayune*, June 21, 1922; Houston *Colonel Mayfield's Weekly*, October 7, December 30, 1922, May 5, 1923; Fort Worth *Star-Telegram*, August 1, 8, 1922; Galveston *Daily News*, December 17, 1923. The size of the donation left by Klansmen varied with the size of the local Klan, but donations as large as $300 were not uncommon.

[9] Denison *Herald*, April 3, 1922; Austin *Statesman*, August 15, 1922; Little Rock *Arkansas Gazette*, August 23, 1923; New Orleans *Times-Picayune*, July 3, 1923.

[10] Shreveport *Journal*, May 15, 1924.

against the preacher, they were families of the Ku-Klux
organization . . . [But] everybody that was against the
Ku-Klux was with the preacher." The anti-Klanners won
the balloting, and the harassed divine stayed on with his
troubled church.[11]

Undoubtedly many Protestant ministers sighed thank-
fully when the Klan disintegrated in their communities and
they no longer had to endure the vicissitudes of pastoring
a congregation rent by the Klan issue. But during its heyday a large number of them had embraced the secret society. The Klan looked like an ally to "fire and brimstone"
clergymen engaged in the exorcism of liquor and vice. Such
ministers agreed with a Wichita Falls, Texas, pastor, who
declared that "there has never been a time . . . when there
was so much freedom among the sexes . . . and so much
light thinking, frivolous thinking about the serious things
in social life and moral life."[12] They perhaps even con-
curred with the minister who "bless[ed] God that men of
high standing and clean and cool judgment have banded
themselves in an order that demands law enforcement and
local reforms."[13]

Some Protestant clergymen left their congregations and
became itinerant lecturers for the Klan. These included,
in Texas, J. T. Renfro (Methodist) of Dallas and Alonzo
Monk (Methodist) of Arlington; in Oklahoma, Stephen B.
Williams (Presbyterian) of Muskogee; in Louisiana, William McDougald (Presbyterian) of New Orleans; and in
Arkansas, Harry G. Knowles (Disciples of Christ) of Little

[11] Testimony of W. H. Castles in *Senator from Texas. Hearings before a Subcommittee of the Committee on Privileges and Elections,
United States Senate,* 67th Congress, 1st and 2d Sessions (1924),
994-96.

[12] The Reverend H. D. Knickerbocker, pastor of the First Methodist Church in Wichita Falls, quoted in Houston *Colonel Mayfield's
Weekly,* December 10, 1921.

[13] The Reverend Harry G. Knowles of the First Christian Church
in Little Rock, quoted in Little Rock *Arkansas Gazette,* April 3, 1922.

Rock and John H. Moore (Baptist) of Pine Bluff. The traveling evangelists of the day, men like B. B. Crimm, Bob Jones, Charlie Taylor, and "faith healer" Raymond T. Richey, frequently devoted part of their messages to laudation of the Klan. Even Billy Sunday, the greatest revivalist of the early twentieth century, spent some time praising the Klan and accepting contributions from prosperous chapters.[14]

Several of the best known leaders of the Klan in the southwestern states were ordained Protestant ministers. Dr. A. D. Ellis, rector of St. Mark's Episcopal Church in Beaumont, briefly held the office of Grand Dragon of the Realm of Texas. The Reverend A. C. Parker of the Forest Avenue Christian Church in Dallas served as Exalted Cyclops of Dallas Klan No. 66. Dr. E. L. Thompson of the Central Christian Church was Cyclops of Shreveport Klan No. 2, while the Grand Kludd (state chaplain) in Louisiana was the Reverend C. C. Miller of Kenner Memorial Methodist Church in Baton Rouge. Dozens of other clergymen held local and district offices in the southwestern states. A pro-Klan newspaper editor was so impressed with the Klan's standing among the ministers of Texas that he wrote enthusiastically: "I find the preachers of the Protestant faith almost solid for the Klan and its ideals, with here and there an isolated minister . . . who will line up with the Catholics in their fight on Protestantism, but that kind of preacher is persona non grata in most every congregation in Texas."[15]

The cordial relationship obtaining between Protestant ministers and the Klan was mutually profitable, if at times a bit risky for both parties. The Klan espoused a literal interpretation of the Bible and gave encouragement and

[14] For a good description of an appearance of both Klansmen and members of the Women of the Ku Klux Klan at a Sunday revival, see Shreveport *Journal*, March 29, 1924. On Sunday's relation to the Klan, see William G. McLoughlin, *Billy Sunday Was His Real Name* (Chicago, 1955), 274-76.

[15] Houston *Colonel Mayfield's Weekly*, December 8, 1923.

financial rewards to theologically intransigent preachers. But as the Klan devoted an increasing amount of attention to politics, an even more profitable area of activity, the monetary favors, if not the moral support, dwindled steadily. Politics eventually obscured every other form of Klan endeavor, but before southwestern Klansmen became thoroughly embroiled in political enterprises, the order had spread goodwill as a philanthropic institution.

When William J. Simmons wrote into his constitution for the Klan an article stipulating that the order was to "exemplify a practical benevolence," he was simply following the philanthropic tradition of other adult fraternal orders.[16] Like the Masons, Odd Fellows, Knights of Pythias, and other societies, the Klan carried on a fairly large amount of charity work wherever it was organized. Imperial Klan headquarters announced that local chapters gave more than one million dollars in charity during the year 1921; the figure was probably a fairly accurate estimate. Imperial Wizard Simmons maintained that Klan aid had been a major factor in helping many communities, schools, and families through the depression of that year. "The pursuit of charity has become a paramount issue with members of the Ku Klux Klan," proclaimed Simmons, "and whenever the organization is active, assistance will be rendered to the needy."[17]

The Klan's national leaders ordinarily left charitable undertakings to the state and local units. Consequently the great bulk of Klan philanthropies involved gifts to local persons or agencies. These contributions were distributed among a wide variety of "worthy" organizations and individuals; they ranged from modest donations to widows and sick people to ambitious fundraising drives for the con-

[16] *Constitution and Laws of the Knights of the Ku Klux Klan* (Atlanta, 1921), art. II, sec. 1. While the Klan constitution bears the copyright date 1921, the Imperial Klonvocation, or national convention, did not ratify the document until November 1922.

[17] Quoted in Tulsa *Tribune,* January 27, 1922.

struction of hospitals or orphans' homes. Klansmen were anything but silent Samaritans. They invariably publicized their acts of benevolence, frequently leaving the recipient of the gift instructions to report the deed to the local newspaper. The Klan in almost every case made an investigation of the character of an individual before contributing to his welfare. When Fort Smith Klan No. 15 played Santa Claus to 120 needy families at Christmas (a favorite occasion for Klan benevolence), the chapter informed the public that Klansmen had checked the relief rolls in the Arkansas city to prove the worthiness of each family and to avoid duplication with other organizations. The Houston Klan announced that each family which received one of its Christmas baskets had undergone investigation to determine whether the head of the family were vagrant or just luckless. A shiftless husband meant that the family was eliminated from consideration.[18]

Some local Klans went to great lengths to display the spirit of giving at the organizational level. Alexandria Klan No. 12, in Louisiana, created a relief fund of nearly $2,000 for victims of a tornado at Pineville. In Arkansas, El Dorado Klan No. 92 initiated a fundraising drive for an "Arkansas Oil and Gas Field Klan Hospital," to cost $125,000 and to be open to patients of all religious denominations. Donations came in from Klansmen over the country, but not a brick of the hospital building was ever laid. Fort Worth Klan No. 101 pledged $1,000 toward the construction of a new Y.M.C.A. building in the city; San Antonio Klan No. 31 contributed $2,500 in gold for a new "Y" building in the Alamo City; and the Houston Klan gave $2,000 to a Baptist hospital fund in Houston. In the spring of 1925 Little Rock Klan No. 1 financed a charity circus which played before a separate group of handicapped children for

[18] Fort Smith *Southwest American,* December 25, 1923; Houston *Post,* December 25, 1922.

a week, all proceeds going to a fund for the children. Later that year the Little Rock chapter of the Women of the Ku Klux Klan dedicated a fourteen-room children's home on Woodlawn Avenue. But the home, crippled by a split in the local chapter membership and general apathy, made little contribution to the city's welfare problem.[19]

A much more elaborate and somewhat more successful undertaking was Hope Cottage, an institution for homeless children financed and built by the largest chapter in the Southwest, Dallas Klan No. 66. In May 1923 the Dallas Klan collected enough money to begin construction on Hope Cottage by staging a blackface minstrel show. In October, Klansmen from Texas, Arkansas, and Oklahoma gathered in Dallas to witness ground-breaking and dedication ceremonies, and the following March the Dallasites inaugurated a "Kolossal Klan Karnival" to raise funds for the operation and maintenance of the finished orphans' home. The lavish and well-attended carnival served to advertise the essential goodness of the Klan in general and Klan No. 66 in particular.[20]

In 1925 the Realm (state) organization assumed control and management of Hope Cottage, changing its name to "Klanhaven." The Klan secured a charter from the state for its operation by an agency called the "Texas Klanhaven Association." But financial difficulties, brought on by a rapidly declining membership in Texas, plagued Klanhaven from its inception. In the late twenties the Klan turned the orphans' home over to the city, which renamed the institu-

[19] New Orleans *Times-Picayune*, April 12, 1923; Shreveport *Journal*, July 13, 1923; Fort Worth *American Citizen*, April 13, 1923; Fort Worth *Star-Telegram*, July 11, 1922; Dallas *Texas 100 Per Cent American*, November 10, 1922; Houston *Colonel Mayfield's Weekly*, July 8, 1922; Little Rock *Arkansas Gazette*, March 23, 24, December 21, 1925.

[20] Houston *Colonel Mayfield's Weekly*, May 26, 1923; Dallas *Morning News*, October 25, 1923; Dallas *Texas 100 Per Cent American*, March 21, 1924.

tion Hope Cottage. This move ended the Klan's connection with what had been the biggest single charitable enterprise of Klansmen in the Southwest.[21]

During the late 1920s a dwindling Klan membership made it hard for local Klans to secure funds for philanthropic work. As a consequence, Klan beneficences became rare. These acts had given the movement a touch of respectability it would not otherwise have obtained. As larger and larger amounts of Klan moneys were diverted to political ventures, however, charity, like the order's donations to the Protestant churches, came to be neglected. Failure in politics, apathy, and dissension ravaged the membership of the Klan in the Southwest, and the order ceased to "exemplify a practical benevolence."

The Klan might be many things—philanthropic agency, militant arm of the church, terrorist organization, political machine, business corporation—but it was just another lodge for many respectable businessmen who joined the organization. In fact, the Kleagles commonly began their solicitations in a town by calling on the local Masonic lodge. In 1923 the Klan claimed that 500,000 Masons were citizens of the Invisible Empire.[22] Both Simmons and his successor as Imperial Wizard, Evans, were Masons, and so many Masons joined the Klan that in some communities the Masonic lodge became simply an adjunct of the local Klan unit. Speaking before the Grand Lodge of Texas in 1922, Grand Master D. Frank Johnson denied that there was any connection between Freemasonry and the Klan, although he admitted that the activities of Kleagles among Texas Ma-

21 Dallas *Morning News,* September 11, 1925. The writer has been able to obtain only vague and general information regarding the history of Klanhaven and the Klanhaven Association in the late twenties. An ex-Klansman who was a director of the association, interviewed May 18, 1959, could give little specific information, stating simply that Klanhaven eventually went bankrupt and that the home had to be turned over to the city of Dallas.

22 Atlanta *Searchlight,* November 3, 1923.

sons had caused so many factional disturbances that a split
in the Grand Lodge almost had occurred.[23] Some Masons
eventually voiced disapproval of the Klan, but Masons were
never officially advised not to join the hooded fraternity.

The prominent men of a community, provided they were
Protestants, were special targets for the Klan's Kleagles.
And in many places, membership in the Klan became quite
a status symbol. When a highly respected Klansman died,
the local Knights had an opportunity to ape the other fraternal orders by performing ritualistic graveside services.
Klansmen often appeared while a brother was peacefully returning to dust, laid a "fiery cross" of red roses on the grave,
and then knelt for a moment of prayer.[24] If an especially
well known civic figure died as a Klansman, the Klan might
use his death to publicize the good repute of the order.
Tulsa Klan No. 2, for example, placed a notice in the Tulsa
newspapers memorializing E. Rogers Kemp, prominent
banker, churchman, and philanthropist, as "the exemplar
of real Klansmanship." The notice, in the form of a resolution, read in part: "We commend the spirit of our Fellow
Klansman to the tender keeping of the Perfect Emperor of
the Invisible Empire of the Soul, and the fervent fellowship
of his fellow Klansmen."[25]

The literature of the Klan repeatedly emphasized that the
Klan was a fraternity and that Klansmen were obligated to
practice fraternalism or, in Klan parlance, "Klannishness."
In an economic sense this concept meant that Klansmen
were supposed to trade with other members of the order
as much as possible. Simmons once defined the practice
of "vocational Klannishness" as: "Trading, dealing with and
patronizing klansmen in preference to all others. Employ-

[23] Little Rock *Arkansas Gazette,* December 6, 1922.
[24] See, for example, Shreveport *Journal,* December 21, 1921; Tulsa
Tribune, March 22, August 21, 1922; New Orleans *Times-Picayune,*
January 30, 1923.
[25] Tulsa *Tribune,* June 18, 1922.

ing klansmen in preference to others whenever possible. Boosting each other's business interests or professional ability; honorably doing any and all things that will assist a klansman to earn an honest dollar, thereby adding to his material wellbeing, lightening the burden of life for him and constantly succoring him with new strength and refreshing encouragement."[26] Many businessmen joined the Klan simply to take advantage of the trade of its members. Klan newspapers carried advertisements for places of business with names like "Klean Kut Kleaners" or "Klansman's Kafe." *Colonel Mayfield's Weekly,* published in Houston, continually called on members of the organization to: "Trade with klansmen, there is a klansman in every line of business in every community; trade with klansmen, and see that all of your friends do the same." On other occasions readers were assured that "if you will trade only with klansmen for 30 days, you will have the Kikes grovelling at your feet in 30 days."[27]

Men of enterprise outside the Invisible Empire were not above soliciting the favors of Klansmen. Railroad lines sometimes offered reduced fares to Klansmen and ran extra trains to take the sheeted Knights to their special Konklaves.[28] October 24, 1923, was "Ku Klux Klan Day" at the State Fair of Texas, so designated by the Fair Association. That day some 75,000 Klansmen, wives, and children from Texas, Oklahoma, and Arkansas thronged Fair Park in Dallas for the festivities, climaxed by an address by Imperial Wizard Hiram W. Evans. The next March the directors of the Southwestern Exposition and Fat Stock Show in Fort Worth set aside a day for the enjoyment of the

[26] William J. Simmons, *The Practice of Klannishness* (Atlanta, 1918), 3, pamphlet in M. S. Newsom and Family Papers, Merrit M. Shilg Memorial Collection, Department of Archives, Louisiana State University, Baton Rouge.

[27] Houston *Colonel Mayfield's Weekly,* April 17, June 23, 1923.

[28] See the New Orleans *Times-Picayune,* June 17, 1923; Little Rock *Arkansas Gazette,* November 3, 1923, July 5, 1924.

hooded Knights. Klan Day in Fort Worth, however, was not nearly so well attended as the October gathering in Dallas.[29]

With all the other money making devices the Klan's leaders dreamed up, it would have been surprising if some enterprising Klansman had not taken advantage of the excellent prospects the order offered for the sale of insurance benefits to the faithful. In 1923 Grand Dragon Z. E. Marvin of Texas originated a plan for a national fraternal insurance company and had the Klorero, or state convention of chartered Texas Klans, endorse the idea. Marvin and his associates secured a charter from the state of Texas, and by the end of the year the company supposedly had sold about one million dollars worth of insurance. Early in 1924 Imperial headquarters in Atlanta assumed control of the company, rechartering it under the laws of Missouri and naming it the Empire Mutual Life Insurance Company, with home offices in Kansas City. National headquarters set up an Insurance Department to administer the affairs of the Empire Mutual, which began operations with a capital stock of $100,000 and a surplus of $25,000. While the insurance company was designed for national operations, most of its work was confined to Missouri, Arkansas, Kansas, Oklahoma, and Texas. By the fall of 1924 its directors claimed to have three million dollars worth of insurance in force. Very little is known about the history of the Empire Mutual after 1925. The business was probably in existence only about four years before it fell into arrears and dissolved.[30]

[29] Dallas *Morning News*, August 13, October 25, 1923; Fort Worth *Star-Telegram*, March 14, 1924.

[30] *Proceedings of the Second Imperial Klonvocation, Held in Kansas City, Missouri, September 23-26, 1924* (Atlanta, 1924), 131-32. The writer was able to ascertain only that the Empire Mutual ceased operations "around 1928." A former member of the Klan, interviewed May 18, 1959, commented that the company never had capable management and that a few large claims and the depletion of Klan membership were sufficient to cause its dissolution.

One of the biggest inducements for becoming a Klansman was the opportunity to participate in the order's manifold social functions. The regular chapter meetings were important social events for most members, with Klansmen in their white robes and hoods exchanging the mysterious SOG (Sign of Greeting) with their fellow Knights and going through the heavily ritualistic opening and closing ceremonies. The Klan outdid all the other lodges in secrecy, ritual, and weird nomenclature. Then there were the cross burnings, the parades, the initiations, the picnics for the Klansmen and their families. Such fraternal doings were especially popular with the rural-minded folk who flocked into the Klan. The hooded order became the biggest thing in the social life of most people who left the "alien" world and became "citizens of the Invisible Empire."

Parades and initiations were the most spectacular and widely publicized social events staged by the Klan. These demonstrations, often held on the same night, constituted displays of strength and brotherhood and required much planning and preparation. The size of the parades and the grandeur of the initiations depended on the occasion and the strength of the local Klans, but most of the demonstrations followed roughly the same procedure. The big Konklave held in September 1923 at Shreveport furnishes an example. Klansmen from all over Louisiana and from southern Arkansas and eastern Texas packed the local hotels on Saturday, the day of the festivities. A capacity crowd already sat in the grandstand at the fairgrounds stadium when, at 6:00 P.M., an aerial bomb exploded over the throng. More explosions followed at thirty-minute intervals until 8:00, when the membership of Shreveport Klan No. 2, over 3,000 strong, joined by robed Klansmen from other towns and surrounding states, paraded around the racetrack of the stadium. At 8:15 Klan No. 2 staged "naturalization ceremonies" for a class of aliens, featuring a human square formed by Klansmen and the singing of

"Onward, Christian Soldiers." After the initiation, Imperial Wizard Evans, Imperial Kligrapp H. Kyle Ramsey (a native of Shreveport), and J. K. Skipwith of Morehouse Parish fame all spoke on the tenets, aims, and struggles of the Klan. At 10:00 came a fireworks display and then the climax of the evening—the igniting of a thirty-foot-tall wooden cross covered with oil-soaked rags. As the giant symbol of the Klan burst into flames, the assemblage sang "The Star-Spangled Banner."[31]

There were some occasions when Klansmen encountered hostility to their plans for staging fraternal pageants. The nationally famous riot at Lorena, Texas, in October 1921 has been mentioned earlier.[32] A few months later, at Laredo, a heavily Catholic and Mexican-American town on the Rio Grande, county and town law officers armed about one hundred special deputies and set up a machinegun to prevent an announced Klan parade. In December of 1922 a rock-throwing battle and fist fight broke out during a Klan parade in the north Texas town of McKinney. The city council of Alexandria, Louisiana, adopted an ordinance to prohibit masked parades in the city limits, although the people of the town later voted to rescind the ordinance. When anti-Klanners placed a notice in the Bartlesville, Oklahoma, newspaper proclaiming that "the American flag will not be permitted to be carried down the streets by a masked mob tonight," the local Klan went ahead with its parade, 272 Klansmen marching with the usual flags, banners, and crosses. Klansmen were not so brave in San Antonio. In January 1924 the city commission passed an ordinance forbidding masked parades. That month some 150 fully robed Klansmen from Dallas alighted from a train and formed ranks for a march into the downtown section to advertise a rodeo the San Antonio Klan was going to present. Sheriff John Stevens of Bexar County, his deputies, and three

[31] Shreveport *Journal*, September 15, 1923.
[32] See page 50.

squads of policemen arrived at the railroad station and turned back the Klansmen, some of whom reentrained for Dallas, while others hired taxicabs and went to the local Klavern.[33]

Still, incidents of opposition to Klan functions were rare in the southwestern states. Most of the time the local officials either belonged to the Klan and encouraged the demonstrations, or bowed before the Klan's might in their communities—or were not even consulted before the robed Knights appeared. When Oklahoma, Louisiana, Arkansas, or Texas Klansmen wanted to march, have a picnic, or induct a group of aliens, they usually were not bothered.

As the Klan gained in strength and power during the early twenties, the prospect of organizing a secret women's society to parallel the men's order grew increasingly attractive. Evans was already thinking about creating an organization for women when he took over the Imperial Wizardship late in 1922. After all, if the Klan were to achieve the aims of its political program, it would be necessary to organize the native-born Protestant women as the Klan had done with a large portion of the male population. Then too, a secret society for women would mean new sources of revenue for the Klan—initiation fees, robe sales, taxes, contributions. The Evans administration was making plans for the establishment of an organization to absorb a number of women's patriotic groups in the country when Simmons, now holding the purely ceremonial office of "Emperor," began a movement to regain some of the power and money he had lost by giving up the Wizardship.

In March 1923 Simmons, using a women's group in Oklahoma called the W.A.P. (White American Protestant) Study Club, with chapters in Tulsa, Claremore, and a few

[33] Denison *Herald,* March 20, 1922; Dallas *Morning News,* December 10, 1922; New Orleans *Times-Picayune,* March 25, September 6, 1922; Tulsa *Tribune,* August 28, 1923; San Antonio *Express,* January 23, 26, 27, 1924.

other places, as a nucleus, started organizing a new secret order for women, the "Kamelia." Simmon's move caught the Evans regime off guard, and it was several days before the Wizard moved to quash the Kamelia project by decreeing that Klansmen could in no way participate in or assist the Kamelia or any other women's group. Simmons, now calling himself "El Magnus" of the Kamelia, denied that a Klansman's obligation to the Klan precluded his helping the women's order. The conflict over the Kamelia precipitated an involved legal battle between the Evans and Simmons factions for control of the Klan. A court decision eventually established a compromise whereby the interests of both factions were recognized. In the meantime the founder of the Klan and his organizers busily went about the work of organizing "Kamelia Kourts," mainly in the southwestern states. Units of the Kamelia were formed at Little Rock in Arkansas and at Tulsa, Claremore, Guthrie, and various other towns in Oklahoma, where H. Tom Kight, Blanche Kight, C. W. Beeson, and Rowena Beeson, Simmons' allies, had previously organized chapters of the W.A.P. Study Club.[34]

The Kamelia made some initial progress, but soon Evans' warning to Klansmen to avoid any association with Simmons' new order, together with the quick solidification of the Evansite state administrations behind the Wizard, destroyed the chances of the society. Grand Dragon H. C. McCall of Texas announced that Texas' 140,000 Klansmen and all of the 275 Klans in the Realm were supporting their fellow Texan Evans. A statewide meeting of Arkansas Klansmen, under the control of Grand Dragon James A. Comer, endorsed the Wizard and denounced the Emperor. N. Clay Jewett, Grand Dragon of Oklahoma, and the lead-

[34] Tulsa *Tribune,* March 25, April 1, 5, 1923; Fort Smith *Southwest American,* May 23, 25, 1923; New Orleans *Times-Picayune,* May 25, 1923; Little Rock *Arkansas Gazette,* May 25, 1923; "The Clash in the Klan," *Literary Digest,* LXXVII (April 21, 1923), 13.

ers of the powerful Tulsa and Oklahoma City Klans backed Evans, as did district leaders Paul D. Perkins, Thomas F. DePaoli, and R. Will Germany, the Klan bosses in Louisiana. Klan moguls in other strong Klan states like Indiana and Ohio also repudiated Simmons and lined up with the Evans regime. As a final note, early in May the "Imperial Kloncilium" in Atlanta, the official council and judicial body of the Klan, voted its endorsement of the Texan.[35]

The legal contest and the infighting at Atlanta continued for the remainder of 1923 and into 1924. Highlights of the conflict included the banishment from the Klan of Edward Y. Clarke, the original salesman of the order, by the Evans regime; Simmons' attempt, after the Klan had sanctioned the formation of another women's order, to create the "Knights Kamelia," a "second degree of Klankraft" wherein Klansmen would owe allegiance to him as Emperor; and the murder of W. S. Coburn, the Emperor's attorney, by Klan propagandist and Evans supporter Phillip Fox, for which Fox received a sentence of life imprisonment.[36] In early 1924 the Klan bought out Simmons' interests in the organization for about $146,500, and the father of the Klan, whom Evans once described as "the most impractical man I have ever met," left the Invisible Empire to squander his remuneration on other fraternal projects.[37]

Technically, the Klan did not establish the Women of the Ku Klux Klan, the order formed in June 1923. In a legal

[35] New Orleans *Times-Picayune*, April 10, 1923; Fort Smith *Southwest American*, May 13, 1923; *Minutes of the Imperial Kloncilium, Knights of the Ku Klux Klan, Meeting of May 1 and 2, 1923, Which Ratified W. J. Simmons' Agreement with the Knights of the Ku Klux Klan, Together with Certified Copies of All Litigation Instituted by W. J. Simmons against the Imperial Wizard of the Knights of the Ku Klux Klan* (Atlanta, 1923), *passim*.

[36] See New York *Times*, September 16, 1923, p. 23, November 6, pp. 1, 5, November 7, p. 15, January 3, 1924, p. 3, January 12, p. 1, February 13, p. 5, February 25, p. 17.

[37] William G. Shepherd, "Fiery Double Cross," *Collier's*, LXXXII (July 28, 1928), 48; "Colonel Simmons and $146,500 from K.K.K. to K.F.S.," *Literary Digest*, LXXX (March 8, 1924), 36-40.

sense the Women of the Klan was a separate and distinct organization with its own set of officers and finances; Imperial Klan headquarters only "sanctioned" the enterprise. Yet the women's organization was always so much under the dominance of the men's order as to make it actually an auxiliary body. On June 9 Mrs. Lulu A. Markwell and Grand Dragon Comer headed a group of petitioners who secured a charter for the Women of the Ku Klux Klan in Second Division Circuit Court in Little Rock. The affairs of the women's order were to be administered by a Board of Directors, with national headquarters in Little Rock. The board never really carried out an executive function; like the Klan, power in the Women of the Klan was centered in one office, that of Imperial Commander. Mrs. Markwell became the first Imperial Commander. When the charter was granted, there were already about 2,500 Klanswomen in Little Rock, and eight Kleagles had gone into the field in Arkansas.[38]

At its inception the Women of the Klan benefited from advantages not enjoyed by the Klan in its early years. The new order absorbed various other women's groups organized on a local basis, primarily in the Southwest, like the Order of American Women in Fort Worth, the Ladies of the Invisible Empire in Louisiana and Arkansas, and the Ladies of the Cu Clux Clan in Oklahoma. Then too, there was already in existence a powerful men's organization, which subsidized the Women of the Klan and assisted the work of the women Kleagles. Klansmen were supposed to influence their wives and sisters to join the Women of the Klan, and many relatives of Klan members, as well as other moralistic, nativistic, and race-minded females, paid their five-dollar initiation fees.[39]

Local chapters of the Women of the Klan appeared

[38] Little Rock *Arkansas Gazette*, June 10, 13, 1923.

[39] The best treatment this writer has seen of the national career of the Women of the Ku Klux Klan, with emphasis on one state, is in Loucks, *Klan in Pennsylvania*, ch. x.

quickly in the Southwest. Klanswomen came into the open in Fort Worth only five days after the issuance of the Imperial order sanctioning the organization.[40] Soon women's Klans were thriving in Dallas, Shreveport, Tulsa, Oklahoma City, and Little Rock. By the fall of 1923 organizers for the Women of the Klan were moving into the smaller towns of the Southwest and other parts of the nation; and Klan newspapers, like one in Columbia, Louisiana, were urging "wives, mothers, and daughters of Klansmen, as well as sympathizers," to "make application for membership at once and get in as charter members. . . . Enlist today."[41] Imperial Commander Markwell announced that 250,000 women over the nation had joined the women's order.[42]

The Women of the Klan never possessed the strength in the southwestern states it did in Indiana, Ohio, or Pennsylvania, where the women's state organizations attained a size comparable to the men's order. The organizational drive for the women's society was still gaining momentum when the Klan began declining in the Southwest. Like the men's order, the Women of the Klan hit its peak in the Southwest in 1924, with Oklahoma probably having more Klanswomen than any other southwestern state. The deterioration of the men's order was perhaps the greatest handicap the women experienced in the Southwest; the Women of the Klan simply got underway too late to equal the strength and prestige of the Klan in the region. Factional squabbles, arising mainly from Comer's efforts to make a personal satrapy of the women's organization, also crippled the movement. These internal disturbances, which split the Little Rock women's Klan and damaged the order elsewhere, will be treated in a later chapter. Here it suffices to say that in the Southwest the Women of the Klan made

---

[40] Fort Worth *Star-Telegram*, June 9, 1923. The costumes of the Women of the Ku Klux Klan were quite similar to those of the men's order, except that the women never wore masks.

[41] Columbia *Caldwell* [Parish] *Watchman*, October 26, 1923.

[42] Little Rock *Arkansas Gazette*, October 7, 1923.

little progress outside the cities. After 1924 the membership of the women's Klan declined as precipitately as that of the men's order.[43]

Where women's chapters existed, Klanswomen entered into charitable and social activities with the Klansmen, displaying as much enthusiasm, and frequently more. During 1924 the Klan also set up an organization, the Junior Ku Klux Klan, open to boys 12 through 18 years of age. Unlike the Women of the Klan, the Junior Klan was legally an auxiliary order of the Klan. Not much is known of the junior order except for the appearance of the organization in a few cities over the country. In the Southwest there were chapters of the Junior Ku Klux Klan in Cedar Grove, a suburb of Shreveport; Tulsa; Little Rock; and Arkadelphia, Arkansas. The Junior Klan sometimes took part in the demonstrations staged by the Klan and the Women of the Klan.[44]

All aspects of the Klan's fraternal program, whether economic or social, suffered with the disintegration of Klan membership in the last half of the 1920s. The giant Konklaves cost money, and a depleted membership made increasingly difficult the collection of funds for such displays. Conversely, the infrequency of exciting demonstrations and the disappearance of a merchant's Klannish patronage removed much of the incentive for remaining in the order.

The Klan's rituals, its religious overtones, and its philanthropic activities made it look like one of the familiar lodges in America. This heightened its appeal and helped it to gain acceptance among middle-class Americans who might

[43] Miss Agnes B. Cloud, State Commander of Texas Klanswomen, probably exaggerated when, addressing the first women's Klorero at Dallas in the spring of 1924, she said that 300 delegates were present from 200 women's chapters. Dallas *Morning News*, May 3, 1924.

[44] Shreveport *Journal*, July 5, 1924; Tulsa *Tribune*, September 10, 19, 1924; Little Rock *Arkansas Gazette*, June 1, July 1, August 27, 1924. The Women of the Ku Klux Klan also had an auxiliary order for girls, the Tri-K Club. Apparently no local units of this organization were established in the states of the Southwest.

otherwise have found unacceptable the terror and violence that marked much of its early history. Its religiosity, its charity, and its fraternity also made the Klan more palatable to "aliens," those outside the Invisible Empire. But these activities underwent deemphasis with the evolution of the Klan into a political machine. The money, time, and interest spent in courting ministers, aiding widows and orphans, and staging initiations and parades were diverted to the benefit of aspiring Klan politicos.

On the whole the tremendous growth of the Klan, its many-sided appeal, and its multifarious endeavors furnish a striking commentary on the nature of American society in the 1920s. Its makeup was far too complex and its ramifications were far too sweeping for its career to be dismissed as representing the antics of a few on the lunatic fringe.

6.

A Taste of Victory

At THE BEGINNING of 1922 the Atlanta officialdom, Kleagles, and ordinary Klansmen had plenty of reason to be happy. The Klan had spread over the South and Southwest, had crossed the Mason-Dixon line and the Ohio River and had inaugurated a promising kluxing campaign in the northern states, and had taken in about 500,000 members over the nation. In the Southwest the induction of new Klansmen and the chartering of local Klans proceeded at a feverish pace. Funds from initiation fees and the sale of Klan regalia poured into Atlanta from the South, Southwest, East, Midwest, and Pacific Coast. These were indeed grand times for William J. Simmons, Edward Y. Clarke, and Mrs. Elizabeth Tyler. Simmons, as Imperial Wizard, did little but make speeches and grow wealthier by the day from the two dollars of each initiation fee that went to him. Clarke and Mrs. Tyler made enormous profits, as much as $40,000 a month, from the Klan's Propagation Department, by now their own personal kingdom.

Yet all was not well in the Invisible Empire. The Simmons-Clarke regime was not ambitious enough to suit a

growing number of Klansmen in the strongest Klan states
—Texas, Oklahoma, Arkansas, Louisiana, Georgia. There
were also disgruntled Klansmen in Indiana, where the
Klan was just beginning its expansion. These insurgent
Knights in various states saw the potentialities of the Klan
as a political organization and regarded the woolgathering
Simmons and the cynical Clarke as millstones impending
the order's fulfillment. They also distrusted the financial
practices of the Atlanta coterie. The insurgent group included Nathan Bedford Forrest, Jr., of Georgia, son of the
famous Confederate cavalry general and alleged "Grand
Wizard" of the original Ku Klux Klan; David C. Stephenson and Walter F. Bossert of Indiana; H. Kyle Ramsey of
Louisiana; James A. Comer of Arkansas; Edwin DeBarr of
Oklahoma; and H. C. McCall, Brown Harwood, and Z. E.
Marvin of Texas. Texas was the star Klan state and the
home of the most ambitious Klansmen, politically and otherwise, during the early years of Klan expansion. The leader
of the political-minded Klansmen was Hiram Wesley Evans,
the first Exalted Cyclops of the mighty Dallas Klan No. 66.

During January 1922, Imperial headquarters formally
established the four Realm, or state, organizations for the
Southwest. At the head of each Realm was a Grand Dragon
appointed by Imperial Wizard Simmons; the Realm was
divided into Provinces, or districts, headed by Great
Titans.[1] In Texas, after a brief term served by Dr. A. D.
Ellis of Beaumont, Brown Harwood of Fort Worth became Grand Dragon. McCall of Houston and Evans were
two of the five Titans for Texas. Ramsey of Shreveport was
the Grand Kligrapp, or state secretary, in Louisiana. Comer,
Exalted Cyclops of Little Rock Klan No. 1, became Grand
Dragon of the Realm of Arkansas. The first Grand Dragon
of Oklahoma was DeBarr of Norman, whose background
made him unique among Klan officials. DeBarr held a doc-

---

[1] *Constitution and Laws of the Knights of the Ku Klux Klan* (Atlanta, 1921), art. xvi, sec. 1.

torate of philosophy in chemistry from the University of Michigan. He had come to the University of Oklahoma in the early 1890s as a member of the original faculty. DeBarr was extremely popular on the Norman campus, both as a personality and as a teacher, and by 1922 he had advanced to the vice-presidency of the university.[2] The chemistry professor may have been about the last person one would expect to find in the Klan, but he was nonetheless a zealous Klansman, devoted to the cause of the order and anxious for the secret organization to become a force in state and national politics.

In the spring of 1922, after a short term as Great Titan of Province No. 2 in Texas, Evans came to Atlanta as Imperial Kligrapp (national secretary). Simmons brought the Dallasite to national headquarters partly because he wanted an efficient assistant in the Imperial hierarchy and partly, it seems, to quiet the demands of the disgruntled Texas Klansmen for more representation at Atlanta. But Simmons soon discovered that he had taken a viper to his bosom. Evans immediately began working to turn the Klan into what he called "a great militant political organization." Operating within the two major parties but never on its own, the Klan would control nominations and elections over the nation. This achievement, as Evans conceived it, necessitated the elimination of Simmons and Clarke as powers in the Klan, the regularization of the order's financial practices, and the conversion of the Klan into a "movement" rather than a terrorist organization or a lodge.[3]

Evans was remarkably successful in carrying out his personal program for the Klan. During 1922, under his leader-

[2] For a brief sketch of DeBarr's life, see the article printed at the time of his death in Oklahoma City *Daily Oklahoman*, December 19, 1950. See also Roy Gittinger, *The University of Oklahoma, 1892-1942* (Norman, 1942), 9-10, 59, 92.

[3] Testimony of Robert L. Henry in *Senator from Texas. Hearings before a Subcommittee of the Committee on Privileges and Elections, United States Senate,* 68th Congress, 1st and 2d Sessions (1924), 46.

ship—and with the acquiescence of Clarke and the ineffec-
tual Simmons—the Klan entered local and state political
contests in various parts of the country, scoring some
notable victories. In November, fortified by the Klan's
triumphs in politics, Evans' followers "persuaded" Simmons
to relinquish the Imperial Wizardship and accept the
specially created but powerless position of "Emperor."
Evans was elected Wizard by the delegates to the first
Imperial Klonvocation in Atlanta. "They thrust that Wizard
job on me," was the way Evans later described his ascen-
sion to the leadership of the Klan movement. One of his
first official acts was to cancel Clarke's contract with the
Klan for propagation work. "As long as I wasn't responsible
for Clarke, I was satisfied. . . . But as soon as I became
Wizard I didn't dare take the responsibility of permitting
Clarke to make so much money," recalled Evans.[4]

The removal of Simmons from the Wizardship and the
severance of the Klan's relations with Clarke marked the
beginning of a process by which the original rulers of the
Klan were driven from the order. In 1923, as related earlier,
Simmons' efforts to organize a secret women's organization precipitated a long, involved power struggle with
Evans, fought out both in the courts and within the ranks
of the Klan. By the end of 1923 the Evans regime had
liquidated the influence of the Simmons-Clarke faction,
and in the early part of the next year the Imperial Wizard
banished the founder of the order and its chief salesman.[5]
By that time Evans had also put an end to most of the
Klan's vigilante activities and had seen the organization,
under his direction, become essentially a political machine.

Yet the Klan would probably have evolved into an in-

[4] William G. Shepherd, "Fiery Double Cross," *Collier's*, LXXXII
(July 28, 1928), 48.

[5] See New York *Times*, January 12, 1924, p. 1, February 13, p. 5,
February 14, p. 16. Mrs. Tyler left the Klan early in 1923 and mar-
ried a wealthy Atlantan. She died the next year. Arnold S. Rice,
The Ku Klux Klan in American Politics (Washington, 1962), 10.

strument for gaining political power if there had never been a Hiram W. Evans. The character of the masked order seemed to make some sort of activity in politics inevitable. Church work, terrorism, parades, and charity might serve quite well for a while, but how could the Klan really implement its program if it did not put the "right men" in public office? The Klan had some rather definite objectives. Its program included, at the local level, rigid economy and merciless law enforcement, particularly of prohibition laws and ordinances against gambling, prostitution, and other forms of vice. At the state level the Klan wanted measures to strengthen law enforcement and to outlaw Catholic schools and prohibit Catholics from teaching in public schools. Nationally, the order worked for strict limitation of "undesirable" foreign immigration, federal aid to public education, an isolationist foreign policy, and a host of other demands. These objectives could be realized only if the Klan took to politics, or so the overwhelming majority of Klansmen came to believe.

But Klansmen found it easier to enunciate a sweeping set of objectives than to enact them. A student of early American nativism laid down a principle for movements like the Klan when he observed: "Radical or reactionary political programs advanced by those seeking power . . . are frequently tempered when opportunity and responsibility for execution have been gained."[6] Klansmen controlled hundreds of local governments, but no noticeable moral improvement or decrease of crime occurred in most of the areas ruled by the Klan. The order secured a majority in several state legislatures, but only one genuinely Klan-inspired measure became state law. That statute, a requirement that all school children in Oregon must attend the public schools through the eighth grade, was initiated by the voters of the state, not enacted by the legis-

[6] William D. Overdyke, *The Know-Nothing Party in the South* (Baton Rouge, 1950), 91.

lature.[7] There was some talk that the Klan would outlaw
Catholic schools in Oklahoma if the organization got
control of the legislature, but when it did, no such measure was introduced in either house. Attempts to outlaw
the teaching of evolution in the southwestern states came
from a group much larger than the Klan, and most of the
antievolution bills appeared in the state legislatures after
the Klan had lost the bulk of its influence. At the national
level the Klan claimed credit for the passage of immigration restriction legislation, but sentiment for curbing the
influx of immigrants from southern and eastern Europe
and Asia was almost universal among native-born Americans, many of whom also opposed the Klan.[8]

Thus while the Klan enjoyed considerable success in
politics during the first half of the twenties, its attempts to
carry its policies into effect usually failed. The Klan nevertheless had a program and a set of power-hungry leaders.
The character of the order, with its unified membership
and revivalist spirit, bred political ambitions. During 1922
and 1923 Klansmen turned to politics in states where
Realm organizations had been set up and a chain of command established. By the middle of 1923 the organization
was a potent element, indefinable and feared, in state
and local politics from North Carolina to Oregon and from
Texas to Indiana. In the Southwest the white-robed society
suffered some defeats, but its victories were spectacular
and manifold. Its most publicized battles came in Texas and
Oklahoma. The Klan engaged in scattered contests in
Louisiana during political off years in that state. Arkansas
was the scene of some conspicuous local conquests, including one of the first triumphs the Klan ever scored
in politics.

The Little Rock city election of April 4, 1922, furnished

[7] In 1925 the United States Supreme Court declared the Oregon
law unconstitutional in *Pierce* v. *Society of Sisters*.

[8] See John Higham, *Strangers in the Land: Patterns of American
Nativism, 1860-1925* (New Brunswick, 1955), ch. XI.

a real surprise. Most observers expected this election to follow the usual pattern for elections in one-party Arkansas, with the candidates nominated previously in the Democratic primaries winning easily over the token opposition of a few Republican contestants. This time, however, there was extraordinary heavy voting in the city's fifth ward, where the Klan was especially strong. When the ballots were counted, Charles M. Snodgrass, an "independent" candidate for alderman in the fifth ward and a Protestant, had overwhelmed Edward L. Younger, the Democratic nominee and the only Catholic on the ticket, 1,040 votes to 462. Snodgrass' victory was the work of the Klan. On the night before the city election the Little Rock Klan had held a meeting in the fifth ward. Exalted Cyclops and Grand Dragon Comer instructed Klansmen to scratch Younger, the incumbent, and write in the name of Snodgrass, whom Younger had defeated for the Democratic nomination in the city primary the preceding December. On election day only about one-fifth of the city electorate voted. Late in the afternoon, word of the Klan's tactics got around in Little Rock, but a last-minute rush of Younger supporters proved futile.[9]

The Klan's upset of Younger, the Catholic candidate for alderman, marked the debut of Little Rock Klan No. 1 in politics. For the next few years what transpired in the local Klavern, at 4th and Main streets, had a decisive impact on the political affairs of Little Rock, Pulaski County, and, ultimately, the state of Arkansas. With perhaps 7,800 members, the Little Rock Klan was by far the largest chapter in Arkansas and one of the largest in the nation.[10] Until mid-1924 it was dominated by Comer, an ex-Bull Moose and Republican politician and currently a Little Rock lawyer. As Cyclops of the largest Klan in the state, Grand Dragon of the Realm, and a favorite of Evans,

9 Little Rock *Arkansas Gazette*, April 5, 1922.

10 This was the estimate of the Reverend Harry G. Knowles, a Klan lecturer, reported *ibid.*, February 5, 1923.

he ruled almost absolutely over the fortunes of the Klan in Arkansas.

In the late spring and early summer of 1922 Klan No. 1, under Comer's direction, carefully prepared to nominate a slate of its favorites in the Democratic primaries and thus to win control of the government of Pulaski County. Simultaneously with Texas Klansmen, the Little Rock Knights used a highly effective device called the "elimination primary." Klansmen in Little Rock and throughout the county were mailed ballots along with a request that they indicate their preference among the candidates for each office. The candidate receiving the largest number of votes would receive the united vote of the Klansmen. Finally, on July 26, about two weeks before the Democratic primary, the Little Rock Klan made public the full slate of candidates it was backing for county, district, and state office. Every one of the Klan endorsees running for county or district office and for the state legislature was a Klansman. Anti-Klan elements in Little Rock, led by the former governor George T. Hays, greeted the announcement of the Klan ticket with a denunciation of "Comerism" and "Bull Moose interference" in county politics.[11]

During the week preceding the Democratic primary Klan No. 1 staged nightly political rallies in different parts of Little Rock. In midweek the Klansmen gathered at night in a field outside town, initiated a class of about 170 neophytes, and made arrangements for the county primary. Comer and his followers agreed to have five Klan workers at each polling place in the county and to have available one thousand automobiles to carry voters to the polls. Every night for the remainder of the week saw Klan candidates and lecturers exhort crowds on the principles of the order. An anti-Klan organization called the "Committee of Democrats" also held nightly rallies, always

[11] Little Rock *Arkansas Gazette*, July 15, 18, 20-23, 26, 29, 1922; Fort Smith *Southwest American*, July 29, 1922.

only a short walk and within hearing distance of the pro-Klan gathering. Throughout the state the Pulaski County campaign attracted more publicity than the statewide races. "With red fire and parades," reported the neutral *Arkansas Gazette* of Little Rock on the day of the primary, "one of the most exciting political campaigns in the history of Pulaski County came to an end last night."[12]

On Saturday, August 8, the Klan swept Pulaski County. Every candidate endorsed by the Klan at the county and district level won the Democratic nomination, including Heartsill Ragon, bidding for a seat in the United States House of Representatives. Throughout Little Rock, Klansmen simply scratched through the names of four unopposed candidates for reelection to the county Democratic committee, three of them Jews and one a Catholic. In a few wards anti-Klan poll watchers challenged the ballots of known Klansmen, but the party officials allowed no disqualifications. Comer looked over the results of the county primary and remarked contentedly: "I think the boys did fine." And from the daily *Arkansas Gazette*: "The Klan bloc decided this election. . . . The results of the Pulaski county primary were . . . determined when the Klan held its elimination contests or decided to support this candidate against that one."[13]

The Klan did not make an open fight in other Arkansas counties, although in Faulkner County (Conway) the local Knights offered a reward of fifty dollars for "election crooks and boodlers" while proclaiming their determination "that the will of the people as expressed at the polls in Faulkner county shall prevail and shall not be thwarted."[14]

At the state level the Klan was not a factor in the 1922 races. The Little Rock Klan endorsed a complete state ticket, including ultraconservative Thomas C. McRae, the in-

[12] Little Rock *Arkansas Gazette*, July 31, August 1, 2, 3, 5, 6, 8, 1922.

[13] *Ibid.*, August 9, 10, 1922.

[14] Fort Smith *Southwest American*, August 6, 1922.

cumbent, for governor.[15] Probably not more than one or two of the state candidates endorsed by Klan No. 1 were Klansmen. Apparently Comer and his minions, in lieu of nominating their own slate, simply endorsed the man most likely to win in each of the state races. Comer could therefore claim a Klan victory when all but one of the candidates favored by the Little Rock Klan won the Democratic nomination.

McRae won the renomination as the Democratic gubernatorial candidate and insured his reelection in Democratic Arkansas. Running on a strict law enforcement platform, he polled about four times as many votes as his little-known opponent. McRae was not a member of the Klan, but the order regarded the economy-minded, "bone-dry" governor as a "friendly neutral," and he received the votes of Little Rock Klansmen and most other Arkansas Knights. The governor's private secretary, Clarence P. Newton, belonged to the Little Rock Klan and in 1924 would be elected county judge of Pulaski County on the Klan ticket.[16]

Little Rock Klan No. 1 followed up its successes in the August primary with a victory in a special municipal judgeship election the next month. Its candidate for municipal judge won over two non-Klan opponents by a margin of 5 to 1. In November, Klan No. 1 publicized its official ticket for the upcoming primary for city offices. The ticket, headed by Mayor Ben D. Brickhouse, included choices for municipal judge, city treasurer, nine seats on the board of aldermen, two places on the city school board, and twenty-seven posts on the county Democratic central committee from the city's nine wards. All of the Klan favorites had been chosen in a series of elimination primaries held at intervals during October and November. In the city primary, on December 4, two Klan aldermanic candidates were beaten, but the rest of the Klan ticket

[15] *Ibid.*, July 29, 1922; Little Rock *Arkansas Gazette*, July 26, 1922.
[16] New York *Times*, August 9, 1922, p. 6, November 1, 1923, p. 1.

was nominated. The next spring, before the city election, the Klan threatened once again to use write-in tactics to defeat the two non-Klan nominees for alderman, one a Jew, the other a Catholic. At the last minute Comer called a Konklave of Little Rock Knights and instructed them to vote for all the Democratic nominees, thereby canceling the original plans for a second Klan bolt.[17]

It is impossible to assess the influence of the Klan in the 44th Arkansas General Assembly, meeting in January 1923. To be sure, there were Klansmen in both legislative houses; the Pulaski County delegation, a senator and four representatives, consisted of members of the hooded order. A correspondent for a Fort Smith newspaper commented on the "strong membership of Klansmen" in the legislature.[18] But the senators and representatives spent most of their time dealing with economic matters, and no issues arose to reveal the strength of the Klan.

In a number of local contests during 1923, however, the Klan was clearly the dominant issue. After a heated campaign the candidate of El Dorado Klan No. 92 won the Democratic nomination for mayor of the southern Arkansas oil town. In Fort Smith the forces of Protestant morality, led by the Klan, forced a recall election on Mayor Fagan Bourland, a Catholic, whom the order accused of misappropriation of funds and softness toward bootleggers and prostitutes. The Fort Smith Klansmen and their allies succeeded in recalling Bourland, 1,737 votes to 1,079. At Camden, in the southwestern part of the state, and at Bald Knob, a little town northeast of Little Rock, the Klan even backed candidates for school trustee, and won in both instances.[19] The Bald Knob contest, and Klan versus

17 Little Rock *Arkansas Gazette*, September 30, October 4, November 30, December 5, 1922, April 1-4, 1923; Fort Smith *Southwest American*, April 3, 4, 1923.

18 Fort Smith *Southwest American*, January 10, 1923.

19 Little Rock *Arkansas Gazette*, February 8, May 20, 22, 1923; Fort Smith *Southwest American*, May 16, 18, 25, 1923.

anti-Klan fights in villages throughout the nation, demonstrated that no town was too small, no election too minor, for the Klan to become the preeminent issue.

By the end of 1923 the Klan in Arkansas, under the leadership of Comer, dominated the governments of Pulaski County and the city of Little Rock, had things its own way in Fort Smith and Sebastian County, and was the most powerful element in scores of other towns and several other counties over the state. The Klan had awed most of its opposition into silence. A New York *Times* correspondent, writing in late 1923, quite accurately appraised the status of the Klan in Arkansas: "There is apparently no organized movement under way to challenge the domination of the masked organization."[20] Yet the Klan's political power had not really been tested at the state level. Such a test would not come until 1924, when the Realm of Arkansas made an all-out bid to control the state of Arkansas.

To the south of Arkansas, in Louisiana, the Klan never became the force in state or even local politics that it did in Arkansas, Texas, Oklahoma, or, outside the Southwest, in Indiana, Oregon, Colorado, or Georgia. There was much talk about the Klan's power here and there in Louisiana, but in fact the influence of the organization on politics in the Pelican State was comparatively small. With at least half of the state's population, the Catholic element, flatly opposed to the Klan, the strength of the order was limited to northern and western Louisiana and the "Florida parishes" in the extreme eastern part of the state. The size of the Klan in Louisiana never exceeded about 50,000 members.[21] The Louisiana Klan always lacked the kind of ambitious, ruthless, and capable political leadership that operated in Arkansas under Comer, in Texas under Z. E. Marvin, or in Oklahoma under DeBarr and N. Clay

[20] New York *Times*, November 1, 1923, p. 1.
[21] This estimate is from Washington *Post*, November 2, 1930, sec. I, p. 4.

Jewett. As a result of its sectional concentration within the state, its relatively small size, and its lack of a determined leadership, the Klan's career in Louisiana politics was not notably successful. Nevertheless, as the discussion in a later chapter will show, the presence of the Klan did have some bearing on the 1923-1924 gubernatorial campaign in Louisiana. And during 1922 and 1923, when there were no state or parish elections, the Klan occasionally threw its weight into local campaigns.

The city primaries of the summer of 1922 in Baton Rouge, the state capital, furnish an example of the Klan's activities in local politics in Louisiana. Turner Bynum, a Baton Rouge banker, anti-Klanner, and candidate for the Democratic nomination for mayor in the city primary, charged that his opponent, railroad conductor Ralph Mc-Burney, was a member of the Klan and had the support of the local chapter. In the first primary, a month earlier, McBurney had led the ticket, but since he had not polled a majority over Bynum and a third candidate, McBurney and Bynum had entered a "runoff" primary. McBurney ignored Bynum's charge of membership in the Klan. Baton Rouge Klan No. 3, however, accused the Reverend Leo Gassler of St. Joseph's Catholic Church of instructing his parishioners to vote against the alleged Klan candidate. The stigma of the Klan proved fatal to McBurney's chances in the capital city, where the Klan was fairly strong, but where opposition to the order was stronger. Bynum won the nomination with 1,892 votes to McBurney's 1,749. In a race also centering on the Klan issue an anti-Klan candidate for city judge won the nomination over an opponent generally credited with Klan support. The Democratic nominees were elected in the fall general election, a mere formality in one-party Louisiana.[22]

Beginning in the fall of 1922 and continuing through most of the next year, Governor John M. Parker of Louis-

[22] New Orleans *Times-Picayune*, July 3-5, 1922.

iana carried on a running fight with the Klan in his state. At the height of Parker's feud with the hooded crusaders came one of the few unequivocal Klan versus anti-Klan election contests in Louisiana. Judge R. R. Reid of Amite died in November 1922, leaving a place vacant on the state supreme court from the Fifth Judicial District, in southeastern Louisiana. Columbus Reid, Judge Reid's son; Robert D. Ellis, also of Amite; and District Judge H. F. Brunot of Baton Rouge announced their candidacies for the supreme court seat. A special primary was to be held in March 1923 to choose the Democratic nominee for the seat. Reid and Ellis, admitting that they belonged to the Klan in Tangipahoa Parish, concentrated their attention on the virtues of the Klan and the demagoguery of John M. Parker. Brunot, a Protestant and an avowed opponent of the Klan, drew the support and praise of the governor. Throughout March, Klan and anti-Klan rallies were held in the fifth district. Dean R. L. Tullis of the Louisiana State University law school spoke at a big gathering of Brunot forces held at the Elks Theater in Baton Rouge. On election eve Klansmen from various parishes in the district staged a joint Ellis-Reid rally outside Baton Rouge, where William C. Barnette of Shreveport, general counsel for the Klan in Louisiana and lawyer for the Klansmen in the Morehouse Parish investigations, denounced Parker and "his tool," Brunot. Returns from the special primary gave Brunot a majority of 409 votes over his two Klan adversaries, thus obviating a runoff primary. Reid and Ellis charged fraud and appealed to the state supreme court, which denied their plea.[23]

Brunot's victory over the two Klansmen illustrated a basic lesson for the Klan and other strong minorities seeking political power: United, there was a good chance of winning, but division of voting strength or indecisiveness

[23] *Ibid.*, March 16, 23, 27, 28, 29, April 1, 1923; *Reid* v. *Brunot (Ellis, Intervener)*, 96 So. 43.

in choosing a candidate was fatal. Reid and Ellis divided the sizable Klan vote in the Fifth Judicial District, with the result that Brunot won a clear majority; the combined vote of the Klansmen carried only five of twelve parishes in the district.[24] Perhaps the Klan leadership in the area, headed by Great Titan Thomas F. DePaoli, planned to let the outcome of the first primary determine which Klansman would get the unified support of the Klan in the runoff. But as a result of these foolish tactics, there was no runoff, and the Klan suffered a serious setback just as the Realm and Provincial officials in Louisiana were scheming to make the influence of the organization felt in the coming gubernatorial election. The special primary in the Fifth Judicial District of Louisiana provided an excellent example of the weakness of the Klan's political leadership in the state.

Such fatuity did not characterize the career of the order in Texas politics. During 1922 the Klan was especially successful in the Lone Star State, where the secret society electioneered more openly and on a grander scale than in any other state. From 1922 to 1924 the Klan was the chief issue in the politics of Texas, where the voters, experiencing the apathy of the postwar years, needed issues.

In the spring of 1922, as the Klan prepared for its entrance into Texas politics, local Klans in the Realm of Texas laid aside whatever reservations they had previously had about admitting "aliens" to the Invisible Empire. "They just throwed the doors open, and every man that had the money, they took him in to get his vote," recalled a former member of a north Texas chapter, "and if he did not have any money, they took his note payable in the fall, and the thing then was to get his vote."[25] Such methods swelled the membership of the Texas Klan to perhaps 100,000. During 1922 the efforts of this unified minority sent Klans-

[24] New Orleans *Times-Picayune*, March 29, 1923.
[25] Testimony of W. H. Castles in *Senator from Texas Hearings*, 992.

men to the state legislature; elected sheriffs, attorneys, and judges at the local and district level; and won one of the most important victories in Klan history—the election of Earle B. Mayfield to the United States Senate.

In 1922 the followers of Evans were active in bringing about Klan successes in various states, but Texas was the only state where the Imperial Kligrapp intervened directly. Evans' heavy hand was most evident in the Texas senatorial race, the major statewide contest, since Governor Pat M. Neff, not openly hostile to the Klan, was almost certain to be renominated and thus reelected in overwhelmingly Democratic Texas. When Evans came to Atlanta in April as Imperial Kligrapp, he was unhappy over an agreement reached by the Klan bosses in Texas a few weeks earlier, whereby three Klansmen who had announced for the United States Senate—former Representative Robert L. Henry of Waco, attorney Sterling P. Strong of Dallas, and Mayfield, a member of the Texas Railroad Commission —were to have equal opportunities to bid for the votes of Texas Klansmen. Evans, as one of the Great Titans, had attended the conference in Waco at which the agreement was made and had urged the Klan officials to unite the organization behind Mayfield. At one point Evans turned to Erwin J. Clark, Great Titan of the Waco Province and a booster of Henry, and said: "Erwin, I have a dead one in Dallas [Strong] and you have a dead one here in Waco [Henry]. Mayfield is the man. Now, they are all three Klansmen, and Strong and Henry are both good fellows, and we do not want to hurt their feelings. Let them ride for awhile and at the proper time we will ditch them and concentrate on Mayfield."[26]

After Evans became Imperial Kligrapp, he set out to solidify the Texas Klan behind Mayfield. He held two more meetings with the Texas Klan hierarchy but was unable to persuade, cajole, or pressure Clark into deserting

[26] Testimony of Erwin J. Clark, *ibid.*, 65.

Henry or the ex-congressman into dropping out of the race. In exasperation Evans turned to two of his cohorts in the Realm of Texas, Marvin, his successor as Titan of the Dallas Province, and Grand Dragon Harwood of Fort Worth. Marvin staged an elimination primary in the Dallas Klan, the biggest local in the Southwest, and Mayfield received a majority over Henry and Strong. The leaders of Fort Worth Klan No. 101 conducted a like poll among the large membership of that chapter, and again Mayfield received a majority of preferential votes. Harwood then communicated the action of the two north Texas Klans to the other 240 or so Klans in the state, and within a short time nearly every active Klansman in Texas, including the members of Henry's chapter, Waco Klan No. 33, had accepted Mayfield as the official Klan candidate.[27]

Strong quietly accepted his fate and withdrew from the senatorial race in June. Henry, however, stubbornly refused to withdraw, even though completely abandoned by most of his sheeted brethren. Henry would attract only a handful of Klan votes and would finish last in the Democratic primary, but his public denunciations of the Klan politicos who he felt had betrayed him did much to air the political machinations of the order in Texas.[28]

By July 22, the day of the Democratic primary, Evans and his friends in Texas had united about 100,000 Klansmen behind Mayfield, an advantage that enabled the railroad commissioner to lead five opponents in the senatorial race. Elderly Charles A. Culberson, the incumbent, seeking a fifth term in the national upper house, finished a poor third. Billie Mayfield of Houston (no relation to Earle), editor of a weekly Klan newspaper and a candidate for lieutenant governor, as well as candidates endorsed by the Klan for state treasurer and state superintendent

[27] Testimony of Henry, Clark, and Dave C. McCord, *ibid.*, 55, 423-26, 377. See also pp. 569-70.

[28] Testimony of H. M. Keeling, *ibid.*, 463; Dallas *Morning News*, July 29, 1922.

of public instruction, survived the first primary and entered the runoff campaign.[29]

In the senatorial runoff Earle B. Mayfield faced the most controversial figure in Texas politics, James E. Ferguson of Temple. Ferguson, a demagogic, ruthless politician, was making a comeback after being impeached and ousted from the governorship in 1917 and running a bootless race for President on his own "American party" ticket in 1920.[30] The oracle of the white tenant farmer and day laborer, Ferguson had also become the outstanding antiprohibitionist in the state. Now he locked horns with Mayfield in one of the fiercest campaigns in the history of a state long noted for its vitriolic politics. Although "Farmer Jim," as Ferguson called himself, could find little wrong with the Klan except its political ambitions, he denounced those ambitions and the Klan candidate in the crude but effective fashion for which he had become famous. Among other choice epithets, he referred to Mayfield as a "Klandidate," a "drunkard," and the "crown prince of the Klan." Mayfield completely ignored the Klan issue (he explained that it was "a matter over which the United States Senate has no jurisdiction"), concentrating instead on Ferguson's besmirched public record and his well-known moistness on the liquor question.[31]

When the runoff primary returns were in, Mayfield had won the nomination over Ferguson by a margin of 44,607

[29] On the Klan affiliation of Billie Mayfield, George D. Garrett, candidate for treasurer, and Ed R. Bentley, candidate for state school superintendent, see the testimony of Brown Harwood in *Senator from Texas Hearings*, 558-59.

[30] For a more favorable view of Ferguson, see Ouida Ferguson Nalle, *The Fergusons of Texas* (San Antonio, 1946), written by Ferguson's daughter. For a summary of Texas political history in the twenties, see Rupert N. Richardson, *Texas, the Lone Star State* (2d ed., Englewood Cliffs, N. J., 1958), ch. xx; and Seth S. McKay, *Texas Politics, 1916-1944, with Special Reference to the German Counties* (Lubbock, 1954), ch. iii.

[31] Dallas *Morning News*, August 16, 26, 1922; McKay, *Texas Politics*; Nalle, *Fergusons of Texas*, 162-64.

votes. The Klan had nominated its favorite for senator, but its choices for lieutenant governor, state treasurer, and state school superintendent were beaten by their non-Klan opponents. A large majority of Klan-endorsed candidates in Harris (Houston), Dallas, McLennan (Waco), Jefferson (Beaumont), Tarrant (Fort Worth), Wichita (Wichita Falls), and many less populous counties, however, were nominated.[32] In Atlanta, Evans was jubilant. He had good reason to be happy. His supporters in Texas had done an excellent job of organizing the rank and file, not only behind Mayfield, but behind local candidates. In Dallas, for example, Klansmen set up precinct organizations outside the regular Democratic party machinery, conducted fund-raising drives for local Klan politicians, and perhaps gave money to Mayfield headquarters. The Fort Worth Klan made its members pledge to vote for the Klan ticket in the county primary and suspended two Knights who refused to support the entire slate.[33]

Klansmen and sympathizers controlled the state Democratic convention, held in San Antonio the first week in September, and shouted down all attempts to incorporate an anti-Klan plank in the party platform.[34] After the convention, angry Fergusonites and other Democratic Klan haters, calling themselves "Independent Democrats," bolted the party, fused with the Texas Republican party (which had gone on record against the Klan), and chose George E. B. Peddy, the young assistant district attorney of Harris

[32] Alexander Heard and Donald S. Strong, *Southern Primaries and Elections, 1920-1949* (University, Alabama, 1950), 133; testimony of Jesse Martin in *Fort Worth Grain and Elevator Co.* v. *Alliance Insurance Co.* (No. 1068) (United States District Court, Fort Worth, Texas), reported in Fort Worth *Star-Telegram,* January 2, 1924.

[33] Testimony of E. J. Jones, McCord, J. F. Collier, Keeling, and F. G. Van Valkenburg in *Senator from Texas Hearings,* 364, 373-75, 380, 382, 399-402, 466-77, 533-35; testimony of Martin and T. H. Mills in *Fort Worth Grain and Elevator Co.* v. *Alliance Insurance Co.,* reported in Fort Worth *Star-Telegram,* January 2, 1924.

[34] San Antonio *Express,* September 7, 1922.

County, to oppose Mayfield in the general election campaign.[35]

Peddy's campaign against the Klan in the fall, while less blustering than Ferguson's of the summer, was just as vigorous. But his chances were doomed from the outset. The votes of the Klansmen and their allies the prohibitionists remained solid for Mayfield; the primary pledge worked against the youthful Houstonian; and the secretary of state refused to certify Peddy's name for the November ballot because he had voted in the Democratic primaries. Peddy's supporters were not without legal weapons of their own. They charged Mayfield with excessive campaign expenditures and with being the candidate of a political conspiracy formed by the Klan, and they tried through the courts to have his name barred from the general election ballot. After a bewildering round of litigation, the state supreme court certified the name of Mayfield, the regular Democratic nominee. On November 5 Mayfield was elected senator, with 264,260 votes to 130,744 write-in votes for Peddy.[36] Just before the election, Evans, worried that Mayfield's name might be left off the ballot, may have given a delegation of Texas Klan officials $25,000 to use in educating Klansmen over the state in the proper way to write their candidate's name on the ballots.[37]

Submerged by Mayfield's vote in the general election, Peddy and his backers carried their charges against Mayfield and the Klan before the United States Senate Committee on Privileges and Elections. A subcommittee conducted an extended inquiry into the 1922 campaign in Texas, the Klan's part in the election of Mayfield, and the expenses of the senator-elect. After interviewing a number

35 Dallas *Morning News*, September 18, 1922.

36 Fort Worth *Star-Telegram*, September 26, 1922; Austin *American*, September 29, October 28, November 5, 1922; Dallas *Morning News*, October 3, 1922; Heard and Strong, *Southern Primaries and Elections*, 167-69.

37 Testimony of J. Q. Jett in *Senator from Texas Hearings*, 193.

of Klansmen from Atlanta and Texas and discovering abundant evidence of the solid backing given Mayfield by the Klan, the subcommittee finally voted to recommend his confirmation. On February 3, 1925, the Senate voted unanimously to seat Mayfield.[38]

The election of Mayfield amounted to a striking victory for the Klan, one of the best known and most spectacular of its numerous conquests in the twenties. And there were many more Klan successes in Texas during 1922 and 1923. The order probably had a majority in the house of representatives of the 38th Texas Legislature, which met in January of 1923. In county after county in the eastern two-thirds of the state the Klan's dominance was unquestioned. In 1923, a political off year in Texas, Klan endorsees lost in the city elections in San Antonio and El Paso, but the Klan established its firm control over the governments of Dallas, Fort Worth, and Wichita Falls.[39] At the beginning of 1924 Lone Star Klansmen could boast of the fact that Texas was the number one Klan state politically, and could look forward to even greater conquests that year.

The year 1922 saw the Klan enter statewide contests in four states. In Texas the secret organization elected a United States Senator, although failing in the other races for state office. In Oregon the Klan was responsible for the election of a Democratic governor in a predominantly Republican state, and in Georgia the order was strong enough to turn out a hostile governor and elect its own man to succeed him.[40] Finally, the Klan plunged into the malestrom that was Oklahoma politics in the 1920s and

[38] Dallas *Morning News*, February 4, 1925; *Congressional Record*, 68th Congress, 2d Session (1925), 2929-30.

[39] Austin *Statesman*, February 25, 1923; Fort Worth *American Citizen*, April 13, 1923.

[40] On Klan successes in 1922 in states outside the Southwest, see "Klan Victories in Oregon and Texas," *Literary Digest*, LXXXV (November 25, 1922), 12; Rice, *Ku Klux Klan in American Politics*, 46, 49, 58-63; Waldo Roberts, "The Ku-Kluxing of Oregon," *Outlook*, CXXXIII (March 14, 1923), 490-91.

tried to elect a governor. The Klan lost that contest, but at the local and district level and in the state legislature it built a system of power that would bring about the downfall of a foolhardy governor who had the temerity to join battle with the masked crusaders.

So 1922 was a watershed for the Klan movement. Henceforth, in almost every state where it attained much strength, the Klan would be preeminently a political organization. The paradox of a militant secret society, essentially totalitarian in philosophy and structure, thrusting its way into the democratic processes was obvious to outsiders and to a growing number of Klansmen. The dangers of dissension arising from this paradox would hereafter plague the Klan.

Klan nighttime initiation near Lone Wolf, Oklahoma, ca. 1922. Courtesy Western History Collections, University of Oklahoma Library.

K. K. K.

Election of Officers of Anadarko Klan will be held Tuesday, May 13. All Klansmen are urged to attend. Important.

The Ku Klux Kreed

I believe in God and in the tenets of the Christian religion and that a Godless nation can not long prosper.

I believe that a church that is not grounded on the principles of morality and justice is a mockery to God and to man.

I believe that a church that does not have the welfare of the common people at heart is unworthy.

I believe in the eternal separation of church and state.

I hold no allegiance to any foreign government, emperor, king, pope or any other foreign, political or religious power.

I hold my allegiance to the Stars and Stripes next to my allegiance to God alone.

I believe in just laws and liberty.

I believe in the upholding of the constitution of these United States.

I believe that our free public school is the corner stone of good government and that those who are seeking to destroy it are enemies of our republic and are unworthy of citizenship.

I believe in freedom of speech.

I believe in a free press uncontrolled by political parties or by religious sects.

I believe in law and order.

I believe in the protection of pure womanhood.

I do not believe in mob violence, but I do believe that laws should be enacted to prevent the causes of mob violence.

I believe in a closer relationship of capital and labor.

I believe in the prevention of unwarranted strikes by foreign labor agitators.

I believe in the limitation of foreign immigration.

I believe in the supremacy of the White Race.

I am a native born American citizen and I believe my rights in this country are superior to those of foreigners.

If you believe in the above creed and desire to join an organization standing for and advocating the above principles sign on line below and mail to P. O. Box 30, Oklahoma City, Oklahoma, or hand to some person you know to be a Klansman.

....

P. O. ....

R. F. D. ....

Initiatory Fee $10.   **Annual Dues $5.**

Blackwell, Okla., Klan Distributes Truck Loads of Food and Clothing

BLACKWELL KLAN NO. 44, REALM OF OKLAHOMA, used several trucks to distribute the baskets of food, toys and clothing sent to more than a hundred needy families the day before Christmas. Santa Klaus was in charge of each truck and personally presented the baskets at the door of each home visited. Much credit was given the Women of the Ku Klux Klan for their work of assembling the groceries and gifts and arranging the baskets.

Above: Klan benevolence: members of the Blackwell, Oklahoma, Klan No. 44 joining Santa Claus in delivering food, toys, and clothing to the needy, 24 December 1924. Courtesy Western History Collections, University of Oklahoma Library.

Facing page: Advertisement in Anadarko *American-Democrat,* Oklahoma, 7 May 1924, for a Klan meeting, showing the Kreed and an application to join the Klan. Courtesy Western History Collections, University of Oklahoma Library.

Above: John C. "Jack" Walton, fifth governor of Oklahoma, impeached and removed in 1923 by a largely pro-Klan legislature. Courtesy Western History Collections, University of Oklahoma Library.

Facing page: Advertisement in Anadarko *American-Democrat*, Oklahoma, 23 July 1924, for a Klan rally at local fair grounds. Courtesy Western History Collections, University of Oklahoma Library.

Robed but unmasked members of Dallas, Texas, Klan No. 66's drum and bugle corps members with mounted and unrobed Klansmen and Klanswomen at a rodeo staged in conjunction with the annual Klorero (state Klan convention), San Antonio, Texas, 1924. From the collections of the Dallas Historical Society, reprinted by permission.

Klavern of Little Rock, Arkansas, Klan No. 1, which met on the third
floor of the Dodge and Osborn Building, Main and Fourth Streets.
Photo by Larry Obsitnik, courtesy of the Arkansas Historical
Association.

R. A. "Bob" Cook, Exalted Cyclops of Little Rock Klan No. 1 in 1924. Courtesy of the Arkansas Historical Association.

7.

"Neither Klan nor King"

IN THE EARLY 1920s Oklahoma was in only the second decade of statehood. The Sooner State presented what one writer called "a curious mixture of the Old South, the pioneer West, and hustling modern Rotary Club Babittism."[1] On one hand there was rampant business prosperity based mainly on the state's expanding oil industry; on the other, widespread agricultural distress had given rise to a strong agrarian radical movement. On the liquor question most Oklahomans not only voted dry, but they were willing, as members of the Klan, to take a horsewhip or a razorstrop to suspected bootleggers. By 1922 Oklahoma had had four governors; three of them, together with a lieutenant governor, had been threatened with impeachment by contrary legislatures. The current governor, James B. A. Robertson, was under indictment in a district court in Okmulgee for accepting a bribe from a violator of the state banking laws.[2] Oklahoma already had a tradition of mistrusting its public officials and taking quick action against them, at both state and local levels, if there was any suspicion of misconduct.

In 1922 two potent ingredients were added to the already
spicy Oklahoma political stew—the Klan and the Farmer-
Labor Reconstruction League. The Klan, concerned mainly
with bringing law and order to Oklahoma, infiltrated both
political parties. Oklahoma did have a legitimate two-party
system in the early twenties, although the Republican party
had never elected a governor and had carried the state in
only one presidential election, that of 1920. But the Republicans were in the majority in most of the state's northern
counties, had won control of the state house of representatives in 1920, and usually offered stiff opposition to the
Democrats in all elections. By contrast, the Farmer-Labor
Reconstruction League, organized in September 1921 by
representatives of the Farmer's Union, the state Federation
of Labor, and the Railway Brotherhoods, worked only
within the Democratic party, although it included many
former Republicans and Socialists. On February 23, 1922,
the Reconstruction League, in convention at Shawnee,
adopted a platform emphasizing liberal economic and social
reform. It chose as its gubernatorial candidate in the
Democratic primary John Callaway "Jack" Walton, the
mayor of Oklahoma City.[3]

Walton was in his early forties when he decided to run
for governor. Born in Indiana, he had worked on a railway
construction gang in the Oklahoma Territory and in Mexico
City. He had briefly studied civil and electrical engineering,
worked in Oklahoma City as a salesman for a while, and
then, in 1906, formed a small utilities company. In 1917

[1] Bruce Bliven, "From the Oklahoma Front," *New Republic* XXXVI
(October 17, 1923), 202.

[2] See the Tulsa *Tribune*, September 18, 26, 1922; New York *Times*,
December 3, 1922, sec. i, pt. 2, p. 5.

[3] On the Farmer-Labor Reconstruction League, see Gilbert C.
Fite, "Oklahoma's Reconstruction League: An Experiment in Farmer-
Labor Politics," *Journal of Southern History*, XIII (November 1947),
535-55, and "John A. Simpson: The Southwest's Militant Farm
Leader," *Mississippi Valley Historical Review*, XXXV (March 1949),
563-84.

he had been elected commissioner of public works in Oklahoma City, and two years later he had been elected mayor of the capital city. As mayor, Walton issued a warning to the members of his police force that membership in the Klan would not be tolerated. The city Chamber of Commerce fought him because he supported local packing-house workers during a strike, and Walton, displaying the same penchant for direct action that later characterized his brief reign as governor, threw the Chamber of Commerce president in jail for several hours.[4] Walton's personal appearance, while not unattractive, was unimpressive. An observer described him as "thick set, of medium height, with college-cut brown hair, the rounded, fleshy face of the politician, large protuberant eyes, and a weak mouth."[5] But the mayor, posing as the poor man's friend, had a certain charm which appealed to the Farmer-Labor people and which would help to make him governor of Oklahoma.

In the 1922 gubernatorial campaign most of the liberal and radical sentiment in Oklahoma united in the Reconstruction League and behind Walton. The "progressive" element, meaning the prohibitionist, economy-minded segment of the population concerned principally with honest government and law and order, divided its support between Thomas H. Owen, former chief justice of the state supreme court, and Robert H. Wilson of Chickasha, the state superintendent of public instruction and a Klansman. Sometime in the spring of 1922, probably early in May, Grand Dragon Edwin DeBarr and his associates in the hierarchy of the Oklahoma Klan decided that the Klan should throw its 75,000 or so votes behind Wilson. On May 14 E. B. Howard of Tulsa, a Klansman and a former United States Representative, withdrew from the governor's race. Howard then announced for Congress. With the support of the powerful

[4] Howard A. Tucker, *Governor Walton's Ku Klux Klan War* (Oklahoma City, 1923), 3-6.
[5] Bliven, "From the Oklahoma Front," 203.

Klan organization in Tulsa County, he would be nominated in the Democratic primary and elected in November.[6]

The Klan did not openly campaign for Wilson, but by August 1, the day of the party primaries, the fact that the Klansmen had formed ranks solidly behind the state school superintendent was common knowledge. The Klan heirarchy also sent out word that George F. Short, Democratic candidate for attorney general, must be elected. Short's opponent had called the Klan's outrages "unspeakable and innumerable" and had pointed out that not one night-rider had been brought to justice.[7]

Wilson's strength, and the bulk of the Klan's, lay in the central, northern, and eastern parts of the state. Walton drew his main support from the farmers in the western and southern counties and from the oilfield workers and miners in the eastern and southeastern counties.[8] The Oklahoma City mayor was a colorful campaigner. He carried a jazz band with him in his jaunts over the state while he thundered denunciations of Owen and the Oklahoma City *Daily Oklahoman,* Wilson, the "Marland and Dutch-Shell oil interests," the Oklahoma City Chamber of Commerce, and the Oklahoma Gas and Electric Company. While he did not mention the Klan or Wilson's connection with the secret society, he received the endorsement of thousands of Roman Catholics over the state, along with the enthusiastic support of Patrick S. Nagle, recognized Socialist chief in Oklahoma and editor of the *Oklahoma Leader.*[9]

Two days before the primaries Klansmen circulated

[6] Ernest T. Bynum, *Personal Recollections of Ex-Governor Walton* (2d. ed., Oklahoma City, 1924), 39-40; Victor E. Harlow, *Oklahoma: Its Origin and Development* (Oklahoma City, 1949), 357; Tulsa *Tribune,* May 15, 1922.

[7] New York *Times,* June 18, 1922, sec. VIII, p. 6.

[8] See the county by county survey of the gubernatorial race in Tulsa *Tribune,* July 23, 27-31, 1922.

[9] Oscar Ameringer, *If You Don't Weaken* (New York, 1940), 369-72; Oklahoma City *Daily Oklahoman,* July 16, 1922; Harlow, *Oklahoma,* 358.

model Klan Democratic tickets in many of the Protestant churches of Oklahoma City. Wilson headed the ticket, which included an expression of preference for most state offices and an endorsement of a full slate of candidates for county offices. Shortly before noon on the day of the primaries, the sheriff in Tulsa arrested two election workers for passing out sample Klan ballots for both Republican and Democratic primaries. The Tulsa ticket indicated the Klan's choices among Republican county candidates and Democratic state and county aspirants. Again Wilson headed the Democratic Klan state.[10]

Walton—"Our Jack," as the Reconstruction Leaguers called him—led the Democratic ticket in the August 1 primary. Although he did not have a clear majority over Wilson and Owen, Oklahoma law and party regulations made no provision for a runoff primary, and the trust-baiting mayor won the nomination. Final returns gave Walton 119,504 votes; Wilson, 84,569; and Owen, 64,229. Short won the Democratic nomination for attorney general. Although failing to nominate a candidate for governor, the Klan nominated most of its favorites in both parties for county and district offices in Tulsa, Oklahoma, Okmulgee, Muskogee, Osage (Pawhuska), Washington (Bartlesville), Grady (Lawton), Rogers (Claremore), and other counties.[11] A Tulsa newspaper after the primaries commented that "politicians admit that the Knights of the Invisible Empire have control of the political situation in this county today and must be reckoned with."[12]

Grand Dragon DeBarr now had to reckon with an angry board of regents at the University of Oklahoma. The previous spring the board of regents had instructed faculty members at the University not to take part in "the con-

[10] Oklahoma City *Daily Oklahoman*, July 31, 1922; Tulsa *Tribune*, August 1, 1922.
[11] Oklahoma City *Daily Oklahoman*, August 15, 1922; Tulsa *Tribune*, August 3, 4, 1922.
[12] Tulsa *Tribune*, August 6, 1922.

troversy that exists throughout the state in connection with
the Ku Klux Klan and the Anti-Ku Klux Klan." On August
5 the president of the board, pointing out that DeBarr had
made speeches on Wilson's behalf and had mailed model
Klan tickets to local Klans over the state, charged the
chemistry professor with conduct "in direct violation of the
policy of the university." Claiming that he had been
"greatly misrepresented," the Grand Dragon retorted: "If
thirty years of living and doing in Norman and in Oklahoma
is not sufficient defense, then I have none other to make."
And the Norman chapter of the University alumni association added: "If Dr. DeBarr is a Klansman, then the Klan
is to be congratulated on the high type of its membership."
The board of regents voted to reprimand DeBarr officially.
The professor talked for a time of taking the whole affair
into court, but he eventually accepted the regents' condemnation and stayed on at the University. In the spring
of 1923 he resigned the Grand Dragon's office and was
succeeded by N. Clay Jewett, a handsome Oklahoma City
businessman.[13]

At the state Democratic convention in September, Walton
and his followers stood on the "Shawnee platform" adopted
by the Reconstruction League the previous February and
refused to accept the conservative regular Democratic
platform. The party endorsed the league's proposals, whereupon many Democrats who could not accept the radicalism
of the league and its candidate bolted the Democratic
party and threw their support to the Republican nominee,
spade-bearded John Fields, editor of a conservative agricultural weekly called the *Oklahoma Farmer*. The bolters,
who coalesced around an organization formed in Oklahoma
and Tulsa counties under the name "Constitutional Demo-

[13] "The University of Oklahoma and the Ku Klux Klan," *School
and Society*, XVI (October 7, 1922), 412-13; Oklahoma City *Daily
Oklahoman*, August 6, 7, 16, 1922; Atlanta *Imperial Nighthawk*,
May 9, 1923.

crats," included many Democratic Klansmen, particularly in the industrial counties in eastern Oklahoma. The state Klan organization took no part in the general election campaign, and Wilson endorsed Walton and the Democratic party, thereby inaugurating a short honeymoon between Walton and the Klansmen who remained Democrats.[14]

The general election, on November 7, saw Walton poll 280,206 votes to Fields' 230,469, a surprisingly large total for a Republican candidate for governor. Fields carried Tulsa County, strong Klan territory and usually Democratic; there the rest of the Democratic state candidates piled up majorities averaging about 3,000 votes over their Republican opponents. In Tulsa County the Klan could not lose. In the races for sheriff and county attorney, for example, the nominees of both parties were Klansmen. In the former contest a Democrat was elected, but a Republican was elected county attorney.[15]

On January 10, 1923, Walton began his administration with the biggest barbecue in Oklahoma history, held at the state fairgrounds.[16] He promised to enact the Shawnee platform, but he did not talk about the Klan, claiming that it was a "dead issue." Only a few weeks after his inauguration, however, he ordered Attorney General Short to help the county attorney of Harmon County in his investigation of the whipping of a man near Hollis. The inquiry produced no results, but the Klan-haters among Walton's followers gained assurance that "Our Jack" was not in sympathy with the masked order. Aldrich Blake, a Muskogee publicity agent whom Walton had appointed to the wholly extraconstitutional post of "executive counselor," announced, "The governor is determined that these masked

14 Harlow, *Oklahoma*, 358-59; Bynum, *Personal Recollections of Ex-Governor Walton*, 41.

15 Tulsa *Tribune*, November 8, 1922.

16 Edward E. Dale and Jesse L. Rader, *Readings in Oklahoma History* (Evanston, Ill., 1930), 735-39.

outrages must stop, and he will use every power of the state government to see that persons participating in such mobs are punished."[17]

But Walton was not content to pin his fortunes solely on the following of farmers, laborers, Socialists, and Catholics that had elected him. When he came into office, Walton faced a legislature that, while overwhelmingly Democratic, contained a majority of conservative Klansmen and sympathizers, hostile to the Farmer-Labor movement and "Our Jack." Walton realized that the conservative majority was unwilling to accept more than a few Reconstruction League proposals, that there was strong opposition to him within his own party, and that the biggest single group opposing him was the Klan. So he hopefully turned toward the many prominent Klansmen who flocked to his office in the capitol during the early days of his administration. As Ernest T. Bynum, Walton's campaign manager, confidant, and state banking commissioner, described it: "From the very beginning of his official term friendly relations with the klan increased until his most confidential advisers in the House and Senate appeared to be of that persuasion. Leading appointments were conferred upon members of the hooded order, and not infrequently he would hold long conferences behind locked doors with titans, cyclopses, and kleagles. . . . He wanted to do all he could for his new friends without breaking with the old."[18]

In one of those conferences behind locked doors the governor became a "Klansman at Large." Before Walton took office, Dr. W. T. Tilley, a Muskogee Kleagle, contacted Minor Meriwether of Tulsa, Great Titan of Province No. 3, about the creation of such a designation for the new chief executive. Meriwether wrote Imperial Wizard Hiram W. Evans on the matter; Evans replied that the title Klansman at Large could be conferred by the Realm administration

[17] Oklahoma City *Daily Oklahoman,* January 29, 1923.
[18] Bynum, *Personal Recollections of Ex-Governor Walton,* 71-72.

with the approval of the Wizard on "public officials whose membership is for the good of the order to remain a secret." Meriwether then wrote Kleagle Tilley that he could go ahead with whatever he had in mind for Walton.[19] Sometime in late January, Tilley met in Walton's capitol office with Walton and Dr. A. E. Davenport, the state health commissioner and a Klansman. Walton filled out an application for membership in the Klan as a Klansman at Large and gave Tilley twenty dollars as a klectoken for the special title. Meriwether forwarded the klectoken and the governor's application to Grand Dragon DeBarr in Oklahoma City, together with a recommendation that Tilley be granted life membership in the Klan for "one of the best pieces of work that has been pulled by a Klansman in the history of the state." But, cautioned the Titan, "Governor Walton does not want anyone . . . to know of this. I believe it wise for you not to approach him in any way for the present." Brown Harwood, the ex-Dragon from Texas who had become Imperial Klazik (officer in charge of Realms), wrote Tilley expressing "deep appreciation" for the "splendid feat of service" of securing Walton's application, and on May 5, 1923, Klan Emperor William J. Simmons conferred life membership on the Muskogee man.[20]

While Walton was becoming a Klansman at Large, one of his most ardent followers in the house of representatives, Fred Brydia of Pontotoc County, introduced a bill to require publication of the names of all members of secret

[19] Minor Meriwether to Dr. W. T. Tilley, January 11, 1923, photographic copy in Jack C. Walton Collection, Division of Manuscripts, University of Oklahoma Library, Norman.

[20] Minor Meriwether to Edwin DeBarr, February 14, 1923, Brown Harwood to W. T. Tilley, undated, William J. Simmons to Tilley, May 5, 1923, reprinted in Oklahoma City Oklahoma Leader, December 14, 1923. Copies of correspondence relating to Walton's becoming a Klansman were printed in other newspapers in Oklahoma, but the Oklahoma Leader, the Socialist and Reconstruction League organ edited by Patrick S. Nagle, carried the most complete collection of letters.

organizations operating within the state. Several known Klansmen in the house charged that Brydia was turned down when he applied for membership in the Klan. Brydia heatedly denied the charge. The Walton administration ignored both Brydia and his anti-Klan bill. When the bill came to a vote, the house rejected it, with only the Farmer-Labor representatives, about thirty strong, casting their votes for its passage.[21]

Despite his dalliance with the Klan, "Our Jack" wanted to keep his Farmer-Labor support intact, and he worked earnestly with the Reconstruction League minority in the legislature to put into law the league's program. Some ameliorative measures were passed, but the main planks of the Shawnee platform—a state bank, a state insurance system, a generous soldiers' bonus—died as the session came to a close. By the time the 9th Oklahoma Legislature adjourned, it had listened to a speech by a national lecturer for the Klan, had tacked an antievolution amendment onto the free textbook bill passed during the session, and had blocked most of the efforts of the governor and the Reconstruction League to enact the league's liberal platform.[22]

In the meantime Walton instigated a major shakeup in the administration of the state institutions of higher learning. He removed five of the regents of the University of Oklahoma and appointed five of his friends to fill their places. Under increasing pressure from Walton, the president of the University resigned. Walton removed the president of the Agricultural and Mechanical College and appointed a Socialist politician to the post, a move that brought so much vilification from the alumni of the school and other conservative groups that Walton quickly fired the Socialist and appointed a man with more orthodox

[21] Oklahoma City *Daily Oklahoman,* February 1, 2, 1923; 9th Oklahoma Legislature, *House Journal,* Regular Session, 255, 291, 406, 409, 422, 441, 442.

[22] New York *Times,* March 17, 1923; Tulsa *Tribune,* same date.

economic views. The fumbling governor succeeded in alienating all groups concerned. To make matters worse, he accepted a $48,000 home in Oklahoma City as a "gift" from a well-known oilman, proclaimed that during his administration the practice of capital punishment would be abandoned, and instituted a liberal pardon and parole policy, sometimes setting free convicted criminals before they reached the state penitentiary.[23]

By the spring of 1923 Jack Walton, who had promised so much and accomplished so little, was on the verge of political bankruptcy. He had driven away many of his original followers and virtually destroyed the Farmer-Labor-Catholic-Socialist coalition that had made him governor. And he had not built any real basis of support among the conservative groups, who still distrusted him and wanted to see him out of the governor's chair. It seemed that the legislative session had ended just in time for Walton. There was an increasing amount of talk around Oklahoma City that Walton's opponents might resort to the already traditional Oklahoma practice of bringing impeachment charges against the governor.[24] Walton needed some new issue, a distraction, a device with which to rebuild his collapsing popularity. Once again he turned to the Klan. This time, however, he did not propose an alliance with the hooded order.

During the first few months of 1923 the epidemic of Klan terrorism which had surged over Oklahoma for two years slackened appreciably. Evans, as Imperial Wizard, was working to curb the violent acts of local Klans over the nation, particularly in the Southwest, while the Oklahoma Klan itself was turning away from vigilantism and

[23] Bliven, "From the Oklahoma Front," 204; Harlow, *Oklahoma*, 360; Edwin C. McReynolds, *Oklahoma: A History of the Sooner State* (Norman, 1954), 343-44; Edward E. Dale and Morris L. Wardell, *History of Oklahoma* (Englewood Cliffs, N.J., 1948), 338.

[24] See the analysis of the political situation in the state in Tulsa *Tribune*, June 13, 1923.

devoting more and more of its attention to politics. But there were still some Klansmen who liked to venture into the night to rectify someone's objectionable conduct or settle a personal grudge. As the summer approached, a new outbreak of masked attacks occurred in Oklahoma, although not on nearly so large a scale as the earlier campaign of terrorism. Walton announced that he was going to give the local law officers a chance to stop the masked lawlessness, but that if they failed, he would call out the national guard and see if the state could not protect its citizens. "This is serious and I mean business," said the governor. But he did not specifically attack the Klan.[25]

Attorney General Short admitted that his office had received many complaints describing the activities of hooded bands, but he added that since almost all the communications were anonymous, it was difficult to conduct an effective investigation of the allegations.[26] Walton waved aside the advice of Short and others around him. He decided on a scheme whereby he would substitute general anti-Klan sentiment for the lost support of the Reconstruction League, make himself a national figure, and destroy the credibility of his critics by painting them "with the common brush of Klannishness."[27] He would, in short, declare war on the Klan.

On Tuesday, June 26, acting on a complaint signed by three Okmulgee County citizens that the sheriff was "utterly indifferent" to the presence of mob violence, Walton declared martial law in the county and ordered between 300 and 400 national guardsmen to move into the area and supersede the civil authority. "I am going to stamp mob rule and mob violence out of Oklahoma," snapped Walton, "if I have to put every county under military law. . . . I have tried and tried to get results through the regular civil

[25] Oklahoma City *Daily Oklahoman*, May 14, 1923.
[26] *Ibid*, May 15, 1923.
[27] Bliven, "From the Oklahoma Front," 204.

agencies without success. Local officials are too often allied with these secret, lawless mobs and I have gotten no results. I am determined to get results."[28]

The state troops set up a military court in Okmulgee and invited people who had been abused by masked bands to come forward and testify. Adjutant General Baird H. Markham said that he could see little need for martial law in Okmulgee County. A man identified only as "a prominent citizen of Okmulgee" told a newspaper reporter that the membership of the Klan in the county had declined from a peak of about 3,000 to 1,500, with small attendance at the meetings. An anti-Klan organization called the "True Blues" had ceased to function, and most Klansmen and ex-Klansmen had joined a county peace movement to try to allay strife between the Klan and its enemies.[29]

Only three days after the declaration of martial law Walton, on General Markham's recommendation, withdrew all troops from Okmulgee County except for a small district around the mining town of Henryetta. The military court had uncovered no evidence of mob rule in the county, and it appeared unlikely that it would. A company of troops stayed in Henryetta until July 12, when Walton, after conferring with county officials and reaching what he termed "perfect accord in regard to the Okmulgee County situation," issued an order ending martial law in the Henryetta district and withdrawing the troops.[30] Throughout the entire Okmulgee "war" not one state official had mentioned the name of the Klan.

The Okmulgee enterprise proved a damaging venture. While the state health commissioner was reporting that the governor was on the verge of a nervous breakdown and would have to go into seclusion, Walton went on a house-

[28] Tulsa *Tribune*, June 27, 1923; Oklahoma City *Daily Oklahoman*, same date.
[29] Tulsa *Tribune*, June 28, 1923.
[30] *Ibid.*, June 29-July 1, July 5, 12, 1923.

buying tour in Muskogee. Executive Counselor Blake asserted that as many as 2,500 people had been whipped in Oklahoma during the past year.[31] The newspapers of the state, led by the *Tulsa Tribune*, began training their editorial guns on the governor. "The whole life of the state suffers from the whims of this pitiful child-man," declared the *Tribune* after Walton had pardoned two men convicted of vote fraud in Tulsa earlier in the year. "For his own good, no less than that of the state, he should go, and as soon as possible. The mess he has made of the biggest chance any Oklahoman ever had proves how utterly impossible he is." The Tulsa daily predicted that Walton would almost certainly be impeached at the next session of the legislature.[32] The harassed ex-railway hand doubtless agreed with the *Tribune's* prediction. His military sortie into Okmulgee County had been a failure, mainly because people refused to get excited about Klan lawlessness and because he could obtain no solid evidence against the order. He needed a concrete example of mob violence, something to arouse the people and give him a real excuse to send in the troops.

The excuse for which he had been waiting came the evening of August 9 in Tulsa. Six unmasked men kidnaped suspected narcotic peddler and bootlegger Nathan Hantaman, a Jew, outside the Wonderland Theater, put him in an automobile, took him to a spot on the Sand Springs road, and lashed him unmercifully with a black-snake whip. The next day Walton said that he thought the sheriff and county attorney in Tulsa were investigating the incident well enough without his intervention. But on the eleventh he deputized a Tulsa political hack named Lee Kunsman to look into the whipping, and a day later he received Kunsman and the battered Hantaman in his

[31] Oklahoma City *Daily Oklahoman*, July 19, 1923; Tulsa *Tribune*, July 20, 1923.
[32] Tulsa *Tribune*, August 1, 1923.

executive chambers in Oklahoma City. Late Monday afternoon, August 13, Walton declared the city of Tulsa under martial law and sent about 150 national guardsmen into the oil city. Early the next morning Adjutant General Markham convened a military court of inquiry in a suite in the Hotel Tulsa, while in the lobby downstairs and in the streets outside dozens of men carrying special police commissions from Walton detained passers-by and questioned them about the Klan's activities in the city. On August 15 three companies of guardsmen were in Tulsa as the military authorities took control of the police department and the sheriff's office, forbade criticism of state and military personnel, and prohibited the carrying of firearms in the city limits. Although the military court could find no trace of Hantaman's floggers, it did begin interviewing victims of hooded assaults dating back to 1921. On the afternoon of the fifteenth, guardsmen arrested two men for a flogging that had occurred the previous April.[33]

Press reaction to the imposition of martial law in Tulsa was immediate and mostly condemnatory. "The grounds are not sufficiently clear to warrant martial law," concluded the Ponca City *News*. The Oklahoma City *Daily Oklahoman* criticized the dispatch of troops to Tulsa and pointed out Walton's inactivity during the violent packinghouse strike of 1920 in Oklahoma City. A Pawnee weekly reasoned that "by his [Walton's] very acts, his failure to enforce the simplest laws, his failure to protect life and property, he gives the Klan an excuse for existing in Oklahoma."[34] Only the Tulsa *Daily World*, a Republican paper, sympathized with the governor. "As between the invisible empire and its flagrant disregard of the rights of citizenship," commented the Tulsa journal, "its treasonable and vicious

[33] Tulsa *Daily World*, August 11, 1923; Tulsa *Tribune*, August 12, 14, 16, 1923; New York *Times*, August 14, 1923, p. 5.

[34] Oklahoma City *Daily Oklahoman*, August 15, 1923; Ponca City *News* and Pawnee *Courier-Dispatch*, quoted in Tulsa *Tribune*, August 16, 19, 1923.

defiance of orderly government, as evidenced by the blazing crosses and mob activities, *The World* admits its choice is with Governor Walton."[35]

The days passed with guardsmen patrolling the streets of Tulsa, enforcing a curfew, and bringing more prisoners to the national guard armory for detention. Three admitted Klansmen confessed to participating in a whipping and received two-year sentences from the military court. The night of August 30 Walton heard that another Tulsa resident, a suspected car thief, had been kidnaped within a block of Markham's headquarters. Charging that the civil authorities in Tulsa County were in "secret sympathy with those responsible for mob floggings," he decreed absolute martial law and the suspension of habeas corpus for the entire county. Two hundred more guardsmen entered the city of Tulsa and began strict enforcement of a sundown curfew. Now the civil officers could operate only after securing permission from the military. Walton left Oklahoma City on a speaking tour in the eastern half of the state, where he told his listeners to shoot on sight any masked men who tried to assault them. "I don't care if you burst right into them with a double-barreled shotgun," shouted Walton. "I'll promise you a pardon in advance."[36]

More than three weeks after the martial law edict for Tulsa, Walton finally moved toward an open fight with the Klan. Blake began a series of syndicated newspaper articles describing the mob outrages in Tulsa County and placing responsibility for the deeds directly on the Klan. The Klan leaders in Oklahoma were slow in responding to Walton's declaration of war on their organization, but finally they acted. Jewett retorted that the governor's only interest was persecuting the Klan and that he was trying for the Demo-

[35] Tulsa *Daily World*, quoted in "Masked Floggers of Tulsa," *Literary Digest*, LXXVIII (September 22, 1923), 17.

[36] Tulsa *Daily World*, August 24, 1923; Tulsa *Tribune*, August 31, September 1, 4, 1923; New York *Times*, September 1, 1923, p. 2.

cratic vice-presidential nomination in 1924 (this was the same charge Louisiana Klansmen had made against Governor Parker earlier in the year). Jewett claimed that the Oklahoma City Klan had refused to accept Walton when he had applied for membership. While some of the Tulsa floggers belonged to the Klan, admitted the Grand Dragon, the organization as a whole was not responsible for any mob violence. Then Jewett threw his long-expected challenge at the governor: "Jack Walton and all his cohorts never will be able to break the power of the Klan in Oklahoma."[37]

Now it was Walton's turn. In a speech at the Marshall County fair in Madill he proclaimed that all Klan parades were "banned in Oklahoma from now until the termination of my administration." Walton perhaps hoped that the Klan would defy him and furnish an excuse for more extreme measures; instead, Grand Dragon Jewett complied with the governor's latest edict by issuing an order forbidding local Klans from holding any masked assemblies. From Atlanta, Evans said that the Imperial Klan would not interfere in the Oklahoma troubles because the order wanted to avoid giving Walton an excuse for putting the whole state under martial law.[38]

On the twenty-eighth day of military rule in Tulsa, September 11, Walton came to the oil city to confer with a delegation from the local Chamber of Commerce. There he laid down his terms for the withdrawal of the troops: the selection of a new jury commission and the resignations of the sheriff, the police commissioner, and the police chief. Leaving the businessmen to consider his terms, Walton retired to the Tulsa Country Club for a round of golf. The actions of the Chamber of Commerce delegation were puzzling. On September 12 the group voted to reject

[37] Tulsa *Tribune*, September 7, 1923; New York *Times*, September 8, 1923, p. 15; Oklahoma City *Daily Oklahoman*, same date.
[38] Oklahoma City *Daily Oklahoman*, September 9, 1923; New York *Times*, September 11, 1923, p. 19; Tulsa *Tribune*, same date.

Walton's terms, but the next day the business leaders reported officially: "We find that the Ku Klux Klan is responsible and check it up to them to remove the soldiers from our city." Walton abandoned the negotiations and prepared to return to Oklahoma City. Before his departure he turned angrily on the Tulsa *Tribune,* which had led the criticism of his policies, and fastened military censorship on the paper's editorial page. A day later, under threat of court action by the owners of the *Tribune,* Walton removed the censor.[39]

Now, with the whole state at his mercy, "Our Jack" reached out for more power. He sent an emissary to Muskogee, headquarters of the Eastern Province of the Klan in Oklahoma, to threaten martial law unless Exalted Cyclops W. R. Sampson of Muskogee Klan No. 3 resigned within twenty-four hours.[40] But before he could act on his threats in Muskogee, Walton decided to go one step further in his struggle for political survival. He would declare the whole state under martial law.

On September 13, 1923, to counter growing opposition everywhere, but especially in Oklahoma City, where a special grand jury was about to convene to investigate his misadministration and illegal use of power, Walton proclaimed that military rule was in force in all of the state's seventy-eight counties. Terming members of the Klan "enemies of the sovereign state of Oklahoma [who] shall be dealt with by the military forces of this state," he called up 6,000 additional guardsmen. Walton clamped absolute martial law on Oklahoma County and Creek County (Sapulpa), the latter of which had a particularly obstreperous anti-Walton county administration.[41] The *Daily*

[39] Tulsa *Daily World,* September 12, 13, 14, 1923; Tulsa *Tribune,* September 14, 1923.

[40] Tulsa *Tribune,* September 14, 1923; New York *Times,* September 15, 1923, p. 17.

[41] Tulsa *Tribune,* September 16, 1923; Oklahoma City *Daily Oklahoman,* same date.

Oklahoman advised its readers to remain orderly as the troops moved into Oklahoma City. "This unjustified shame must be suffered in silence while Governor Walton rides his anti-klan war-horse to the end of the road," fumed the most popular daily in the state. "The governor's ambition is a much desired end, but he has no more right to suspend the privileges of citizenship . . . than masked men have to inflict penalty with a split strap."[42]

On Sunday, September 16, as crowds milled aimlessly in the rain in the streets of the capital, guardsmen set up machineguns before the police station, the city hall, and the county courthouse. Ninety-five miles to the east, in Henryetta, Walton told the delegates to the state labor convention that he was going forward with the fight against "invisible government" and would not tolerate the "klan grand jury" in Oklahoma City.[43]

With a machinegun trained on the door of the courthouse, the special grand jury failed to convene in Oklahoma City. While the *Oklahoma Leader*, the Socialist and Farmer-Labor organ, lamented that Walton had acted "in as arbitrary and illegal a manner as ever the klan did," a military court began hearing witnesses brought before it to relate their experiences at the hands of the secret society.[44] Members of the state legislature straggled into the capital and met secretly in different parts of the city. Jewett now eloquently described the Klan as "the peg on which a political bankrupt has hung the tattered habiliments of grotesque failure while making his last frantic bid for public favor."[45]

On September 21 Walton disclosed testimony given before the military court in Oklahoma City, in which the

[42] Oklahoma City *Daily Oklahoman*, September 16, 1923.

[43] New York *Times*, September 17, 1923, p. 1; Oklahoma City *Daily Oklahoman*, same date.

[44] Oklahoma City *Oklahoma Leader*, quoted in Tulsa *Tribune*, September 18, 1923.

[45] Oklahoma City *Daily Oklahoman*, September 20, 21, 1923.

county attorney, the sheriff, and a district judge admitted joining the Klan. The next day, flogging charges were filed against Jewett for participating in the beating of Edward R. Merriman on March 7, 1922. In Shawnee a joint military-civilian court brought charges of flogging against three men, all admitted Klansmen, and the county attorney there said every city officer in the Pottawatomie County town, from mayor to patrolman, was a Klansman.[46]

Legislators continued to gather in Oklahoma City. With the city humming with rumors that members of the house of representatives would convoke a special session on their own to impeace the governor, Walton issued orders to his private army to "shoot to kill" to prevent the "Klan legislature" from assembling. The representatives formulated plans for meeting in the state capitol on Wednesday, September 26. Thousands of people crowded into Oklahoma City to see what would happen when the legislators defied the governor. Among the spectators were a few leaders of the Farmer-Labor Reconstruction League. Breaking completely with the man they had once called "Our Jack," the Reconstruction Leaguers condemned "the sacrifice of constitutional guarantees" by Walton.[47] The Farmer-Labor politicians, along with non-Klan citizens in every part of the state, sent up the cry "neither Klan nor king."

At 9 A.M. on September 26 a company of riflemen met sixty members of the house of representatives before the doors of the house chamber and ordered them to disperse. Wesley E. Disney of Muskogee asked the commanding officer if they were being turned away as individuals or as a legislature. "You are being dispersed as a legislature," he answered. The dissident representatives returned to their headquarters in the Hotel Skirvin to plan their next move.

[46] New York *Times*, September 22, 1923, p. 1; Tulsa *Tribune*, September 22, 23, 1923.
[47] W. D. McBee, *The Oklahoma Revolution* (Oklahoma City, 1956), viii, 50; Ameringer, *If You Don't Weaken*, 386; Oklahoma City *Daily Oklahoman*, September 25, 1923.

Disney and a few others went to the state supreme court and filed suit against Walton for illegally dispersing a legislature.[48]

Now Walton began a legal contest to prevent the holding, on October 2, of an election on the proposition of empowering the legislature to convene without being called by the governor. The election, originally scheduled to cover four proposed constitutional amendments, was broadened to include a fifth, the matter of a special legislative session, as a result of the agitation of thousands of people, Klan and non-Klan, who signed a petition to get the proposition on the October 2 ballot. Walton secured an injunction from a district judge in Oklahoma City to prevent the state election board from placing the special session question on the ballot, but the state supreme court quickly overruled it. The state election board then ordered the election held on the prescribed date, whereupon the governor reconstituted the board to give himself a 2-to-1 majority. The new board issued instructions to the county authorities that the election was not to be held. The day before the election, however, district courts in Ardmore and Oklahoma City granted injunctions against the actions of the new board. Frustrated in his legal fight, Walton turned to the threat of military force. On election eve he proclaimed an indefinite postponement of the referendum and warned the people of Oklahoma, "There may be bloodshed, but there will be no election." He added that his entire national guard force of 6,000 men plus his corps of special state policemen were ready to shoot anyone who violated his decree. In county after county the authorities announced that they intended to ignore Walton's orders.[49]

On election day, balloting took place in all counties except Bryan, Harper, Cimarron, Delaware, and Johnston. As one

[48] Oklahoma City *Daily Oklahoman,* September 26, 1923; New York *Times,* September 27, 1923, p. 1, September 29, p. 9.
[49] Oklahoma City *Daily Oklahoman,* September 29-October 1, 1923; New York *Times,* October 1, 1923, p. 1, October 2, p. 1.

writer described the drama, the state's "most solid citizens
said their family prayers, then buckled on weapons not
used since Indian days, and went solemnly to the polls,
defying Walton and all his armed men to interfere with
their most fundamental right."[50] There was no violence in
any county, but only because Walton's policemen and the
guardsmen did not follow his orders to shoot people who
tried to vote. In Tulsa County the authorities deputized
about two hundred citizens, most of them apparently
Klansmen, to guard the election boxes and preserve order.
The deputies began disarming Walton's special policemen,
scores of whom were in the city. All of the gunmen quietly
gave up their arms and left the courthouse area when
ordered away. In every other part of the state, county and
city law officers swore in citizens, including numerous
Klansmen, to keep the peace and to prevent Walton's men
from interfering with the election. One estimate put the
number of election box deputies operating in the state at
10,000.[51]

The result of the election was a staggering defeat for
Walton. The constitutional amendment to legalize the
assembly of the legislature without his call carried by a
vote of 209,452 to 70,638. About 200,000 people stayed
home from the polls, most of them not wanting to risk
being shot by one of Walton's gunmen or being hit by a
stray bullet from a gun battle. Newspapers over the state
exulted in the triumph. This, by all odds, meant certain
impeachment for Walton when the legislature convened.
But Walton was not through. "I am still governor," he
assured his remaining supporters. "The fight on the invisible
empire has just started in Oklahoma." He called on all
anti-Klan forces in the state to organize and sign cards

[50] Stanley Frost, "The Oklahoma Regicides Act," *Outlook*, CXXXV
(November 7, 1923), 396.
[51] Tulsa *Tribune*, October 2, 1923; New York *Times*, same
date, p. 1.

pledging their allegiance to him. He claimed that his life was in danger. "I am daily in receipt of threats of assassination," he said, "but I had rather die by the hand of an assassin than die the death of a coward."[52]

Walton now realized that his only hope of escaping ouster lay in court action. So in the first days of October, as he looked for legal weapons to use against the legislature, he began slowly withdrawing the troops and abandoning military rule. By October 7 he had disbanded all the military courts in Oklahoma, Creek, Murray, Pottawatomie, and Payne counties. The next day, with only a handful of guardsmen left in Tulsa, Adjutant General Markham received final demobilization orders from the governor. In all, the Tulsa tribunal had heard testimony relating to about 120 floggings in the county. Military authorities had filed bills of information against thirty floggers. Four men had confessed to participation in whipping parties and received prison sentences. Eight accused citizens were released at preliminary hearings, and six were bound over to district court for trial (the state subsequently dropped its charges). Seven men were indicted in neighboring Wagoner County (where the authorities eventually dismissed the indictments).[53]

On October 3 Walton got a temporary injunction in district court in Oklahoma City to prevent certification of the election returns by the state election board. Six days later his application for a permanent injunction was denied. In the meantime, however, he stole a march on the legislature by calling the lawmakers into special session on October 11 "to consider proposed legislation against acts of lawlessness by masked mobs." He declared that he would resign if the legislature enacted the kind of anti-Klan law

[52] McReynolds, *Oklahoma*, 347; New York *Times*, October 3, 1923, p. 1; Tulsa *Tribune*, October 2, 3, 1923.

[53] Oklahoma City *Daily Oklahoman*, October 5, 1923; Tulsa *Daily World*, October 8, 1923; Tulsa *Tribune*, September 21, 1923.

he wanted, which included a membership registration provision in addition to an article prohibiting the wearing of masks in public.[54]

The 9th Oklahoma Legislature convened in special session at nine o'clock on the morning of October 11. Before a full gallery the house of representatives elected W. D. McBee, who was not a Klansman, speaker of the house. Members of the state senate then filed into the house chamber to hear the clerk of the house read Walton's message to the legislature. When the message ended with a request for a stiff antimask law, scattered applause came from the gallery, but on the floor the representatives and senators sat silently. The house then adopted a resolution establishing a committee to investigate the Walton administration. The committee included several Klan solons, but its chairman, Disney, did not belong to the order.[55] In such rapid order the legislature turned away from Walton's appeal for an antimask law and put into motion the machinery for getting rid of the beleaguered governor.

The house investigating committee called Blake and other state officials to appear before it, whereupon Walton fired them all. In a temperate statement Blake called Walton "a man of limitations" who had acted against his advice in putting the state under martial law. Blake said he was finished with Walton but that he intended to continue fighting the Klan. On October 13 Blake testified before the committee, while in the house itself a shouting majority of representatives by voice vote tabled a proposed resolution asking for an investigation of the Klan's strength in the house.[56]

The house committee drew up twenty-two charges against

[54] New York *Times*, October 4, 1923, p. 1, October 7, p. 1, October 10, p. 3; Oklahoma City *Daily Oklahoman*, October 7, 1923.

[55] New York *Times*, October 12, 1923, p. 1; Oklahoma City *Daily Oklahoman*, same date.

[56] Tulsa *Tribune*, October 13, 17, 1923; New York *Times*, October 13, 1923, p. 1, October 14, p. 4, October 16, p. 23.

Walton and presented them to the full membership of the house. Of the charges the first sixteen concerned the corrupt nature of the Walton administration, the governor's personal irregularities, and his general incompetence; and the last six pertained to Walton's declaration of martial law. While the charges were under consideration in the house, there were numerous rumors that Walton was planning this or that drastic action. One of the most widely believed pieces of gossip was that he was about to pardon the entire population of the state penitentiary at McAlester. To counteract whatever measures Walton may have had in mind, the house quickly voted his impeachment on two charges and sent them to the senate, which voted 36-to-1 to suspend Walton pending the outcome of his formal trial. Lieutenant Governor Martin E. Trapp, who once had faced impeachment himself during the Robertson administration, became acting governor.[57]

The house eventually sent the remaining twenty charges to the senate, which accepted them and convened as a court of impeachment on November 1. That same day a special train, carrying hundreds of Oklahoma Klansmen to Dallas for "Ku Klux Klan Day" at the Texas State Fair, pulled into the railroad station at the Texas city bearing a banner that read: "Did we impeach Walton? Hell yes!" As the senate began its trial of Walton, the governor's lawyers asked to challenge the qualifications of each senator by inquiring about his Klan membership. The senate refused the request with a thundering voice vote, and the long trial got underway.[58]

On the eighteenth day of the impeachment proceedings Walton suddenly rose from his chair and told the senators:

[57] New York *Times*, October 24, 1923, p. 1; McReynolds, *Oklahoma*, 348; Frost, "Oklahoma Regicides Act," 396; Dale and Wardell, *History of Oklahoma*, 342-43.

[58] McReynolds, *Oklahoma*, 348; Tulsa *Tribune*, November 1, 1923; New York *Times*, November 2, 1923, p. 1, November 3, p. 6, November 7, p. 15, November 8, p. 3.

"I do not care to stand this humiliation any longer for myself, my family or my honorable attorneys. You may proceed as you see best." Then, followed by his wife and lawyers, he walked out of the senate chamber. Two days later the senate sustained eleven of the twenty-two articles of impeachment, acquitted Walton on five counts, and dismissed the remaining six articles, which related to the imposition of martial law. Ten months and ten days after he took office "Jack the Klan Fighter," as one of the eastern periodicals called him, found himself officially removed from the governorship. He had expected the senate to convict him. It would have been something of a miracle if the upper house had not sustained at least one of the articles, and one was all that was needed to remove him. But he was sorely disappointed when the senate dismissed the charges having to do with his martial law decrees. He and his lawyers had planned a spectacular revelation of Klan activities in Oklahoma, including a description of the alignment of county officials with the order. The senate convicted Walton on charges of collecting campaign funds illegally, padding state payrolls, using the national guard to prevent a lawful grand jury from convening, paying his private chauffeur with state funds, issuing deficiency certificates to place unauthorized employees on the state payrolls, suspending the writ of habeas corpus in violation of the state constitution, making excessive use of the pardoning power, and being generally incompetent.[59]

With Walton safely relieved of the governorship and Trapp firmly implanted in the executive office, the legislature took up the matter for which it had been called in the first place—the passage of anti-Klan legislation. Just as Fundamentalism, racism, nativism, and rigid moralism were much broader than the Klan in Oklahoma, so the movement

[59] New York *Times*, November 18, 1923, p. 2, November 20, p. 1; 9th Oklahoma Legislature, Extraordinary Session, *Transcript of Proceedings of the Senate, State of Oklahoma, Sitting as a Court of Impeachment to Try John C. Walton, Governor*, 1812-930, 1935.

to impeach Walton went far beyond his declared enemy, the Klan. By the time the legislature finally convened, only a relatively small number of diehard farmers and laborers still supported Walton; otherwise, public sentiment was united in the feeling that the power-hungry governor must go. But with Walton out of the way, opinion in Oklahoma began once more to divide on the Klan issue—on the specific issue of what, if anything, the legislature should do about regulating the hooded organization. There was even a division of opinion within the Klan. Early in the special session Grand Dragon Jewett announced the official Klan attitude toward an antimask law: The Klan opposed legislation banning the mask entirely, but did not "object to legislation that would penalize the illegal use of the mask."[60] Some rightwing Klansmen in the legislature were in favor of adjourning without doing anything that would affect the order. Other Klan solons, following Jewett's lead, wanted a mild antimask law. One admitted Klansman, Senator Clark Nichols of Eufaula, favored not only an antimask law, but a law requiring the registration of secret organization membership lists.[61]

Although he was a Klansman, Nichols represented the viewpoint of the new governor, a conservative, quiet man who had never berated the Klan but who nevertheless had strong objections to the white-robed order. The day after Walton's conviction, Senator Tom Anglin of Holdenville introduced the Trapp administration's version of anti-Klan legislation—a law to require that a list of the membership of all secret organizations be filed with state and county officials, and to prohibit the wearing of masks in public places.[62] Such a measure, which would have gone a long

[60] N. C. Jewett, Grand Dragon, Realm of Oklahoma, to All Hydras, Great Titans and Furies, Giants, Exalted Cyclops and Terrors, and All Klansmen, Realm of Oklahoma, October 10, 1923, reprinted *ibid.*, 88-89.

[61] Oklahoma City *Daily Oklahoman*, November 28, 1923.

[62] *Ibid.*, November 20, 1923.

way toward stripping the Klan of its secrecy, had little chance of passing both houses, and this fact pointed up the strength of the Klan in the legislature. The debate over the anti-Klan bill split the parties in the senate. Five Republican senators supported the administration's position, while the remaining six Republicans lined up with Wash E. Hudson of Tulsa, one of the most extreme Klansmen, and the other Klan Democrats. Hudson and his group succeeded in emasculating Anglin's bill and several other strong bills proposed in the senate. At one point in the debate Hudson, who opposed any anti-Klan legislation, delivered a long eulogy of the order. "The Ku Klux Klan cleaned up those leeches on society, those peddlers of dope, sellers of whiskey and traffickers in women [in Tulsa County]," declared the Tulsa Klansman. "I know of only one man who was flogged [who] did not get what he deserved."[63]

The senate finally passed a bill which outlawed public mask-wearing and provided minor penalties for offenses committed while disguised and for sending anonymous threats. The vote on the measure was 27 to 11. The anti-Klan forces, disappointed because the bill did not contain a membership publication clause, denounced the measure as a Klan bill. As the legislature adjourned for the Thanksgiving holidays, Representatives John Miller of Tulsa, Jess Pullen of Sulphur, and Allen Street and R. A. Singletary of Oklahoma City made plans for fighting any legislation regulating the Klan. Speaker McBee, Klan-hater J. P. Callahan of Latimer County, and Disney called on the house members to pass a strong bill.[64]

The Klansmen in the house had a sudden change of heart when the senate bill came before the house and Richard

63 Tulsa *Tribune*, November 23, 25, 1923; New York *Times*, November 24, 1923, p. 3, November 27, p. 21; Oklahoma City *Daily Oklahoman*, November 28, 1923.
64 Oklahoma City *Daily Oklahoman*, November 29, 1923; New York *Times*, November 29, 1923, p. 23; Tulsa *Tribune*, November 28, 1923.

Elam of Osage County offered an amendment to require the registration of the officers of secret societies. Immediately after Elam finished speaking, the rightwing Klansmen proclaimed their support of the simple unmasking bill passed by the senate. Disney pleaded with the representatives "to pass a Klan bill with teeth." "Jack Walton wants this milk and water bill passed by the Senate adopted here," said Disney. He predicted accurately that if a strong bill were not passed, Walton would claim that the Klan dominated the legislature and would run for the United States Senate in 1924. Despite the entreaties of Disney, Speaker McBee, and others, the house passed the senate bill without amendment, 71 to 15.[65]

By the time the bill came to him, Trapp had given up hope of seeing an effective piece of anti-Klan legislation enacted. He finally signed the "milk and water bill" into law on January 15, 1924, with the comment: "The bill is as good an anti-masking measure as I have read." The law, the first statute regulating Klan mask-wearing to be passed in any state, was to go into force ninety days from the date of Trapp's signature.[66] Less than a month after the enactment of the law, however, Trapp brought pressure on the Oklahoma Klan hierarchy to refrain from staging a masked parade at the annual Klorero (state convention) in Oklahoma City. Jewett at first refused Trapp's requests, asserting that the Klansmen would parade in "full regalia," including hood visors worn down. But on the night of February 22, 1924, in a drizzling rain, Jewett rode horseback at the head of a procession of about 4,500 robed, hooded, but unmasked Klansmen and Klanswomen from Oklahoma, Texas, Arkansas, Kansas, and Missouri.[67] In all future demonstrations in

[65] Tulsa *Tribune*, December 5, 1923; New York *Times*, December 6, 1923, p. 3, December 8, p. 15; 9th Oklahoma Legislature, Extraordinary Session, *House Journal*, 379, 397, 399, 538, 549, 583.

[66] Oklahoma City *Daily Oklahoman*, January 16, 1924; *Session Laws of the State of Oklahoma* (Oklahoma City, 1924), ch. II, pp. 2-3.

[67] Oklahoma City *Daily Oklahoman*, February 18, 20, 22, 23, 1924.

Oklahoma, members of the Klan appeared with the visors
of their hoods pinned back.

Jack Walton's fight with the Klan focused the attention
of the whole country on Oklahoma. For months the nation
read of martial law, troop movements, floggings, legal
maneuverings, the expulsion of legislators from the state
capitol, the impeachment of a governor, and the power of
the Klan in the Sooner State. Some writers outside Oklahoma saw Walton as "Jack the Klan Fighter" or "Oklahoma's
Klan-fighting governor."[68] Most Oklahomans, however, both
Klan and non-Klan, came to view their governor as a petty
tyrant and a blustering incompetent.

This writer finds it impossible to believe that Walton
sincerely considered the Klan a menace when he declared
war on the secret order. Walton had ignored the anti-Klan
bill introduced in the house of representatives during the
regular legislative session in 1923. Early in the session he
had joined the Klan as a "Klansman at Large" in an attempt
to win the favor of the organization. When the rank-and-
file Klansmen refused to embrace him and when his Farmer-
Labor following began to fall apart, Walton picked up the
Klan as the issue with which to recoup his crumbling
fortunes. His irresponsible actions brought the state close
to civil war. Perhaps Walton's greatest sin was that he
forced people who did not like the Klan to choose between
the hooded order and a despotic governor. To rid the state
of Walton, the non-Klan segment of the electorate joined
forces with the Klan. As a result the Klan received the
boost it needed for the Oklahoma political wars of 1924, a
presidential election year.

[68] For national periodical coverage of the martial law period in
Oklahoma, see, for example, "Masked Floggers of Tulsa"; H. J.
Haskell, "Martial Law in Oklahoma," *Outlook*, CXXXV (September
26, 1923), 133; "Oklahoma's Uncivil Civil War," *Literary Digest*,
LXXVIII (September 29, 1923), 10-11; "Jack, the Klan Fighter in
Oklahoma," *ibid.*, LXXIX (October 20, 1923), 38-44; Aldrich Blake,
"Oklahoma's Klan-Fighting Governor," *Nation*, CXVII (October 3,
1923), 353.

8.

A Sortie at Presidential Politics

BY 1924 THE KLAN was, more than anything else, a political organization. However much its leaders, including Hiram W. Evans, might protest that the Klan was not "in politics," the fact remained that in state after state the order was the most powerful single element at work. Evans, as Imperial Wizard, was the unchallenged ruler over three to five million Klansmen, citizens of an Invisible Empire that, while no longer invisible, was certainly imperial.[1] During 1922 and 1923 the Klan helped to elect governors in Oregon and Georgia, a United States Senator in Texas, Representatives in several states, and local officials—sheriffs, attorneys, judges, mayors, police commissioners—in every part of the nation. In 1924 the order enjoyed even greater success, electing governors in Colorado and Maine, winning almost complete control of the state of Indiana, and joining with its sympathizers to elect governors in Ohio and Louisiana and a United States Senator in Oklahoma. Equally important, the Klan for the first time threw its weight into national politics. There its main accomplishment was to influence the process by which the Democratic party adopted a platform and nominated a presidential candidate.

At the beginning of 1924 the Klan was strongest politically in those states where the Democratic party was in the majority. That year the organization scored its principal victories by working within the Republican party, while in Texas and Arkansas, predominantly Democratic states, the order was beaten. Considering the whole political history of the Klan in the 1920s, however, the secret society wielded its greatest power in the Democratic party. This was especially true at the national level when the parties chose presidential candidates and tried to elect them.

In 1924, for example, Imperial Wizard Evans and his "board of strategy" were on hand at the Republican national convention in Cleveland, but the Klan played a minor role throughout the boringly harmonious gathering. Even in delegations from strong Klan states like Indiana and Oklahoma there was little evidence of Klan influence. In the sessions of the platform committee, Rene B. Creager, the Republican leader in Texas, and a few other Klan-haters argued for a statement denouncing the Klan by name. But the committee, and the delegates to the convention as a whole, wanted above all else to avoid or soften potentially dangerous issues. Consequently the platform submitted to the delegates and adopted without opposition contained an innocuous plank in which the party pledged "its unyielding devotion to the Constitution and to the guarantees of civil, political, and religious liberty therein contained."[2] The placid state of affairs at the Republican convention was nowhere to be found at the Democratic national con-

[1] The estimate of three to five million Klansmen in 1924 seems to represent a consensus of membership estimates given by observers during the 1920s.

[2] Arnold S. Rice, *The Ku Klux Klan in American Politics* (Washington, 1962), 74-75.

vention in New York. There the presence of the Klan issue brought about the longest deadlock in the history of American political parties and almost tore the Democratic party in two.

The Klan's national objectives in 1924 were threefold: to block either major political party from condemning the Klan *by name* in its party platform; to help win the Democratic presidential nomination for William Gibbs McAdoo of California; failing to nominate McAdoo, to prevent the nomination of Alfred E. Smith, the Catholic, antiprohibitionist governor of New York, or Oscar W. Underwood, the anti-Klan United States Senator from Alabama. The achievement of half of the first objective turned out to be easy for the Klan when the Republican convention refused to go on record against the organization. Attainment of the rest of the Klan's goals, however, was much harder. One of them, the nomination of McAdoo by the Democratic party, proved impossible.

The reasons for the Klan's attachment to McAdoo are not wholly clear. The Californian was a native of the South, born in either Georgia or Tennessee (both states claimed him). He had been one of the outstanding figures in the administration of Woodrow Wilson, serving both as Secretary of the Treasury and director general of the railroads during World War I. He was an unequivocal advocate of prohibition, and his economic views had apparently grown increasingly conservative in the postwar years. During the early months of 1924 the disclosure of his association with oilman Edward L. Doheny, implicating him in the celebrated Teapot Dome scandal, cut into his popularity with many Democratic progressives.[3] But McAdoo remained attractive to the Klan because he was a Protestant,

[3] See David H. Stratton, "Splattered with Oil: William G. McAdoo and the 1924 Presidential Nomination," *Southwestern Social Science Quarterly*, XLIV (June 1963), 62-73.

a dry, and noncommittal on the Klan issue.

Of McAdoo's two principal opponents for the Democratic nomination, Smith was a Catholic, a wet, a friend of the hated Tammany political machine in New York City, and a foe of immigration restriction. Underwood was a dry, southern Protestant conservative, but also a determined enemy of the Klan. The secret order probably centered its attention on McAdoo because, quite obviously, he was the least objectionable serious candidate for the Democratic nomination. Some of McAdoo's stanchest supporters, like Democratic national committeeman Thomas B. Love of Dallas, pointed to "the parochialness and bigotry of that organization [the Klan]" and urged him to "disassociate your name from alleged adhesion to the K. K. K."[4] But McAdoo acquiesced in the Klan's adoption of him, silently accepted its help, and never publicly took a stand against the order. Thus historians are justified in concluding: "It could not be doubted that at least in some sense that McAdoo was the Klan candidate."[5]

Smith's strength was concentrated in the populous eastern states, which sent large delegations to the Democratic convention. In the South and Southwest, Smith was anathema, not only to Klansmen, but to most other people in those areas, who held basically the same attitudes as the Klan on the questions of religion, city machine politics, foreign immigration, and prohibition. By contrast, Underwood had a rather strong following in the southern and southwestern states. In the contest for convention delegations carried on in the states of the South and Southwest, it was Underwood who presented the stiffest opposition to

[4] Thomas B. Love to William Gibbs McAdoo, October 23, 1923, Thomas B. Love Papers, Archives of the Dallas Historical Society, Dallas. On the McAdoo movement nationally, see Lee N. Allen, "The McAdoo Campaign for the Presidential Nomination in 1924," *Journal of Southern History*, XXX (May 1963), 211-28.

[5] David B. Burner, "The Democratic Party in the Election of 1924," *Mid-America*, XLVI (April 1964), 100.

McAdoo's, and the Klan's, plans for capturing the state delegations.

Arkansas was the first of the southwestern states to choose a delegation to the national convention. The Klan hierarchy in Arkansas was not particularly enthusiastic over McAdoo or any other Democrat, a condition that perhaps resulted from the apparent apathy of Grand Dragon James A. Comer, a nominal Republican, toward national affairs in the Democratic party. Comer was very much interested in Democratic politics inside Arkansas, and in 1924, under his leadership, the Klan would have a candidate for governor of the state. Since there was not a strong McAdoo movement in Arkansas, it seems that most Arkansas Klansmen inclined toward the favorite-son candidacy of United States Senator Joseph T. Robinson as a means of blocking the Underwood backers in the Democratic State Central Committee. One of the leading Robinson supporters was Klansman Virgil C. Pettie, secretary of the state committee and a highly respected Democrat.[6]

In Arkansas the meeting of the state central committee at Little Rock in April served as the state convention. Before the meeting there was some speculation about an open fight between Underwood and Robinson committee members, but all was tranquil when the state committee chose delegates to cast the state's eighteen votes at the Democratic national convention. Although the delegation was officially uninstructed, the committee adopted a resolution "requesting" the delegates to vote for Robinson. Pettie was one of the delegates-at-large from Arkansas.[7]

Contrasted with the absence of an effective McAdoo organization in Arkansas and the peaceful nature of the state convention was the contest for the twenty national convention votes of Oklahoma. In the Sooner State there

[6] On the Klan membership of Virgil C. Pettie, see the New York *Times*, June 22, 1924, p. 3.

[7] Little Rock *Arkansas Gazette*, April 23, 24, 1924.

was never any solid sentiment in favor of an Underwood delegation, but at the county convention a fight shaped up between the non-Klan and anti-Klan supporters of the Trapp administration, working for an uninstructed delegation, and McAdoo's following, which included most Klansmen. In some respects the fight was a ramification of the split developing in late 1923 between Governor Martin E. Trapp and the Klansmen in the state legislature over the passage of a bill to regulate the Klan.[8]

Klan-haters and "moderates" controlled most of the county conventions in Oklahoma. Of 1,082 delegates at the state Democratic convention in Oklahoma City, only about one-third favored an instructed McAdoo delegation. In Stephens County (Duncan), home of the embattled Speaker W. D. McBee, a thoroughgoing anti-Klan group won control of the convention, whereupon a number of Klansmen walked out. Compromise was the keynote at the state convention, held in early May. Henry S. Johnston of Perry, a Klansman and Grand Master of the Oklahoma Masonic Lodge, was elected convention chairman, but most of the important committee posts went to non-Klan men and women. The convention, with the Klan in the minority, voted to send an uninstructed delegation to New York. To keep the Klansmen and Klanswomen happy, however, the delegates adopted a resolution endorsing McAdoo for the presidential nomination. Most of the votes against the resolution came from anti-Klan delegations from eighteen small counties.[9] Grand Dragon N. Clay Jewett, not satisfied with the compromising spirit of the convention, which made it possible for the Klan to exercise some influence without being vilified, attempted to block the reelection of Scott Ferris of Lawton as national committeeman and secure the post for his friend Edward M. Seamans, outgoing state

[8] See pp. 155-57.
[9] Tulsa *Tribune*, January 21, 1924; Oklahoma City *Daily Oklahoman*, April 30, May 7, 1924.

Democratic chairman. But Ferris was elected by a large majority.[10]

Across the Red River in Texas, a straightforward McAdoo versus Underwood, Klan versus anti-Klan struggle occurred. The Texas McAdoo movement, fostered mainly by the Klan, was extremely well organized; the Klan probably reached the zenith of its political power in the state during the contest for the forty votes at the national convention. The Klan and its allies easily controlled an overwhelming number of the poorly attended precinct conventions in Texas, and thus the conventions in most of the state's 254 counties. After the precinct battles, Underwood's supporters realized that they had lost the Texas delegation to the national convention. W. E. Lea of Orange, campaign manager for Underwood in Texas, charged that the Klan was responsible for McAdoo's victory in the precincts, and that the order went so far as to distribute handbills in the local gatherings instructing those who attended to vote for a McAdoo delegation to the county conventions.[11]

The Klan was the dominant element at the state Democratic convention, held in Waco late in May. Perhaps two-thirds of the delegates at the state meeting were Klansmen, Klanswomen, and Klan sympathizers. Prior to the convention the Democratic State Executive Committee first endorsed Governor Pat M. Neff for the presidential nomination, but then reversed itself and voted its endorsement of McAdoo. At the state convention a large majority voted for an instructed McAdoo delegation.[12] The delegation included

[10] Klansman [Carlton Weaver] to N. C. Jewett, Grand Dragon of the Ku Klux Klan, Realm of Oklahoma, November 1924, Carlton Weaver Collection, Division of Manuscripts, University of Oklahoma Library, Norman. See also Tulsa *Tribune*, July 30, 1924.

[11] Dallas *Morning News*, May 4, 6, 1924.

[12] Lee N. Allen, "The Democratic Presidential Primary Election of 1924 in Texas," *Southwestern Historical Quarterly*, LXI (April 1958), 474-93. There is a copy of the minutes of the meeting of the Democratic State Executive Committee, including the initial endorsement of Neff, in the Thomas B. Love Papers.

such prominent Texas Klansmen as Earle B. Mayfield, a
delegate-at-large; Mike T. Lively of Dallas; and Marvin A.
Childers of San Antonio.[13]

In Louisiana the Klan had only a small part at the state
Democratic convention in Baton Rouge, which voted to
send an uninstructed delegation to the national party con-
clave. Before the convention Swords R. Lee of Alexandria,
the outstanding Klansman in central Louisiana, stated flatly
that "there will not be any attempt on the part of the klan
to control or in any way interfere with the state Democratic
convention." The Klan was evidently as good as Lee's word.
The state convention went along with the current vogue
for "harmony and peace" in Louisiana politics. The few
Klan delegates at the convention acquiesced in the domination of the convention by an alliance of upstate politicians
and industrialists, led by a former governor, Jared Y.
Sanders, and the New Orleans machine under the leadership
of Martin H. Behrman. In the sessions of the platform
committee a small group of anti-Klanners tried to incorporate a denunciation of the Klan in the platform, but the
committee voted down the proposed plank, 13 to 4. The
anti-Klanners carried their fight to the floor of the convention, where a motion to table their substitute resolution
carried with a roar of "yeas." The Louisiana delegation,
with twenty votes, was led by Sanders, Behrman, Governor
Henry L. Fuqua, and former Governor Ruffin G. Pleasant of
Shreveport. Only two known Klansmen, Lee and Jeff B.
Snyder of Tallulah, went to New York as members of the
delegation.[14]

The Democratic national convention met on June 24 in
the sweltering confines of New York's Madison Square
Garden. The first candidate for the presidential nomination
to have his name placed before the convention was Underwood. When Forney Johnston of Alabama, making the

[13] Dallas *Morning News*, May 27, 1924.
[14] New Orleans *Times-Picayune*, May 28, June 6, 1924.

nominating speech for Underwood, referred to the Klan by name and condemned its "un-American and un-Democratic political action," the Underwood and Smith delegates staged a wild demonstration.[15] Some Louisiana delegates joined in the parading and shouting, but the delegations from Texas, Arkansas, and Oklahoma sat silently along with groups from Georgia, Indiana, California, Missouri, and other states. The Arkansas delegation paraded after favorite son Robinson's name was placed in nomination. When James D. Phelan of California presented McAdoo's name to the convention, nearly all the Oklahoma delegates joined the line of march, together with all but three or four of the Texas delegates and alternates.[16]

After the nominating and seconding speeches for McAdoo, Smith, Underwood, and a number of minor candidates, the convention delegates steadied themselves for the struggle over the adoption of the party platform. Here the Klan issue emerged with a vengeance. Evans and his Klan "board of strategy" had come to New York from Cleveland and had set up headquarters on the fifteenth floor of the Hotel McAlpin. The board included Grand Dragons Nathan Bedford Forrest of Georgia, Walter F. Bossert of Indiana, James Esdale of Alabama, Comer of Arkansas, Fred L. Gifford of Oregon, Jewett of Oklahoma, and Z. E. Marvin of Texas, as well as publicity man Milton Elrod of Indiana, United States Senator-elect Mayfield of Texas, and Pettie of Arkansas, the last two being delegates-at-large.[17]

Evans and his minions began organizing their forces and lining up the Klan delegates for the expected fight against

[15] Democratic National Committee, *Official Report of the Proceedings of the Democratic National Convention Held in Madison Square Garden, New York City, June 24, 25, 26, 27, 28, 30, July 1, 2, 3, 4, 5, 7, 8, and 9, 1924* (Indianapolis, 1924), 102.

[16] Dallas *Morning News*, June 26, 1924; Oklahoma City *Daily Oklahoman*, June 25, 26, 1924.

[17] New York *Times*, June 22, 1924, p. 3; Rice, *Klan in American Politics*, 80.

naming the Klan in the Democratic platform. The New York *World* estimated the number of Klansmen in the state delegations at 300. In the southwestern delegations perhaps 80 percent of the delegates from Texas and Arkansas were Klan-oriented, while the non-Klan forces had a slight majority in the Oklahoma group and were clearly in control of the representation from Louisiana.[18]

The majority report of the Democratic platform committee, one of whose members was Klansman Alva Bryan of Waco, Texas, did not mention the Klan by name, containing only an ambiguous condemnation of mob violence and religious and racial strife. The minority report, presented by William R. Pattangall of Maine, an Underwood man, pledged the party "to oppose any effort on the part of the Ku Klux Klan . . . to interfere with the religious liberty or political freedom of any citizen, or to limit the civic rights of any citizen . . . because of religion, birthplace, or racial origin." A rancorous debate followed over the minority plank. At one point during the speechmaking, rowdy Smith and Underwood supporters on the floor and in the balcony shouted down the patriarch of the party, William Jennings Bryan, as he spoke in rambling fashion against naming the Klan in the party platform.[19]

In the early morning hours, amid shouts, handclapping, laughter, and boos, Permanent Chairman Thomas J. Walsh called for a vote on the minority report. There were repeated polls of delegations and frequent vote changes. The delegations from Texas, Louisiana, Arkansas, and Oklahoma all voted under the unit rule at the convention. All four delegations cast their votes against the minority report and the naming of the Klan. A Louisiana man demanded a poll of his state's delegation; the poll showed that the Louisiana

[18] Rice, *Klan in American Politics*, 81; New York *Times*, June 22, 1924, p. 3.

[19] *Proceedings of the Democratic National Convention*, 279-309; New York *Times*, June 29, 1924, pp. 1-8.

delegates stood 18 to 2 against the minority report. The final vote on the platform issue almost rent the Democratic party. A preliminary count gave the opponents of the Klan, the advocates of the minority report, a one-vote majority over the pro-Klan element and the proponents of harmony. But during a recount a Georgia woman changed her mind and voted against the minority plank, thus giving Klansmen and those who wanted to compromise the Klan issue the victory, 543 3/20 votes to 542 7/20. By a margin of less than one vote the Democrats rejected an unequivocal anti-Klan plank, made possible the adoption of a harmless affirmation of personal liberties, and averted an almost certain split of the party.[20]

With one crisis past, the convention delegates began the onerous work of choosing a presidential nominee, a task that set an alltime endurance record for national party conclaves. The two strongest aspirants before the convention were McAdoo and Smith, and pro- and anti-Klan forces coalesced as they had in the platform battle. For nine hot days the delegates deadlocked between Smith and McAdoo. The Californian led in the balloting, but his total was always short of the two-thirds majority needed to secure the nomination. Again and again, for 100 ballots, McAdoo failed to obtain the necessary majority, and his fight with Smith became increasingly hopeless. Oklahoma's twenty votes went to McAdoo until the 43d ballot, when the delegates switched to Robinson of Arkansas. On the 62d ballot the Oklahoma votes went to the state's Democratic United States Senator, Robert L. Owen, but a few ballots later, Oklahoma was back with McAdoo. On the 96th ballot the Oklahoma delegation swung to John W. Davis, a New York corporation lawyer and a native of West Virginia. Although technically uninstructed, the Arkansas delegation

[20] *Proceedings of the Democratic National Convention,* 279-334; Tulsa *Tribune,* June 29, 1924; Dallas *Morning News,* June 30, 1924; Burner, "Democratic Party in the Election of 1924," 99-100.

cast every ballot for Robinson, its favorite son. On the first ballot Louisiana gave its twenty votes to Senator Pat Harrison of Mississippi; the Pelican State delegation, voting under the unit rule, then threw its votes to first one minor candidate and then another before swinging to Davis on the 67th ballot. Texas' forty votes, bound by the unit rule and pledged to McAdoo, remained with the Californian until he released his delegates after the 100th ballot. The Texas vote then went to Davis.[21]

After McAdoo and Smith withdrew by mutual agreement at the end of 100 fruitless ballots and released the delegations pledged to them, the convention took only three more ballots to choose a candidate for president. On the 103d ballot the delegates gave the necessary two-thirds majority to the respected but colorless Davis, whose views on the Klan were not known.[22] After sixteen strife-ridden days the exhausted Democrats packed their bags and returned to their homes. Their party was still intact, but the facade of unity erected after weeks of battling over the Klan, and to a lesser extent over prohibition and the League of Nations, was indeed precarious.

With the two major party conventions, one boisterous, the other placid, now part of Democratic and Republican history, the parties turned to the business of getting their candidates elected. Neither the states of the Southwest nor the Klan was especially significant in the story of the 1924 presidential campaign. At the election in November the southwestern states went Democratic, as they usually did, while the strong Klan states of the Midwest went Republican, as they usually did. The Klan issue never figured prominently in the campaign, nor, for that matter, did any other issue of much importance. Both Davis, the Democrat, and Vice President Calvin Coolidge, the Republican nomi-

[21] For the balloting on the presidential nomination, see *Proceedings of the Democratic National Convention*, 338-979.

[22] *Ibid.*, 963-75; Burner, "Democratic Party in the Election of 1924," 100-105.

nee, largely ignored each other, spending most of their darts on Robert M. LaFollette, the candidate of the ill-fated farmer-labor protest movement organized as the Progressive party. The Klan also concentrated its fire on LaFollette. Evans called him a "radical" and "the arch enemy of the nation," referring to his advocacy of liberal economic reforms and his opposition to American participation in the war. Evans termed Coolidge and Davis "nationals and Americans, aides of the Klan in the attempt to 'Americanize America,' and for this reason the Klan will take no part in the political struggle as far as they are concerned."[23]

Evans' remarks about Davis came before the Democratic candidate made his famous attack on the Klan in a speech at Sea Girt, New Jersey, on August 22. In that address Davis implied that the Klan "raises the standard of racial and religious prejudice" and therefore "does violence to the spirit of American institutions and must be condemned." Davis invited Coolidge to declare himself on the Klan issue, but the dour man from Massachusetts treated the Klan as he did most controversial matters—he simply gave no sign that he knew it existed. But his runningmate, Chicago banker Charles G. Dawes, mildly attacked the Klan's bigotry and its extralegal attempts at law enforcement.[24]

In the Southwest the fact that Davis denounced the Klan, and thus alienated the order's national leadership, had little effect on the actions of Klansmen. In Oklahoma the publicity director for the Democratic State Committee charged that Grand Dragon Jewett, a Republican, was traveling around over the state trying to line up local and district Klan leaders for Coolidge and that he would hold a conference of Klan bosses in Oklahoma City the night

[23] New York *Times*, August 23, 1924, p. 3. On the Progressive party of 1924, see Kenneth MacKay, *The Progressive Movement of 1924* (New York, 1947).

[24] New York *Times*, August 23, 1924, p. 1; Burner, "Democratic Party in the Election of 1924," 105-13.

before the election. State Democratic chairman R. L. Davidson joined in, predicting that each of the 216 local Klans in Oklahoma would receive instructions that Klansmen should, for the good of the order, vote for Coolidge. Jewett denied that any meeting of Klan leaders would be held before the election or that the local Klans would hold special political Konklaves before November 3.[25]

The Grand Dragon of Oklahoma did not openly work against Davis, to be sure. But after the election, in which the Democratic candidate carried Oklahoma and the "Solid South" but lost everywhere else, the *Fiery Cross,* the official weekly newspaper of Realm headquarters published in Oklahoma City, ran a long editorial denouncing Davis for his stand against the Klan and placing responsibility for the Democratic failure on the fact that Davis had attacked the hooded order. In response to the editorial an unhappy Klansman wrote Jewett an angry letter in which he accused the Grand Dragon of working for Coolidge in Oklahoma. Jewett's maneuverings, concluded the Klansman, "ought to cost the Klan half its strength in Oklahoma."[26]

In Arkansas, about two months prior to the election, Klansman H. N. Street, president and general manager of the Central & Gulf Railroad at Lonoke, decided to do what he could to swing the heavily Democratic state to Coolidge. Street enthusiastically wrote Harmon L. Remmel, longtime Republican leader and collector of internal revenue in Arkansas, that as a result of Davis' Sea Girt speech the Republicans had a chance to carry Texas, Oklahoma, Tennessee, Kentucky, and Arkansas. Remmel thanked the Klansman for his "very patriotic letter" but expressed doubt that Coolidge could carry Arkansas, whereupon Street got more specific as to how this reversal of form could be brought about. "I would advise that you personally go and

[25] Tulsa *Tribune,* October 27, 28, 30, 1924.
[26] Klansman [Carlton Weaver] to N. C. Jewett, November 1924, Carlton B. Weaver Collection.

have a heart to heart talk with Mr. J. A. Comer, Grand Dragon, of the Realm of Arkansas," wrote Street. "In this talk lay before him the proposition of carrying Arkansas for the National Republican Ticket. . . . I am going to suggest the matter of expediency too—it is this—Comer is an old Republican—later a Bull Mooser—as a matter of expediency be carefull [*sic*] of your steps."[27]

Remmel was intrigued by the possibility presented by a Klansman of obtaining the 50,000 or so votes of the Klan in Arkansas, which might be enough to give the state to Coolidge. He did in fact talk to Comer. The Arkansas Dragon predicted that Coolidge would poll more votes in the state than had Warren G. Harding in 1920 and that more Arkansans would vote Republican than ever before, although he doubted that the Republicans would carry Arkansas. Remmel urged C. Bascom Slemp, Coolidge's private secretary, to arrange an interview with Comer in order to discuss Republican prospects in Arkansas; Slemp cooly replied that he would not be able to see the Grand Dragon.[28]

In October, Imperial Wizard Evans, Comer, and other Klan moguls met at the Blackstone Hotel in Chicago. Comer wired Remmel that he should come to Chicago and talk over "matters political" with the Klansmen. Remmel was reluctant to make the trip, but when Comer sent him another telegram stating that the "subject [is] too important to write or talk on phone," Remmel answered that he was on his way.[29] What transpired when the Republican boss in Arkansas met with the Grand Dragon of Arkansas and

[27] H. N. Street to Harmon L. Remmel, September 5, 1924, Remmel to Street, September 8, Street to Remmel, September 12, Harmon L. Remmel Papers, General Library, University of Arkansas, Fayetteville.

[28] Remmel to C. Bascom Slemp, September 15, 1924, Slemp to Remmel, September 18, *ibid*.

[29] James A. Comer telegram to Remmel, October 15, 1924, Remmel telegram to Comer, same date, Comer telegram to Remmel, same date, Remmel telegram to Comer, October 16, *ibid*.

the Imperial Wizard of the Klan is not known, for Remmel's records of his dealings with the hooded order end abruptly with his telegram informing Comer that he was coming to Chicago. But whatever happened did not alter the fact that Arkansas was a Democratic state. In November, Davis carried Arkansas with 87,743 votes to 40,036 for Coolidge, whose percentage of the vote was smaller than that of Harding in 1920, when there was no Klan issue. After the election Remmel wrote Republican James S. McConnell, an attorney at Mineral Springs, and asked him whether he thought the Klan vote in Arkansas was of any real help to Coolidge. McConnell replied that while there was "no concerted support" of the Republican by Klansmen, some Knights voted Republican, but that "a far greater number simply stayed at home and hoped for his election and many others voted the Democratic ticket, also hoping for his election."[30]

Democratic Klansmen in the other states of the Southwest may also have hoped that Davis, who had denounced their organization, would be beaten, but there is no evidence that their sentiments brought any significant shift of votes to the Republican ticket. Davis carried Oklahoma by about 35,000 votes, whereas in 1920 Harding had won the state's electoral votes. Texas went Democratic in both elections, but Davis polled nearly six times as many votes as Coolidge, while James M. Cox, the Democratic candidate in 1920, did not quite double Harding's vote. In Louisiana the results of the election indicated a similar absence of Klan influence on presidential politics. In 1920 Cox had about three times as many votes as Harding; in 1924 Davis received about four times as many votes as Coolidge in the Pelican State.[31]

[30] James S. McConnell to Remmel, November 15, 1924, *ibid.*

[31] Eugene H. Roseboom, *A History of Presidential Elections* (New York, 1957), 406-17; Edgar E. Robinson, *The Presidential Vote, 1896-1932* (Stanford, Calif., 1947), 21-24; Svend Petersen, *A Statistical History of the American Presidential Elections* (New York, 1963), 86-88, 120, 133, 150, 157.

The year 1924 marked the first essay of the Klan into national politics. The order was a negligible factor in the contest for delegates preceding the Republican national convention and was not much in evidence at the convention itself. In the Democratic party, however, the Klan worked effectively, if covertly, in several southern and southwestern states to win state delegations for its adopted favorite, McAdoo. And at the epic Democratic national convention the presence of the Klan, both in body and in spirit, brought the party close to disaster. Once the conventions were over and the campaign began, the Klan ceased to figure prominently. In Louisiana, Texas, Arkansas, and Oklahoma the secret organization had little if any bearing on the presidential campaign and seems to have exerted scant influence on the relative strength of the parties in the four states.

But it was at the local and state level that a well-organized minority like the Klan was able to wield its political power most effectively. In 1924 the Klan almost everywhere reached the apex of its career. The order became the critical issue in a series of unprecedentedly hard fought state campaigns. The outcome of those struggles would decide the course of the Klan's history, not only in the southwestern part of the Invisible Empire, but throughout the nation.

9.

Uncertain Victories, Bitter Defeats

THE YEAR 1924 marked the climax of the Klan movement, and the beginning of the end. In that year the white-robed order reached the peak of its power, numerically and politically, in practically every state. It was a year of victory for the Klan in such widely scattered states as Maine, Indiana, Georgia, and Colorado. The secret society strode into the arena of national politics and, at the Democratic national convention, raised its head for all to see. The Klan electioneered more openly than it ever had, or ever would again, in the Southwest, where its political enterprises gave a Klan versus anti-Klan flavor to numerous state and local races. The political machinations produced disastrous setbacks in Texas and unquestioned defeat in Arkansas. In Oklahoma and Louisiana the Klan scored apparent victories. Yet they were also Pyhrric victories, for they brought disappointment and strife which speeded the downfall of the Klan in those states. After 1924 the Klan ceased to be the overriding element in southwestern state politics.

There are few better illustrations of the anomalous nature of Louisiana politics than the statewide campaign of 1923-1924. In the twenties Louisiana remained virtually untouched by the agrarian protest and progressive reform movements that had swept almost every other state in the generation before the First World War. The state continued to be ruled by an ultraconservative hierarchy comprised of the sugar, rice, and cotton planters; the lumber, railroad, and sugar refining interests; the oil interests centering in the all-powerful Standard Oil Company; the upstate political leaders who managed the dry, Protestant vote; and the New Orleans political machine under Martin H. Behrman—the "Old Regulars" or the "Choctaw Club."[1] Whenever all or most of these elements struck a balance on one candidate, that candidate was usually elected. The year 1920 provided an exception to this political law of Louisiana. In that year John M. Parker, an ex-Bull Moose, won the governorship behind an alliance of insurgent "New Regulars" in New Orleans and dissatisfied upstate leaders. A "reform" ticket overturned Choctaw dominance in New Orleans. But by 1923-1924 Behrman and his Old Regular organization, together with their business and financial allies, were ready to reestablish the old order in the Crescent City and in the state government at Baton Rouge.[2]

Into the oligarchial setup that was Louisiana politics in the twenties came the Klan, representing a voting potential of perhaps 54,000 dedicated native-born white Protestants.[3]

[1] T. Harry Williams, "Gentleman from Louisiana: Demagogue or Democrat," *Journal of Southern History*, XXVI (February 1960), 9; Allan P. Sindler, *Huey Long's Louisiana: State Politics, 1920-1952* (Baltimore, 1956), 22-26.

[2] George M. Reynolds, *Machine Politics in New Orleans, 1897-1926* (Columbia University Studies in Economics, History and Public Law; New York, 1936), 212-16, 218-19; Sindler, *Huey Long's Louisiana*, 40-45.

[3] Since the Klan's membership rolls were secret, it is impossible to give more than approximations of the order's strength at a particular time. The estimate of 54,000, by all odds a rather accurate guess, is from Robert L. Duffus, "The Ku Klux Klan in the Middle West," *World's Work*, XLVI (August 1923), 364.

But this voting potential was never realized, and the Klan leaders in Louisiana apparently never made a serious attempt to marshal it. This fact furnishes the outstanding characteristic of the Klan's history in Louisiana. For rather than organizing the Klan as an independent force in state politics, as happened practically everywhere else, the Louisiana Klan leadership plunged the order into the delicate process of maneuvering, bargaining, and jockeying that decided each election. Thus in the only statewide campaign in which it figured prominently, the 1923-1924 races, the Klan became simply one more element to be reconciled, one more faction in the prevailing political hierarchy. The Louisiana Klan's lack of unity and purpose in the campaign, the fact that its leaders horse-traded Klan votes here and there, evidently for their own benefit, caused dissension within the order in the state, made possible the passage of stiff anti-Klan legislation, and led to punitive measures by an angry Imperial Klan leadership. The account of the regulatory laws of 1924 and the troubles with the national organization relate primarily to the decline of the Klan in Louisiana. Here the main concern is with the Klan's role in the political contests of 1923-1924.

As early as March of 1923 several prominent Louisiana Klansmen from different parts of the state met in New Orleans to talk about the approaching gubernatorial campaign. This was the only such meeting the Klan moguls in Louisiana ever held. The Klansmen realized, quite correctly, that they could not with any hope of success put an avowed Klan candidate in the race for the governorship. As the daily New Orleans *Item* pointed out, "nobody could possibly be elected to general office in this state without pledging himself against [the Klan's] Secrecy-and-the-Mask."[4] The Klan's best chance of making its presence felt

---

[4] New Orleans *Item*, undated clipping in Huey P. Long Scrapbooks, vol. I (December 1923-September 1925), Department of Archives, Louisiana State University, Baton Rouge. The *Item* supported Huey P. Long in the 1923-1924 campaign.

in the gubernatorial contest was to solidify behind a non-Klan, Protestant candidate. But the Klan leaders could not agree on a man, and the New Orleans Konklave broke up with the Klansmen divided into two opposing factions.[5]

The larger group, led by Great Titan Thomas F. DePaoli of New Orleans, a member of the state legislature, and farm demonstration agent Paul D. Perkins of Lakes Charles, Great Titan of the southwestern Louisiana Province, favored the candidacy of Henry L. Fuqua of Baton Rouge, general manager of the state penitentiary. The other faction was headed by Swords R. Lee of Alexandria. In 1920 Lee had backed Parker in his campaign for the governorship, but he had broken with the governor after his assault on the Klan. Lee's choice for the governorship in 1923 was the explosive young chairman of the Louisiana Public Service Commission, Huey P. Long. Long had plans for giving the state an adequate system of roads, highways, and publicly owned bridges. Lee, as a construction contractor, was especially interested in Long's roadbuilding program; and he perhaps saw an opportunity to further his own economic well-being by swinging part of the Klan vote to Long, getting him elected, and thus establishing a priority on lucrative highway contracts.[6]

The factionalization of the Klan leadership in Louisiana meant not only that the order would fail to have a candidate of its own for the governorship, but that it would not officially endorse any non-Klan aspirant. William C. Barnette of Shreveport, general counsel for the Klan in Louisiana, laid down the official Klan position on the gubernatorial race when he said that the Klan had no candidate for governor and endorsed no candidate. He called on all Klansmen to vote for the man they thought would best

[5] New Orleans *Times-Picayune*, March 2, 1923.

[6] T. Harry Williams to writer, March 2, 1962, in the writer's possession. Professor Williams, of the Department of History of Louisiana State University, is presently at work on a biography of Huey P. Long and has had access to the hitherto-closed Long papers.

serve the state regardless of his religious affiliation.[7] The leaders of the Klan, however, still felt free to engage in the traditional Louisiana sport of trading blocs of votes.

Three men bid for the Democratic nomination for governor of Louisiana in 1923-1924. One of them, Long, was making a premature venture into gubernatorial politics. In 1924, he was still a sectional candidate, with his following concentrated mainly in the dry, Protestant, northern and central Louisiana parishes. He had not yet developed the statewide appeal that would enable him to carry the rural Catholic parishes in 1928, sweep him into the governorship, and inaugurate the most tempestuous era in the history of the state. In 1924 he ran for governor on a platform calling for extensive social welfare measures and the curbing of big business. Long alternately straddled and ignored the Klan issue in an effort to win votes from both Klan and anti-Klan, Protestant and Catholic. He had the support of many disgruntled citizens in the rural areas of north Louisiana, mostly small farmers and day laborers; the Klan faction led by Lee in Rapides and Ouachita parishes; and an "Independent Regular" group in New Orleans which had splintered from the Behrman machine.[8]

A second candidate whose appeal was primarily sectional was Lieutenant Governor Hewitt Bouanchaud of New Roads, Pointe Coupee Parish, a Catholic and a fierce, uncompromising opponent of the Klan. Bouanchaud's strength lay in the heavily Catholic, wet, southern Louisiana parishes, which comprised the most populous portion of the state outside of New Orleans and Shreveport. He also had the support of the "New Regular" organization in New Orleans.[9]

Fuqua, the third gubernatorial candidate, alone had a real statewide following. His candidacy rested on a power-

[7] Shreveport *Journal,* September 25, 1923.

[8] New Orleans *Times-Picayune,* June 24, September 6, 1923; Sindler, *Huey Long's Louisiana,* 48.

[9] New Orleans *Times-Picayune,* October 11, 1923.

ful alliance consisting of the Old Regular organization in New Orleans, most of the large industrial interests, the Protestant leaders in northern Louisiana and the eastern "Florida parishes," and the followers of Klan leaders De-Paoli and Perkins. Thus the Old Regular machine, sustained mainly by Catholic voters, partly by immigrants, and led by the Jewish Behrman and several Catholics, became a partner in a statewide coalition which included a large portion of the Klan membership in Louisiana.[10] No more striking tribute could be paid to the enervating character of Louisiana politics than the absorption of the Klan into such an incongruous political grouping.

During the gubernatorial campaign Long avoided the Klan issue. Both Bouanchaud and Fuqua went on record against the hooded order and in favor of legislation to abolish "secrecy and the mask." Fuqua did his best to play down the Klan issue, whereas Bouanchaud threw charges of Klan influence in every direction—at Fuqua, the Old Regulars, the upstate Protestant politicians, and Long. But neither he nor those who spoke in his behalf, including Governor Parker, could arouse a great deal of interest in an anti-Klan crusade. The New Orleans *Times-Picayune*, which endorsed Bouanchaud as the only candidate not tainted by the Klan, admitted that its survey showed that the Klan was the principal issue in only seventeen of the sixty-four parishes in the state.[11]

The outcome of the race depended on the efficacy of the different political alignments. Fuqua, who pleaded for "peace and harmony in the state," was the strongest candidate with the backing of a solid Old Regular-neutral Protestant-industrialist-Klan combine. Long, with some Klans-

[10] Reynolds, *Machine Politics in New Orleans*, 219; Jared Y. Sanders, "The Ku Klux Klan," typescript in Jared Y. Sanders and Family Papers, Department of Archives, Louisiana State University, Baton Rouge.

[11] New Orleans *Times-Picayune*, September 30, October 3, 18, 20, 21, 30, November 8, 1923.

men supporting him, urged poor people throughout Louisiana to take up their ballots against Standard Oil and the other business giants; but business prosperity, the Klan issue, and the fact that the agricultural depression was not as severe as it would become in a few years, blunted much of his appeal. Bouanchaud had a strong following in the thickly settled southern Louisiana parishes where Catholic citizens predominated, but he had few supporters in other parts of the state.

From all indications a substantial majority of the Klansmen in Louisiana voted for Fuqua.[12] A few days before the Democratic primary an Alexandria daily newspaper carried an advertisement supposedly paid for by "friends and supporters" of Fuqua. The advertisement consisted of a denunciation by Carey P. Duncan, of Shreveport, the little-known Grand Dragon of Louisiana, of rumors being circulated in the central part of the state to the effect that Long had once become a "Klansman at Large." "Our judgment is that this is a bold and bald attempt to use the Klan for the purpose of advancing the political interests of a candidate and as such should be resented by all loyal Klansmen," wrote Duncan. "I wish to impress on you and all other Klansmen that the organization is not a political one and should not be used to further the interest of any candidate." But at the bottom of the advertisement Klansmen were urged to vote for Fuqua and "Be guided by facts, not hearsay."[13]

At the Democratic primary, on January 15, Bouanchaud, drawing almost all the anti-Klan votes in the state, led the gubernatorial candidates, polling 84,162 votes to 81,382 for Fuqua and 73,985 for Long. A runoff was optional, not mandatory, under Louisiana law and party regulations. Since it was obvious that most of the Long vote would go to Fuqua, many quarters, including the New Orleans *Times-*

---

[12] T. Harry Williams to writer, March 2, 1962.
[13] New Orleans *Times-Picayune,* January 13, 1924.

Picayune, called on Bouanchaud to withdraw and concede the nomination. But Bouanchaud would not bow to the inevitable; instead he began a round of negotiations for the endorsement of Long's Independent Regular following in New Orleans. He even appropriated the free textbook plank in Long's platform as an added inducement to Huey's rural backers. The Independent Regular organization eventually gave its endorsement to Bouanchaud, but Long refused to commit himself on the runoff contest, and the bulk of his upstate retinue, including his Klan partisans in Ouachita and Rapides parishes, went to Fuqua.[14]

On February 19 the "Fuqua ticket," the slate of state candidates endorsed by the Choctaws, most Klan leaders, and some local Klans, swept the state. Fuqua carried New Orleans by nearly 15,000 votes and won six of the eight congressional districts in the state. The parishes carried by Long in the first primary went almost solidly for the penitentiary manager. Fuqua's margin over Bouanchaud was about 33,000 votes. The other members of the Fuqua ticket, which listed two Catholics, also were nominated and thus assured of election in November. The candidate of the Fuqua coalition for attorney general piled up a big majority over Adolph V. Coco, the incumbent and the chief prosecutor of the Klansmen in the Mer Rouge cases a year earlier.[15]

A few days after the primary Hiram W. Evans was in Dallas, his hometown, where he was asked about the extent of the Klan's involvement in politics. The Imperial Wizard answered that in Louisiana most Klansmen voted for Fuqua, even though Fuqua was not a Klansman.[16] Evans went

[14] *Ibid.,* January 18, 19, 20, 23, February 1, 2, 6, 7, 9, 1924; Alexander Heard and Donald S. Strong, *Southern Primaries and Elections, 1920-1949* (University, Alabama, 1950), 69.

[15] New Orleans *Times-Picayune,* February 18, 20, 21, 1924; Heard and Strong, *Southern Primaries and Elections,* 69.

[16] Fort Smith *Southwest American,* February 23, 1924. This was one of the very few occasions when Evans admitted to the Klan's open participation in politics.

on to boast that the Klan had helped to nominate the next governor of Louisiana. His estimate of the situation was generally correct. Nevertheless, it is clear that the Klan leaders did not deliver a solid vote for Fuqua in 1924, that in fact the Louisiana Klan hierarchy was incapable of delivering a solid bloc of Klansmen to any statewide candidate that year or any other year.[17]

The Louisiana Klan always lacked political unity beyond the area of the legislative district. This condition, together with the diverse ethnic complexion of the state, ruled out independent action in state politics. In the legislative districts, parishes, and towns of northern, eastern, and central Louisiana, however, the Klan was sometimes capable of mustering the same power that it did in other states. During the winter and spring of 1924 local Klans got involved in political fights in several parishes. Candidates backed by the Klan were successful in only about half of these contests.[18]

Despite occasional setbacks, by the spring of 1924 the Klan in Louisiana was, on the surface, in a rather enviable position. It shared credit for defeating a Catholic candidate for governor and electing a conservative, Protestant advocate of "peace." In the new state legislature, to convene in May, about fifteen Klansmen or pro-Klan solons sat in the house of representatives, while about ten Klansmen and close sympathizers were in the senate.[19] A new era of harmony and tranquility supposedly was dawning in Louisiana politics. Yet the Klan remained divided in the Pelican State, split between the Klansmen who had supported Long in the first primary and those who had backed Fuqua and thus

[17] T. Harry Williams to writer, March 2, 1962.

[18] New Orleans *Times-Picayune*, November 1, 14, 16, 1923, April 6, 7, 12, 23, 1924.

[19] *Ibid.*, May 4, 1924. Great Titan Thomas F. DePaoli, state representative from the twelfth ward in New Orleans, was defeated when he tried for a second term by Fred J. Oser, independent Democratic candidate. See *ibid.*, January 16, 1924.

tacitly accepted the new governor's plans for anti-Klan legislation. This split became evident when the legislature met and took up the question of regulating the Klan. The subsequent fight over the bills introduced by the Fuqua administration to curb the order intensified the factionalism within the Realm of Louisiana and contributed to the disintegration of the Klan's power in the state.

Contrasting with its sectional character in Louisiana, the Klan thrived in every part of Arkansas—in the Delta country along the Mississippi, in the prairie counties in the southern and central portions of the state, and in the mountains to the west and north. There was nothing to prevent the Arkansas Klan from electioneering on a statewide basis, and as soon as the order was strong enough, it ventured into politics. In 1922 the political activities of the Klan in Arkansas centered in Little Rock Klan No. 1, which won control of the government of Pulaski County, endorsed a slate of candidates for state office, and claimed victory when all but one of its endorsees won the Democratic nomination. Two years later the all-powerful James A. Comer, Grand Dragon of the Realm and Exalted Cyclops of the Klan in Little Rock, had more grandiose designs. With the venerable Thomas C. McRae refusing to run for a third term as governor, the field was wide open for gubernatorial candidates. Comer was determined that one of the candidates would be a Klansman and that he would receive the votes of the 45,000 to 50,000 Knights of the Invisible Empire in Arkansas.[20]

In the early months of 1924 Virgil C. Pettie, secretary of the Democratic Central Committee, looked like the best bet to become the gubernatorial candidate of the Klan. Pettie was one of the leading Democrats in Arkansas, an active Klansman, and along with Comer, a member of Evans' trusted inner circle of political advisers. In April, however,

[20] The estimate of Klan membership in Arkansas is from Duffus, "Ku Klux Klan in the Middle West," 364.

Pettie announced that he would not run for governor.[21] Comer had to look around for another promising Klansman. He found such a man in Lee Cazort, former speaker of the state house of representatives, former president pro tempore of the senate, and now a thirty-six-year-old gentleman farmer at Lamar, Johnson County.[22]

The Grand Dragon realized that a show of democracy was necessary in the form of a statewide Klan elimination primary, the device used so effectively in the Pulaski County races of 1922. So on the night of May 28, as a driving rainstorm swept almost the entire state, the local Klans staged their elimination polls. By rising vote, rather than by mailed ballots, the Klansmen signified their choices for governor and for all the other state offices as well. The rainstorm severely cut attendance at the Klavern meetings, and this evidently benefited Cazort. The number of Klansmen voting in the Klaverns ranged from 40 in the Pocahontas Klan to 2,000 in Little Rock. Cazort piled up a 4-to-1 margin over the only other Klansman bidding for the blessing of the order, Commissioner of Mines, Manufacturing, and Agriculture Jim G. Ferguson. Ferguson carried only four small Klans, as less than five thousand Knights voted in the chapter primaries.[23] Klansmen throughout Arkansas, especially Grand Dragon Comer, now waited quietly for Ferguson to withdraw from the gubernatorial race, as all the candidates had supposedly agreed to do if they failed to obtain the Klan nomination. But the days and weeks passed, and still Ferguson did not withdraw.

In the meantime, Arkansas Klansmen had been busy choosing slates of candidates in the county races. From February through July, Little Rock Klan No. 1 held primaries by mail for the various county and district offices,

[21] Little Rock *Arkansas Gazette*, April 8, 1924.
[22] Fort Smith *Southwest American*, January 5, 1923.
[23] Little Rock *Arkansas Gazette*, May 28-30, 1924.

so that by the time of the Democratic primary in August, the Klan in Pulaski County had once again chosen a full slate of county and legislative candidates, plus a candidate for the state railroad commission from the Little Rock district.[24]

The Klan's prospects for giving Cazort the Democratic nomination looked better and better as the governor's race moved into the summer months. There were six candidates contending for the gubernatorial nomination, and since in 1924 there were no laws or party rules providing for a run-off, one candidate could win the nomination with a relatively small percentage of the total vote. Cazort and his benefactor, Comer, ostensibly commanded a bloc of nearly 50,000 Klansmen and Klanswomen. The other prominent candidates were Ferguson, the Klansman rejected in the Realm-wide elimination primary; former secretary of state Tom J. Terral of Little Rock; and John E. Martineau, judge of chancery court in Little Rock. Of all the aspirants, only Martineau openly opposed the Klan, and then only its "secret politics" and its "Republican Grand Dragon," not its nativism and racism and its history of violence. He charged that "if Cazort is elected, you will have a Republican Governor just as effectively as you would if Comer were elected."[25]

Cazort campaigned as an avowed Klansman. He appeared at Klan local and district meetings in different parts of the state, affirming his membership in the secret order and promising to uphold its principles if elected. At El Dorado, the free and easy oil town, he told his listeners that "what we need is not more laws but more satisfactory law enforcement." And at a big Fourth of July initiation ceremony in Little Rock he shouted that he was "carrying

[24] *Ibid.*, February 13, 20, March 21, 1924.
[25] John E. Martineau for Governor broadside, David Y. Thomas Papers, University of Arkansas General Library, Fayetteville.

the Klan's battle flag into this campaign, not as an individual but as a Klansman."[26]

A month before the Democratic primary, Ferguson, who had not mentioned the Klan since his defeat in the Klan elimination poll, suddenly blasted the secret order. "I have no fight against the Klan and the principles for which it stands," proclaimed Ferguson in a full-page advertisement in daily newspapers over the state, "but I am against the Little Rock crowd into whose hands the destiny of the order has fallen." Among other things he accused Comer of changing the original date for the Klan primary from May 16 to May 28 so that Cazort could have more time to campaign among Klansmen, and of denying him a mailing list of all the Exalted Cyclops in the state. Ferguson said that fewer than 5,000 Klansmen and less than half of the local Klans in Arkansas participated in the primary, and that Comer's office had never given out any specific returns from the primary, announcing only that Cazort won by a big margin.[27]

Ferguson's charges threatened to split the Klan vote in Arkansas. Comer and the officials of the Little Rock Klan angrily called a meeting of the chapter. On Thursday night, July 17, the Klansmen in Little Rock voted to suspend Ferguson and two other Klan politicians who had refused to withdraw after losing in the elimination primaries. Then, to shore up the cracks of dissension in the walls of the chapter and to whip up enthusiasm just before the August 12 Democratic primary, the Little Rock Klan began holding a series of political rallies, addressed by the Klan candidates for Pulaski County offices and by some of the Klan choices for state offices.[28]

Two days before the party primary, on Sunday, August 10, Klan No. 1 of Little Rock presented its political piece

[26] Little Rock *Arkansas Gazette*, June 17, 26, July 4, 5, 1924.
[27] *Ibid.*, July 13, 1924.
[28] *Ibid.*, July 19, August 6, 1924.

de resistance—a big advertisement published in the daily
Arkansas Gazette headed "Sour Grape Candidates for Governor." In the advertisement the Klan said that four candidates for governor had asked for the endorsement of the
order during the course of the campaign. Cazort, "the political grape-picker of 1924," got the Klan nomination, while
the other three—Ferguson, Terral, and Jacob R. Wilson of
El Dorado, a minor candidate—were turned down as being
unworthy of the Klan's favor. Ferguson was, according to
the Klan statement, a sower of strife who had refused to
abide by the Klan's selection of Cazort. Terral's application for membership had been rejected by the Little Rock
Klan three times and by the El Dorado Klan once. Afterward, Terral had joined the Klan in Morehouse Parish,
Louisiana. Then he came back to Little Rock and showed
his card to Comer, who demanded that he return it. But
Terral refused and stayed in the governor's race.[29]

So the Democratic voters of Arkansas went to the polls
to choose a gubernatorial nominee, and the next governor,
amid charges by Ferguson that the Arkansas Klan was a
Republican machine, by the Klan that nearly all the candidates had sought its favor, and by Martineau that Terral
was "a Klansman, but without a Klan home" and that thousands of individualistic Klansmen were going to vote for
him.[30] To almost everyone's surprise, Terral took a slender
early lead, added to it as the tabulation of votes proceeded,
and won the nomination. The final returns gave Terral
54,553 votes; Cazort, 43,466; Martineau, 35,438; and Ferguson, 27,155. The results showed clearly that general dissatisfaction with Comer's regime, and particular unhappiness over the questionable manner in which Cazort had
become the Klan candidate, had vitiated the political unity
of the Arkansas Klan. The Klan once again displayed its
power in Pulaski County, carrying all the county races. But

[29] *Ibid.*, August 10, 1924.
[30] Martineau broadside, Thomas Papers.

the Klan failed to carry the county for Cazort; Martineau, the popular chancery court judge, polled 3,843 votes in Pulaski to the Klansman's 3,744.[31]

Cazort led in only 16 of the 75 counties in the state. He lost not only Pulaski County, but other counties where the Klan was supposed to be in the saddle, like Clark (Arkadelphia), Arkansas (Stuttgart), and Phillips (Helena).[32] The Klan simply had not united behind the avowed Klan candidate for governor. A Klansman from Lonoke gave an accurate post mortem on the contest when he wrote: "Look at Cazort's vote . . . Judge Martineau was the anti-Klan candidate. Yet, he got lots of Klan votes. So did Terrall [sic]—they elected him. They did not want Cazort. I did not & voted for Martineau; because I liked him *personally.*"[33]

Hence widespread dislike of Comer, his methods, and his candidate proved fatal to the chances of the Arkansas Klan to elect a governor. Ferguson's barbs had done their work, along with two years of growing resentment against Comer in the Realm and in the city of Little Rock. The Grand Dragon knew when he was beaten. In a note of congratulations he assured Terral that the Klan would make no fight against the Democratic nominee at the general election in November. Ferguson, although also beaten, was reasonably happy over the course of events. He claimed to have drawn enough Klan votes away from Cazort to prevent his nomination. In a letter of resignation sent to Little Rock Klan No. 1 (significantly, he waited until after the primary to resign from the Klan), Ferguson proclaimed: "The defeat of Comerism at the polls last Tuesday signifies that Democracy wants no meddling with Democratic rule in Arkansas

31 Little Rock *Arkansas Gazette,* August 13, 14, 29, 1924; Heard and Strong, *Southern Primaries and Elections,* 23-24.

32 Little Rock *Arkansas Gazette,* August 13, 1924.

33 H. N. Street to Harmon L. Remmel, September 12, 1924, Harmon L. Remmel Papers, University of Arkansas General Library, Fayetteville.

by the Little Rock crowd of election manipulators that has seized control of the Ku Klux organization in this state."[34]

Most of the other candidates for state office endorsed by the Klan in its May elimination primary won their contests, but the Klan was not an issue in any of the state races except the gubernatorial campaign. Pulaski County was about the only place where the Klan held a firm grip on the county government. In late August, however, enemies of the Klan controlled the Pulaski County Democratic convention, which adopted a resolution barring from the Democratic ballot any candidates henceforth nominated in special "pre-primary elections." The next month anti-Klan Democrats secured a majority at the organization meeting of the county central committee. Klan-haters were elected to the controlling offices of the party agency.[35]

The state Democratic convention met in mid-September in Little Rock. Just before the opening of the convention, the state central committee wrote into the rules of the state party a restriction similar to the one adopted by the Pulaski County convention—a provision barring from the party primary any candidate who previously participated in any "run-off or primary other than a run-off or primary held under the authority of the Democratic party." The next day, however, the resolutions committee of the convention rejected a proposal to denounce the Klan's political activity and its religious prejudice, adopting instead a platform plank that simply affirmed "obedience to the orderly processes of law" and condemned "any effort to arouse religious or racial dissension." Outside the committee room, before the assembled delegates, former United States Senator Walter F. Kirby, the keynote speaker, shouted that "there is no room in the Democratic party for an invisible empire." And on the floor Robert A. Cook, who had succeeded Comer as Cyclops of the Little Rock Klan, added that he agreed with

[34] Little Rock *Arkansas Gazette*, August 15, 24, 1924.
[35] *Ibid.*, August 16, 27, September 6, 7, 1924.

Kirby. "What the Ku Klux Klan should do," said Cook, "is to pay less attention to politics and more to constructive work. . . . It is time for us to quit quarreling and get back to the original purposes of Klankraft."[36]

After failing with Cazort, and except for a short detour into the Little Rock city primaries of late 1924, Klansmen in Arkansas pretty well held their course on the "original purposes of Klankraft" and stayed out of politics. Comer retained his post as Grand Dragon for several more years, but antagonism toward him continued to mount until it eventually brought about a split in the Little Rock Klan. The Klan's one brief venture into statewide politics in Arkansas proved a failure, not because Klansmen over the state lacked dedication to the mission of the order, but because they wanted an honest chance to choose their own candidate for governor without Comer's dictating the choice to them. Klansmen in Texas wanted the same thing, and they also protested when their Grand Dragon employed similar autocratic methods.

Observers of Texas politics agreed that the Klan would have a candidate for governor in 1924. In a sense the election of Earle B. Mayfield to the United States Senate in 1922, and other Klan victories of that year, were only a prelude to 1924, when the order was expected to make an all-out drive for the governorship. By 1924 the Klan in Texas was a highly organized, efficient minority. Working quietly and mysteriously, this minority nearly controlled the political life of the state. Perhaps as many as 400,000 Texans had belonged to the Klan at one time or another. The membership of the order in Texas was quite fluid, as it was everywhere else, but in 1924 there were between 97,000

[36] *Ibid.*, September 10, 11, 1924; Henry M. Alexander, "The Double Primary," *Arkansas Historical Quarterly,* III (Autumn 1944), 225-26; *Platform of the Democratic Party of Arkansas, Adopted September 11, 1924,* Thomas C. McRae Papers, University of Arkansas General Library, Fayetteville.

and 170,000 paid-up Klansmen in the state.[37] In the spring the Klan demonstrated its power, if any further demonstration was needed, by dominating the precinct, county, and state Democratic conventions and thus the Texas delegation sent to the Democratic national convention. The Klan was already having internal difficulties in Texas, however. Early in 1924 dissension broke out in the Realm over the selection of a gubernatorial candidate.

In Houston, Billie Mayfield, an ex-colonel in the Texas National Guard and the unsuccessful Klan candidate for the lieutenant governorship in 1922, published a crudely moralistic, pro-Klan weekly newspaper. In the first weeks of 1924 he began exhorting Klansmen in the columns of his newspaper to unify behind Dallas attorney V. A. Collins as the Knight to go forward with the cause of 100 percent Americanism and moral reform in the coming gubernatorial race.[38] Collins, an active member of Dallas Klan No. 66, had served in the state senate, where he had been an ardent advocate of the statewide prohibition legislation passed during the First World War and a member of the senate committee that wrote the verdict removing Jim Ferguson from the governorship. When *Colonel Mayfield's Weekly*, Billie Mayfield's paper, endorsed Collins, the Dallas lawyer had never seen an issue of the paper or met its editor. Mayfield nevertheless boomed Collins as if the two were old friends.[39]

Mayfield actually had little influence in Texas Klan circles, or at least among those who counted—the Realm officials. This hard truth he soon discovered when the Collins boom collided with the wishes of Z. E. "Zeke" Marvin of Dallas, a wealthy native of Indiana who had risen through

[37] Washington *Post*, November 2, 1930, sec. I, p. 4; New York *Times*, February 21, 1926, sec. VIII, p. 1; Duffus, "Ku Klux Klan in the Middle West," 364.

[38] Houston *Colonel Mayfield's Weekly*, January 19, 1924.

[39] V. A. Collins to writer, February 24, 1962, in the writer's possession.

Texas Klan ranks to the office of Grand Dragon. Marvin
was a good friend and a leading disciple of Imperial Wizard Evans. With Evans and the Dallas Klan, about 13,000
strong, behind him, Marvin ran matters virtually as he
pleased in the Realm. Like his counterpart in Arkansas, the
Texas Dragon had his own candidate in mind for the governorship—District Judge Felix D. Robertson, a member of
the Dallas Klan and, like Collins, a zealous prohibitionist.
In late January, Marvin announced from Realm headquarters
in Dallas that Robertson would be the official candidate of
the Klan in the coming gubernatorial primary.[40]

"I am not ready, and the Klan is not ready," exploded
Billie Mayfield in Houston, "to accept as its governor the
call boy of an individual man in Texas no matter what
exalted position he holds within the Klan."[41] Mayfield began a running editorial fight with Marvin and the weekly
Texas 100 Per Cent American, organ of the Dallas Klan and
thus of the Grand Dragon. Mayfield's attacks apparently
aroused enough Klansmen to worry Marvin. The Grand
Dragon visited the Waco, Fort Worth, Houston, and San
Antonio Klans to assure the hooded Knights that Robertson
had been selected very simply and democratically. Robertson had been nominated by the executive committee of the
Realm, comprised of seven officials from each of the five
Provinces, plus five additional Klansmen from each Province, making a total of sixty. The Klorero, or state convention, of October 1923 had stipulated the makeup of the
executive committee. Marvin neglected to add, however,
that as Grand Dragon he exercised direct or indirect ap-
pointive power over every member of the executive committee and over all of those attending the Klorero.[42] The

[40] Interview of the writer with an ex-Klansman, Dallas, May 18,
1959.
[41] Houston *Colonel Mayfield's Weekly,* February 2, 1924.
[42] Dallas *Texas 100 Per Cent American,* February 15, 1924; *Constitution and Laws of the Knights of the Ku Klux Klan* (Atlanta,
1921), art. xviii, sec. 7.

nomination of Robertson by the state Klan executive committee hardly expressed the voice of the rank and file.

Klansmen in Fort Worth and Waco endorsed Robertson, but Houston and San Antonio Klansmen rebelled against Marvin's dictation and rejected his proposal. Billie Mayfield, intensifying his attacks on the Realm leaders, charged that during 1923 Marvin sold large amounts of whisky illegally through his chain of drugstores in Dallas. Trading Klannish blows with the *Texas 100 Per Cent American*, Mayfield demanded a Realm-wide elimination primary. Finally, yielding to the din raised by Mayfield and others, Marvin decreed that each of the 300 or more local Klans in Texas could hold its own elimination primary to decide between Robertson and Collins. Mayfield, while continuing to push Collins' candidacy, congratulated himself on his successful fight for democracy in the Realm and announced that all was well in Klandom. "Slip me your hand, Zeke, it's all over now," wrote the Houston Klansman. "We are going singing into the battle together, and the fighting can't start any too soon for me."[43]

Klansmen over Texas, perhaps fearing that the Evans-Marvin clique would bolt the Klan if they did not abide by the wishes of the Grand Dragon, overwhelmingly approved Robertson by standing vote in the local primaries in March. Marvin and his cohorts, however, were still not quite sure that Mayfield could be trusted. So they brought the Klan editor to Dallas for a conference. Mayfield spent the better part of a day talking with Marvin and the leaders of the Dallas Klan. After the conference Mayfield saw an angry Collins and told him that Marvin had presented a "great inducement" to the Houstonian to cease supporting Collins and swing to Robertson in his editorials.[44] When he got back to Houston, Mayfield did a neat about-face, condemn-

[43] Houston *Colonel Mayfield's Weekly*, February 16, 23, March 1, 1924.

[44] *Ibid.*, March 22, 1924; V. A. Collins to writer, February 24, 1962.

ing Collins for trying to promote strife and assuring his readers he would not follow the Dallas attorney in a bolt.[45]

Collins hit the campaign trail to tell the voters how "a tyrannical conspiracy" of Klan leaders had betrayed his candidacy. His only sin, he said bitterly, was announcing for the governorship without the consent of the Realm hierarchy. After his announcement, Marvin had begun a systematic campaign of vilification within the Klan and finally had had him suspended from the order.[46] Collins, appearances became less and less frequent during the course of the campaign. He still says, "I had never sought the Klan support or asked any member of the Klan to support me, but . . . was just running as a private citizen on my merit."[47] His fate was to be the same as that of Robert L. Henry in 1922.

The Texas Klan remained united and its opposition disunited at the first Democratic primary in July. The Klan vote enabled Robertson to lead eight candidates for the governorship, with 192,508 votes. His nearest opponent, polling about 46,000 fewer votes and entering the runoff against the Klansman, was Mrs. Miriam Amanda "Ma" Ferguson, the wife of James E. Ferguson.[48]

In 1924 Ferguson had vowed a fight to the death with the Klan. After removing him from the governorship in 1917, the legislature had barred Ferguson from contending for state office. But the advent of woman's suffrage made it possible for a Ferguson to run for governor again—except that in 1924 it was Ferguson's wife. From the beginning of the campaign "Pa" Ferguson, as he now referred to himself, doing most of his wife's speechmaking, concentrated his

[45] Houston *Colonel Mayfield's Weekly*, March 22, 1924.
[46] Fort Worth *Star-Telegram*, March 10, 1924; Dallas *Morning News*, April 11, 1924; V. A. Collins to writer, February 24, 1962.
[47] V. A. Collins to writer, February 24, 1962.
[48] Dallas *Morning News*, July 29, 1924; Heard and Strong, *Southern Primaries and Elections*, 136-38.

choice invective on the Klan. He stepped up his attacks in the runoff campaign, which featured four weeks of the worst vituperation in Texas political history. Ferguson described his wife's opponent as "the great grand gizzard mouthpiece of the Grand Dragon," while Robertson called the ex-governor a "whisky-throated politician," a "thief," and a "liar."

In the runoff all the defeated gubernatorial candidates of the first primary, including Collins, gave their endorsement to Mrs. Ferguson, as did most of the daily newspapers in the cities and such prominent Texans as former United States Senator Joseph W. Bailey, former Governor Oscar B. Colquitt, and Alvin Owsley, national commander of the American Legion. By August 23, the day of the second primary, Robertson and the Klan faced a heterogeneous but powerful coalition of loyal Fergusonites, principally "wets," tenant farmers, small farmers, and day laborers; people who sincerely disliked the hooded order on moral and ideological grounds; and nervous politicians who wanted to end the disruptive presence of the Klan in state politics.[49]

The combination was too much for the Klan. Mrs. Ferguson amassed a vote of 413,751 to 316,019 for Klansman Robertson. The anti-Klan coalition also gave Barry Miller of Dallas, a bitter foe of the Klan, the nomination for lieutenant governor over Will C. Edwards, the Klan candidate. District Attorney Dan Moody from Georgetown, who had sent a Klansman to prison for a flogging in 1923, took the nomination for attorney general from Edward B. Ward of Corpus Christi, generally supported by the Klan. After the runoff primary Dallas and Tarrant counties were the only major

[49] Fort Worth *Star-Telegram*, August 22, 1924; Waco *Times-Herald*, August 14, 1924; Dallas *Morning News*, August 20, 1924; Sam H. Acheson, *Joe Bailey, the Last Democrat* (New York, 1932), 394; V. A. Collins to writer, February 24, 1962; Ouida Ferguson Nalle, *The Fergusons of Texas* (San Antonio, 1946), 168-80; Charles W. Ferguson, "James E. Ferguson," *Southwest Review*, X (October 1924), 30-31.

counties in Texas still under the dominance of the Klan, as in many counties, large and small, slates of anti-Klan candidates were nominated. The final setback of the summer for the Klan came at the state Democratic convention, held in Austin early in September. With forces hostile to the Klan controlling roughly 90 percent of the county delegations, the convention endorsed the nomination of Mrs. Ferguson, denounced the Klan as un-Christian and un-American, and demanded the public registration of secret organizations and an antimask law.[50]

In the general election campaign thousands of Texas Democrats, decrying "Fergusonism" and "government by proxy," left the dominant party and threw their votes to the Republican candidate for governor, Dr. George C. Butte, dean of the University of Texas School of Law. The only group formally bolting the Democracy was an organization called the "Good Government Democratic League," formed under the leadership of national party committeeman Thomas B. Love of Dallas.[51] But most Klansmen, it seems, also voted for Butte, who received almost three times as many votes as any previous Republican candidate for governor in Texas. Butte showed his greatest strength in Dallas, Harris (Houston), Tarrant (Fort Worth), Jefferson (Beaumont), McLennan (Waco), and other counties that were both Klan hotbeds and Democratic citadels. The massive, if unofficial, backing the Klan gave the Republican candidate was a last-ditch effort to stop the hated Fergusons. The bolt entailed going over to a party that had con-

[50] Austin *Statesman*, August 25, September 3, 4, 1924; Fort Worth *Star-Telegram*, August 31, 1924; C. V. Terrell to Oscar B. Colquitt, August 28, 1924, Oscar B. Colquitt Papers, University of Texas Archives, Austin; Heard and Strong, *Southern Primaries and Elections*, 136-38. For a Klan ticket circulated by the Abilene Klan endorsing Felix D. Robertson, Will C. Edwards, and Edward B. Ward, see *Congressional Record*, 68th Congress, 2d Session (1924), 94.

[51] See the folder headed "Good Government Democratic League," Thomas B. Love Papers, Archives of the Dallas Historical Society, Dallas, for material on the anti-Ferguson movement.

demned the Klan in both its 1922 and 1924 state platforms. The influence of the secret society in a Republican state administration would have been negligible. Yet even this desperate crossing of party lines proved futile. There were enough determined anti-Klanners and do-or-die Democrats left in the state to give Mrs. Ferguson 422,588 votes to Butte's 294,970.[52]

The failure of the Klan to win the Democratic nomination for Robertson, then to block the Fergusons in the general election; the loss of nearly all the counties it had formerly dominated; and the election of a legislature that was preponderantly anti-Klan—these developments signaled the passing of the Klan as a force in Texas politics. "It was all over," recalled a former Klansman. "After Robertson was beaten the prominent men left the Klan. The Klan's standing went with them."[53] By the end of 1924 Texas, once the most cherished prize of the men who ran the Klan, was no longer the number one state in Klandom. Other states—Indiana, Ohio, Alabama—became more important than Texas in Klan affairs. Oklahoma, too, superseded Texas in the Invisible Empire, for in the Sooner State the Klan managed to stave off a shattering political defeat, cling to a bit of its prestige, and thus make possible its survival for several more years.

The Klan's fight with Jack Walton in 1923, carried to a triumphant—and legal—conclusion, was quite a boon to the order in Oklahoma. The Klan was evidently losing strength in the summer of 1923, when Walton set out to crush the organization. By the end of the year, however, with Walton ejected from the governorship by an alliance of Klansmen, neutrals, and anti-Klan citizens unable to tolerate Walton, the Oklahoma Klan was stronger than ever. At the beginning of 1924 more than 100,000 Oklahomans held citizen-

[52] Dallas *Morning News*, November 9, 18, 1924; Heard and Strong, *Southern Primaries and Elections*, 136-38.

[53] Interview of the writer with an ex-Klansman, Dallas, May 18, 1959.

ship in the Invisible Empire.[54] Despite the presence of some dissension among Klansmen over the passage of the antimask law, the Klan in Oklahoma was a well-defined bloc of determined voters, ready to proceed to greater conquests in 1924 and, specifically, to renew the fight with its prime enemy, Walton.

In the spring the Klan fortified its power by sweeping to victory in several hard-fought city elections in northeastern Oklahoma. Tulsa, Okmulgee, Muskogee, Sand Springs, and other towns continued under the dominance of the Klan element.[55] As the summer approached, the Klansmen readied themselves for the race for United States Senator, in which, again, the Klan faced Walton. As Wesley E. Disney had predicted, the ex-governor, charging betrayal in that he was "elected by a majority of 50,000 and put out by 40," returned to the political wars in search of the Senate seat being vacated by the retiring Democrat Robert L. Owen.[56]

From the outset Walton's campaign speeches consisted almost solely of harangues against the Klan. His especial targets were the pro-Klan Protestant ministers in the state. "If they would preach love and neighborliness instead of this vicious doctrine," declared the Klan-fighter, "we wouldn't be in the state we're in now."[57] The Klan matched him barb for barb. While he was speaking at Heavener, in southeastern Oklahoma, several hundred Klansmen interrupted him and marched for half an hour around the platform on which he was standing. The white-robed but unmasked Klansmen carried a banner reading "We'll have no Jack in the Senate." After the demonstrators tired, Walton finished his speech.[58]

[54] Duffus, "Ku Klux Klan in the Middle West," 364.
[55] Tulsa *Tribune,* February 29, March 4, 8, 13, 19, April 2, 8, 9, 1924.
[56] Oklahoma City *Daily Oklahoman,* December 1, 1923.
[57] Tulsa *Tribune,* July 12, 1924.
[58] New York *Times,* June 28, 1924, p. 7.

From either Klan or anti-Klan vantage points it soon became apparent that Walton was running a strong race. It looked as if many Oklahomans who could not wait to oust Walton the previous fall now felt that he would be less objectionable in Washington than in Oklahoma City. If they were going to beat back this new threat from Walton, the Klansmen had to form ranks behind one of Walton's two principal opponents, Representative E. B. Howard, a Klan member and elected with the help of the Tulsa Klan in 1922, or Charles G. Wrightsman, also of Tulsa, a reform-minded millionaire oilman. Wrightsman received the endorsement of the remnants of the Farmer-Labor Reconstruction League, whose leaders now thoroughly repudiated Walton. One of the favorite diversions of political observers in the state was guessing whether Howard or Wrightsman would get the official nod of the Klan. Most of the bets were on Howard, an admitted Klansman. On the night of July 29, with N. Clay Jewett out of the state, a group of Klan officials, headed by Exalted Cyclops William Shelley Rogers of the Tulsa Klan, listened to a speech by Howard in a park outside Oklahoma City. The Klansmen then adopted a resolution declaring their support for the Tulsa Representative. The next day, however, Jewett denounced the resolution as completely unauthorized and meaningless. "The Klan is not placing its endorsement on any man," said Jewett. "There is not a single candidate running in the Democratic primary upon whom the Klan felt it could put its approval."[59]

Only two days before the primaries, on August 2, the weekly *Fiery Cross*, published in Oklahoma City as the official organ of state headquarters, came out officially for Wrightsman. The editorial, while specifying that Wrightsman was not a Klansman, urged members of the order: "Don't split the votes Tuesday. [The nominee] will be

[59] Oklahoma City *Daily Oklahoman*, July 18, 29, 1924; Tulsa *Tribune*, July 29, 1924.

Jack Walton unless the electorate swings solidly to Charles J. Wrightsman. He is the best man in the race. Why not support him?" This had all the appearances of the long-awaited Klan endorsement. But then, to the amazement of hooded Knights over the state, on the eve of the primaries Jewett sent telegrams to every local Klan in the state, ordering Klansmen to vote for Howard. "Howard is a Klansman," read the telegrams. "We stand with him because we believe he can win." The Grand Dragon's edict came too late for most Klansmen to make a statement, but Cyclops W. R. Sampson of the Muskogee Klan announced that he would continue to back Wrightsman.[60]

What was behind Jewett's confusing maneuvers? The bulk of the evidence indicates that the Grand Dragon, a devout Republican, deliberately used the power of his office to befuddle obedient Klansmen, cripple the Klan's chances of beating Walton, and thus strengthen the chances of Okmulgee oilman W. B. Pine, the unopposed Republican senatorial candidate, at the general election in November. And this was precisely the result of Jewett's turnabout. With the Klan vote disrupted, Walton, pulling heavy majorities in the rural areas and in Oklahoma County, won the nomination with 91,510 votes to 83,922 for Howard. Wrightsman finished a poor fourth behind Thomas B. Gore, the blind former United States Senator. In the county primaries, however, the Klan managed to sustain its unity, thus perpetuating its control in many counties, including the two most populous, Tulsa and Oklahoma.[61]

The daily newspapers over the state were nearly unanimous in expressing their disgust over Walton's nomination and blaming the indecisiveness of the Klan for his triumphant return. "Say what he will and damn the Klan as he

[60] Tulsa *Tribune*, August 3, 4, 1924; Oklahoma City *Daily Oklahoman*, same dates.

[61] Oklahoma City *Daily Oklahoman*, August 2, 6, 1924; Tulsa *Tribune*, August 8, 1924; Edwin C. McReynolds, *Oklahoma: A History of the Sooner State* (Norman, 1954), 350.

will," grumbled the Oklahoma City *Daily Oklahoman*, "the best political friend that J. C. Walton ever had, the only political asset that he has today is the Invisible Empire."[62] The Tulsa *Tribune*, which had endorsed Wrightsman, observed that "All Jewett accomplished . . . was the nomination of Walton, and the injection of the Klan issue into the final [general election] campaign."[63] Attacked from all sides, the Grand Dragon tried to answer the angry Klansmen and other anti-Walton voters who suddenly found Walton leading the Oklahoma Democracy into the November election. Jewett's mouthpiece, the *Fiery Cross*, claimed that Jewett had the Klan weekly initially sanction Wrightsman only as a trial balloon. The Dragon then discovered that most Klan members favored Howard, whereupon he began trying to line up the Democratic Klansmen behind the Tulsa Representative. "The Grand Dragon merely desired to get the opinion of the majority and abide by their decision," reported the official publication of state headquarters. "In this instance the majority wanted Howard. The state office merely carried out the wishes of the majority."[64]

This explanation failed to satisfy most Klansmen. An especially incensed group of Knights was concentrated in Tulsa and was led by State Senator Wash E. Hudson, an enemy of Jewett since the special legislative session of the previous fall. Hudson called for a renunciation of "partisan politics" and a return to the Klan's "great mission of patriotism, brotherly love and Christianity." Proclaiming "We will be God's men or Jewett's slaves," the florid Hudson formed a "Klansman's Klean-up Kommittee" to purify the Oklahoma Klan. Jewett announced his suspension from the Klan as Hudson began holding a series of conferences in Tulsa with about 350 Klansmen from over the state.[65]

[62] Oklahoma City *Daily Oklahoman*, August 9, 1924.
[63] Tulsa *Tribune*, August 15, 1924.
[64] Oklahoma City *Fiery Cross*, quoted *ibid.*, August 8, 1924.
[65] Tulsa *Tribune*, September 1, 8, 17, 18, 22, 24, 1924.

On September 24 Hudson and the rebellious faction drew up a list of demands and sent them to Grand Dragon Jewett, who was in Kansas City attending the second Imperial Klonvocation, the biennial national convention of the Klan. The disgruntled Klansmen demanded the withdrawal of the Klan from politics and the institution of more democracy into the Klan's rigidly hierarchial structure. Jewett termed the demands "amusing." Imperial Wizard Evans quickly gave Jewett a vote of confidence and denied that the Hudson faction had the right to submit anything to the Wizard or the Klonvocation. Before the delegates in Kansas City, however, Evans announced that hereafter his appointment of a Grand Dragon would have to be ratified by all the local Klans in a state. In Tulsa, Hudson was jubilant. This, he enthused, was the first step toward the democratic reform of the Klan.[66]

As the Klonvocation adjourned, William Shelley Rogers, the Tulsa Cyclops and another foe of Jewett, told reporters that harmony again reigned in the Oklahoma Klan and that all Klansmen who were Democrats would vote against Walton in November. This made official what most people had expected since the August primary—that Oklahoma Knights of the Invisible Empire, like their brethren in Texas, were preparing to bolt the Democratic party. Walton's place at the head of the state ticket caused not only Klansmen, but many other Democrats, to do a good deal of soul-searching. The state central committee refused to draw up a party platform for the November contest. With obvious trepidation it endorsed Walton for the senatorship. As one newspaper described it, "Holding its nose, shutting the eyes and making one big gulp of the bad medicine, the Democratic state central committee yesterday swallowed Jack Walton."[67]

In the general election campaign "Democrats for Pine"

[66] *Ibid.*, September 25, 26, 27, 1924.
[67] *Ibid.*, August 10, September 26, 1924.

clubs sprang up throughout the state, and a number of hitherto stanchly Democratic newspapers joined the Klansmen and other ballot-splitting Democrats. Walton also had his loyal followers. A bipartisan "Anti-Klan Association of Oklahoma" tried its best to unify Klan-haters behind the Democratic nominee. Governor Martin E. Trapp announced that he was supporting Walton as the lesser of two evils. To minimize vote fraud he ordered all county election boards to appoint an equal number of Klan and anti-Klan representatives to the precinct returning boards.[68]

The first returns made it clear that enough Democrats had crossed party lines to crush Walton's hopes for going to Washington. As the rest of the Democratic ticket, including presidential candidate John W. Davis, swept Oklahoma, Pine piled up an enormous lead over Walton, finishing with 339,646 votes to 196,417 for the ousted governor. Pine became the state's second Republican Senator. Walton carried only ten counties, most of them in the southern and southeastern part of the state. The Democrats retained control of most of the county governments and sent a large majority of Democratic representatives and senators, many of them still Klan-oriented, to the state legislature.[69]

After the election, in which Democratic Klansmen had helped mightily to send a Republican to the United States Senate, Grand Dragon Jewett congratulated the Oklahoma Klan on turning back the menace of Walton. "But now that our most pressing duty to country is fulfilled," concluded Jewett, "it is but the part of wisdom that we turn our attention to our second duty, that of building up and strengthening the order. We have been busy being citizens

[68] *Ibid.*, September 9, 1924; Oklahoma City *Daily Oklahoman,* September 15, October 13, November 3, 4, 1924; Eufala *Indian Journal,* September 11, 1924. On the origins of the Anti-Klan Association of Oklahoma, see the Oklahoma City *Daily Oklahoman,* December 1, 2, 9, 1923, February 23, 29, 1924.

[69] Oklahoma City *Daily Oklahoman,* November 5, 7, 1924; New York *Times,* November 6, 1924, p. 1; McReynolds, *Oklahoma,* 351.

of Oklahoma. Now let us get busy being citizens of the INVISIBLE EMPIRE, KNIGHTS OF THE KU KLUX KLAN."[70]

But with the election past and their enemy at least temporarily banished, many Democrats in the Klan, who could not forget Jewett's political meanderings before the Democratic primary, turned their wrath on the Grand Dragon. One prominent Klansman put into words what numerous other Oklahoma Knights were thinking.

Carlton Weaver, a newspaper publisher in Wilburton and head of the local Klan, wrote a letter of resignation to Jewett. In the letter Weaver took the Dragon to task "for degenerating the organization in Oklahoma, into a political machine with a Republican Engineer at the throttle, purpose to discredit, disrupt and demoralize the Democratic party in the state." Weaver charged that Jewett deliberately "gummed up" the senatorial race with his bewildering tactics before the Democratic primary. "A ten year old school boy should have had sense enough to know that this procedure served to divide and confuse the Klan vote, rather than unite and solidify it," wrote the bitter Klansman, "and as a result of your mehtod [sic], many Klansmen in Oklahoma believed that your purpose was to promote the nomination of Jack Walton in order to insure the election of a Republican in November." Weaver went on to accuse Jewett of working clandestinely to swing Oklahoma to Calvin Coolidge in the presidential election. "I love the Democratic party next to my church," said Weaver as he bade farewell to the Invisible Empire, "and I do not want a Republican dictating to it and enforcing himself in its counsels and organizations. . . . Oklahoma has ridden itself of Jack Walton. . . . I submit to you that the next best accomplishment for the people of this state will be to kick the Klan out of Oklahoma politics, that it may function as a fraternal organization with its members voting as their

[70] Oklahoma City *Fiery Cross*, November 12, 1924.

conscience dictates and not as they are advised by a partisan dragon."[71]

The bizarre events of 1924, climaxing in Pine's landslide victory over Walton, did not mark the last of the Klan's dabbling in Oklahoma politics, but henceforth the order was seldom capable of acting as an independent force in primaries and elections. Jewett, the Republican Grand Dragon, may have got his wish with the election of a second Republican to the United States Senate from Oklahoma, but in the process his influence in Sooner State Klan affairs was destroyed.

The Klan in the Southwest never again brandished the power at the state or even at the local and district level that it did from 1922 to 1924. Although more significant as an issue than as an organization in the 1923-1924 gubernatorial campaign in Louisiana, the Klan still represented a potent faction to be absorbed, mitigated, and exploited in the prevailing political equilibrium. With its leadership and its votes divided between two candidates, the Louisiana Klan lost much of its crusading spirit and defensive solidarity, a development heralding its downfall. In Arkansas the determination of the Grand Dragon to see his favorite get the Klan's endorsement for governor led to a division of Klan voting strength and the frustration of its political ambitions. The Realm of Texas, ruled by an equally stubborn Dragon, was also plagued by dissension over the Klan's choice of a candidate for governor. No formal split occurred in the ranks of Texas Klansmen, but an anti-Klan coalition sent the Klan candidate to defeat at the hands of an impeached governor's wife. It is almost a certainty that the Grand Dragon of Oklahoma, like the Realm leader in Arkansas a Republican, purposefully confused Klansmen

71 Klansman [Carlton Weaver] to N. C. Jewett, Grand Dragon of the Ku Klux Klan, Realm of Oklahoma, November 1924, Carlton Weaver Collection, Division of Manuscripts, University of Oklahoma Library, Norman.

before the Democratic primary so that Walton would win
the Democratic nomination for United States Senator and
thus make possible the election of a Republican to the Senate in November. To turn back Walton, Democratic Klansmen dutifully followed their Grand Dragon into the Republican party, but after the election the Oklahoma Knights
felt free to denounce and repudiate their Republican
leader.

The political struggles of 1924 illumined the perilous path
that a secret society like the Klan had to follow in its evolution from a vigilante body into a militant, yet more respectable and less cohesive, political organization. The clash between the personal ambitions of politicians and the democratic ideal on one hand, and the ramrod tactics of the Klan
autocrats on the other, severely and irreparably crippled the
order in Texas, Arkansas, Oklahoma, and Louisiana. In the
years after 1924 disillusionment, decline, and disintegration
were the main characteristics of Klan history in the Southwest.

10.

The Road to Obscurity

DURING THE LAST HALF of the 1920s the Klan fell apart in the states of the Southwest, and nearly everywhere else. There were many reasons for this collapse, some of which will be noted in the succeeding chapter. One of the greatest maladies was dissension. Inner strife, beginning in 1924 on a critical scale and continuing for several more years, sapped the order in each of the southwestern states. Only in Oklahoma did the Klan retain anything like its old vigor, and even there the organization speedily fell into disrepute. By 1926 each political party in Oklahoma was trying to saddle the other with the onus of Klanism. The decline of the Klan in the Southwest roughly paralleled the ebbing of the Klan tide in other parts of the nation. Klan activity virtually ceased in such once-strong states as Indiana, Pennsylvania, Ohio, Colorado, and even Georgia, the mother state of the Klan. By 1928 the Klan in Louisiana, Arkansas, Texas, Oklahoma—and almost everywhere except Alabama—was a hollow and unfrightening shell of the powerful body that had existed a few years earlier.[1]

In Louisiana the process of decomposition began as far

back as the spring of 1924. "Peace" was the keynote at the opening of the second regular session of the Louisiana General Assembly, on May 12, 1924.[2] Henry L. Fuqua, nominated in February and elected in April by an alliance of the New Orleans machine, most of the Klan vote, most of the industrial and planter interests, and the majority of the non-Klan Protestant politicians, came into office on a platform emphasizing peace and harmony, and very little else. Fuqua had, however, pledged that his administration would enact laws to regulate the activities of secret organizations; and in supporting the Baton Rouge man for governor many Klansmen, including several in the state legislature, had obligated themselves to work for such legislation or at least to acquiesce in it. This was the dilemma confronting the Louisiana Klan as the legislature convened and undertook the organization of the senate and house of representatives.

Compromise was the order of the day in Louisiana government and politics, and the Fuqua administration achieved its objectives. A "moderate" Klansman from Shreveport, a Fuqua worker, was elected speaker of the house; a Catholic supporter of Hewitt Bouanchaud in the recent primaries became president pro tem of the senate; and a former Klansman, Oramel H. Simpson of New Orleans, sat in the lieutenant governor's chair. As the New Orleans *Times-Picayune* remarked facetiously, "Peace, peace, beautiful religious peace, envelops the Louisiana legislature tonight."[3]

[1] Alabama presents something of a case of arrested Klan development. The order began to grow and attract attention in that state only when it was declining almost everywhere else. The Alabama Klan was probably more important in the anti-Al Smith movement in 1928 than the Klan organization in any other state. On Klan history in Alabama in the late twenties, see Arnold S. Rice, *The Ku Klux Klan in American Politics* (Washington, 1962), 88-99; and R. A. Patton, "A Ku Klux Klan Reign of Terror," *Current History*, XXVIII (April 1928), 51-55.

[2] The legislative session of 1924 was the second regular session under the Louisiana constitution of 1921.

[3] New Orleans *Times-Picayune*, May 13, 1924.

211

Little more than a week of the legislative session had passed when three antimask and secrecy bills were introduced simultaneously in the house and senate. A Catholic presented the bills to the members of the house, while an admitted Klansman brought the measures before the senate. The bills provided for the publication of the membership of all secret organizations operating within the state in December of each year, a 1-to-5 year penitentiary sentence for masked assaults, and a misdemeanor penalty for appearing publicly while disguised, the Mardi Gras holiday excepted. Monroe Klan No. 4 telegraphed its endorsement of the bills to the state senator and the two representatives from Ouachita Parish. Great Titan Paul D. Perkins of Lake Charles commented that the bills were sound and should pass the General Assembly unanimously.[4]

Not all Klansmen, however, were so enthusiastic over the anti-Klan bills. Throughout north Louisiana and in the legislature there were Klansmen who had backed Huey P. Long in the first Democratic gubernatorial campaign, had reluctantly swung to Fuqua in his runoff race with Catholic Bouanchaud, and now recognized no obligation to accept legislation inimical to their organization simply to fulfill a political bargain made by some of their fellow Klansmen. Dr. E. L. Thompson, for example, pastor of the Central Christian Church and leader of the Klan in Shreveport, blasted the whole legislative attempt to regulate the order as a Catholic plot. The publication of the Klan's membership rolls, the pastor predicted, would lead to boycotting of Klan businessmen throughout the state and retaliatory boycotting by Klansmen against Catholic and Jewish merchants.[5]

Opposition to the attempt to regulate the Klan, both inside and outside the legislature, centered on the membership registration measure. On June 2 the Louisiana house

[4] *Ibid.*, May 21, 23, 28, 1924.
[5] *Ibid.*, May 30, June 1, 1924.

passed the three administration bills—by a vote of 91 to 3 on the prohibition of mask-wearing, 97 to 0 on the outlawry of masked assault, and 80 to 17 on the registration requirement. All of the representatives who voted against the antisecrecy bill were from the central and northern Louisiana parishes. The senate passed the bill to restrict mask-wearing by a vote of 37 to 2; the bill to make masked assault a felony passed 36 to 3. An acrid debate broke out over the membership registration bill. It finally passed the senate by a vote of 28 to 11. Again the opposition to the bill came mainly from the upstate Klan and pro-Klan legislators who had not ridden the Fuqua bandwagon in the gubernatorial campaign. Governor Fuqua signed the three bills into law on June 12, 1924.[6]

The Imperial hierarchy in Atlanta was highly indignant over the passage of the bills. The membership registration law particularly alarmed Atlanta because one of the Klan's greatest assets, one of its most effective weapons, was the secret character of its membership.[7] What upset Hiram W. Evans and his associates most was the fact that some allegedly devout Klansmen inside and outside the Louisiana legislature, including most of the state Klan officials, had actually encouraged and advocated the measure. This the Imperial Klan could not tolerate. Evans named an "Imperial Representative" to discover what was behind the betrayal of the Klan's most sacred tenet. The representative, James Murray of Shreveport, announced that the Klansmen

[6] *Ibid.*, June 3, 12, 13, 1924; Louisiana General Assembly, *House Journal*, Second Regular Session (1924), 55-56, 74-75, 89-90, 115-16, 126-28, 137-40, 285-88, 314-15; *Senate Journal*, 84-85, 92-93, 125-26, 128-29, 170-72, 181-83, 184-85.

[7] The Louisiana membership registration law followed by a year the passage of a similar law by the assembly of the state of New York. That law required organizations not incorporated in the state to file membership lists and other records. See "The Klan Defies a State," *Literary Digest*, LXXVII (June 9, 1923), 12-13; New York *Times*, May 5, 1923, p. 3, May 28, p. 1, June 2, p. 13, June 23, p. 13, July 12, p. 1, July 24, p. 1, August 20, p. 2.

who had helped push the anti-Klan laws through the legislature would soon be expelled from the order.[8]

In late July, when he came to Shreveport for the second Klorero, or state convention, of the Klan in Louisiana, Evans did not mention the rumored banishment of the Klan leaders or the anti-Klan laws, except to remark darkly: "The honest people of Louisiana can be depended upon to care for those who came in sheep's clothing and betrayed the organization that relied on their promises." While he was in Shreveport, however, as he had promised, Evans carried out the fraternal execution of the errant Klansmen whose deviation from true Klankraft had aroused his anger. The Klorero was in the midst of choosing delegates to the Imperial Klonvocation, to be held in Kansas City in September, when Evans walked into the meeting room in the Youree Hotel. Without fanfare he announced the expulsion of Grand Dragon Carey P. Duncan; Great Titans Thomas F. DePaoli, R. Will Germany, and Perkins; Grand Kludd (state chaplain) C. C. Miller of Baton Rouge; and Grand Kligrapp (state secretary) Clayton P. Spring of Shreveport. This broke up the formal session of the Klorero and left the Louisiana Klan without a state hierarchy.[9]

From Shreveport, Evans and his retinue went to Alexandria, stronghold of the Klan supporters of Long. There the Wizard met with about fifty or so prominent Klansmen still in his favor. He named a three-man committee, consisting of William C. Barnette of Shreveport, Robert D. Ellis of Amite, and Swords R. Lee of Alexandria, to govern the Realm.[10]

Having purged the Klansmen who had cooperated with the Fuqua administration, Evans turned to the matter of circumventing the law requiring publication of the Klan's

[9] Shreveport *Journal,* August 11, 1924; New Orleans *Times-Picayune,* August 12, 1924.
[10] New Orleans *Times-Picayune,* August 17, 1924.

[8] New Orleans *Times-Picayune,* June 14, 1924.

membership rolls. His strategy was rather simple. He had all the local Klans in Louisiana, together with the district and state offices, transfer their records membership lists, and regalia to Atlanta. All Klansmen relinquished their old membership cards and received new cards designating them "Imperial Klansmen" rather than Klansmen in the Realm of Louisiana. Each local Klan retained a skeletal membership consisting of its officers and perhaps one or two other leading Klansmen. Thus while the chapters and their officers remained under the jurisdiction of the state of Louisiana, the great majority of Klansmen in the state, by joining the "back to Atlanta" movement, escaped the provisions of the membership registration law. The same procedure was followed for the Women of the Ku Klux Klan, so that by the end of 1924 practically all the Klansmen and Klanswomen in Louisiana were of the Imperial stripe.[11]

In December the Klan and Women of the Klan filed their membership lists with the secretary of state. The list for the women's order showed eighteen chapters and 191 members in the state organization. The list for the Klan, sworn to by Barnette as "chairman of the state committee," named sixty-one local Klans and 432 Klansmen as still belonging to the state organization.[12] The New Orleans Klan, Old Hickory Klan No. 1, did not appear on the membership list. Perhaps it had been disbanded. Or because of De-Paoli's close association with it, perhaps its charter had been revoked.

Hence by making most of the members of the Klan in Louisiana "Imperial Klansmen" the order managed to evade the provisions of the state registration law and escape having its membership in the Pelican State brought into public view. The great wave of boycotting which the Reverend

---

[11] *Ibid.*, November 15, December 31, 1924.

[12] Shreveport *Journal*, December 18, 30, 1924; New Orleans *Times-Picayune*, December 29, 1924, January 1, 1925.

Dr. Thompson and others had predicted never occurred; indeed the registration requirement scarcely affected the activities of the Klan in Louisiana. "The anti-klan forces . . . took good aim, pulled the trigger, and now find they hit every organization in the state except the one they were shooting at," observed the *Times-Picayune*.[13] The effect of the antimask law was also negligible. As the membership of the order continued to decline, the Klansmen found few occasions for staging their famous mass demonstrations. On February 24, 1925, Mardi Gras, hooded and masked Knights and Klanswomen paraded and frolicked in several towns over the state.[14] The next year Mardi Gras passed without any Klan activity.

After 1924 the Klan declined rapidly in Louisiana. The second membership list filed by the Klan, made public early in 1926, showed fifty chapters in the state, a loss of eleven since the previous registration. When Evans returned to Shreveport, a reporter asked him about the condition of the Klan in Louisiana and in the nation as a whole. By this time the Wizard's attitude was a far cry from his embullient mood of a year and a half earlier. "The Klan is a secret organization that minds its own business," was Evans curt reply. And a federal prohibition agent recalled that during the height of Klan power in Louisiana government agents freqently received information from Klan sources about bootlegging activities in the northern part of the state. "Nowadays nothing indicates Klan inspiration of informants," said the federal man. By mid-1926 probably no more than 6,500 Klansmen were still active in Louisiana. What about Morehouse Klan No. 34, whose violent deeds were detailed in virtually every daily newspaper in the country during 1922 and 1923? "Klan activities in Morehouse Parish appear to have subsided," wrote an Arkansas

[13] New Orleans *Times-Picayune*, November 15, 1924.
[14] Shreveport *Journal*, January 7, February 24, 25, 1925.

observer in the late summer of 1926, "and the name of
Captain Skipwith, head of the local Klan, seldom is
mentioned."[15]

Within two or three years after the passage of the
anti-Klan laws and the outbreak of strife within the Realm
hierarchy, the Louisiana Klan had folded up except in
Shreveport and a few other places. The Realm organization
was still alive. Murray, Cyclops of Shreveport Klan No. 2,
served as Grand Dragon during 1926; in February of the
next year Rush H. Davis, also of Shreveport, was appointed
Dragon by the Imperial Wizard. But now only occasional
lectures or social events comprised the business of the
scattered chapters. "Members of the Ku Klux Klan and
their families were guests at a watermelon feast at the
fair grounds Thursday night," read a typical report on
Louisiana Klan doings in the late twenties. "After the feast
a musical program, including songs and specialty numbers[,] was rendered at the dance pavilion."[16] There were
only a few Klansmen left to raise the cry of battle when Al
Smith ran for the presidency in 1928, but together with
ex-Klansmen and sympathizers they could make a fairly
loud noise.

In Arkansas the disintegration of the Klan was even more
rapid. The outbursts of Jim G. Ferguson against the James
A. Comer regime, the split of the Klan vote, and the con-
sequent defeat of Lee Cazort in the 1924 gubernatorial
primary—these elements debilitated the Klan in Arkansas
and contributed to its breakup in the last half of the
twenties. In the fall of 1924 Comerites and anti-Comer
Klansmen in the Little Rock Klan managed to unite to put
over the Klan ticket in the city primary. Charles E. Moyer,
outgoing county judge, won the mayoralty nomination

[15] *Ibid.*, January 7, 16, 1926; New York *Times,* February 21, 1926,
sec. VIII, p. 15; Washington *Post,* November 2, 1930, sec. I, p. 4;
Little Rock *Arkansas Gazette,* September 6, 1926.

[16] Shreveport *Journal,* February 17, 19, September 7, 1927.

from an infuriated Ben D. Brickhouse, who had been elected with Klan support two years earlier, but who had since broken with the secret order. In April 1925, at Stuttgart in the Arkansas rice belt, the Klan ticket piled up a 3-to-1 margin in the city election. But in Fort Smith, where the Klan vote had ousted a hostile mayor in a recall election in 1923, the list of candidates endorsed by the Klansmen lost to the ticket of the local anti-Klan faction in a contest that drew the largest vote in the city's history.[17]

The city primaries and elections in the winter and spring of 1924-1925 were the last political adventures of the Klan in Arkansas. Thereafter the local Klans had all they could do to hold their memberships together. The backbone of the Arkansas Klan, Little Rock Klan No. 1, broke under the strain of its running fight with Grand Dragon Comer. The fight had its origins in the gubernatorial campaign of 1924 and in the charges that Comer was trying to "Republicanize" Arkansas. Troubles during the summer of 1925, stemming largely from developments within the Women of the Ku Klux Klan, aggravated the bad feeling between the Grand Dragon and Klan No. 1.

From its inception the Women of the Ku Klux Klan was something of a protectorate of Comer. In mid-1923, when Imperial headquarters sanctioned the formation of a women's order, Comer put $8,000 into the Women of the Ku Klux Klan to get it started. The national offices of the Women of the Klan were established on the second floor of the Ancient Order of United Workmen hall in Little Rock, where Comer closely supervised the affairs of the new organization. Mrs. Lulu A. Markwell of Little Rock was the first Imperial Commander. In June 1924 Mrs. Markwell resigned abruptly, probably because of difficulties with Comer. Miss Agnes B. Cloud of Dallas, as Imperial

[17] Little Rock *Arkansas Gazette*, November 8, 21, December 8, 16, 1924, April 8, 1925.

Vice Commander, was the heiress apparent to the leadership of the women's order. Instead Miss Robbie Gill of Little Rock, the Imperial Secretary and a close acquaintance of Comer, became Imperial Commander and moved the order's national offices to a palatial home which she dubbed the "Imperial Palace." A year later Miss Gill, an attractive, dark-haired woman in her thirties, married Grand Dragon Comer.[18]

Within a few weeks Miss Cloud and two other Dallas Klanswomen, accusing the newlyweds of waste, extravagance, and misappropriation of funds, filed suit against them in chancery court in Little Rock. Miss Cloud asserted that legally she was supposed to have succeeded Mrs. Markwell as Imperial Commander, and that Mrs. Comer was a usurper. The Imperial Commander and Grand Dragon's wife notified the three rebellious Klanswomen that they were suspended from the women's order, while Evans telegraphed her and Comer that they had his full support in the upcoming power struggle. In September the plaintiffs filed an amended petition setting out their specific charges: that Mrs. Comer, as Imperial Commander, had received $17,850 in salary which should have gone to Miss Cloud; that Mrs. Comer bought an expensive sedan for her husband, using funds of the women's order; that she bought an "Imperial Crown" worth $750; and that Comer had received $18,000 in legal fees as Imperial Klonsel (attorney) for the Women of the Klan. On October 3, 1925, Chancellor John E. Martineau, who had run for governor primarily as an anti-Klan candidate in the summer of 1924, refused to review the plaintiff's charges, holding that he lacked jurisdiction in the dispute. He did rule that the plaintiffs could examine the books of the Women of the

[18] Emerson H. Loucks, *The Ku Klux Klan in Pennsylvania: A Study in Nativism* (Harrisburg, 1936), 150, 160; Little Rock *Arkansas Gazette,* June 30, 1925.

Klan and file another amended petition setting out further charges against the Comers.[19]

A few weeks later Little Rock Klan No. 1 and Rose City Klan No. 1, the women's chapter, broke with the Grand Dragon. The night of November 5, 1925, the members of the men's chapter adopted a resolution expressing a lack of confidence in Comer, citing their unsuccessful efforts to persuade him to resign, and proclaiming the secession of the Little Rock chapter from the Klan and the formation of a new organization. "His [Comer's] usefulness was at an end and had been for many months, on account of inactivity as leader of the state organization, and because of loss of prestige," read the resolution. The new organization was to feature "greater secrecy" and "utter banishment of the spirit of monetary gain." Four days later the rebels chartered their organization, the "Independent Klan," under the laws of Arkansas. On November 11 most of the membership of Rose City Klan No. 1 voted to follow the men from the Invisible Empire and to organize as an auxiliary to the Independent Klan. In their "ordinance of secession" the women assailed Comer's dictatorial methods and the dominance of the Women of the Ku Klux Klan by Klansmen, most notably by Comer.[20]

The secession of the Little Rock Klansmen and Klanswomen added more litigation to the dockets of the courts in the city. Little Rock Klan No. 1 filed replevin suits in circuit court for the regalia and records taken by the "Independent" Klansmen when they seceded, and also for the use of a tabernacle which had been the meeting place of the men's and women's chapters for some time. The Imperial Klan filed an injunction suit in chancery court to restrain the splinter group from using the name "Klan."

[19] Little Rock *Arkansas Gazette*, August 30, September 1, 7, 8, 16, October 1, 4, 1925.
[20] *Ibid.*, November 6, 8, 10, 11, 1925.

The secessionists got around this last dispute simply by changing the name of their organization to the "Mystic Knights of Arkansas." The circuit court judge decided the replevin suits by awarding the records and regalia to the Little Rock Klan and having the chapter pay Robert A. Cook of the Mystic Knights $315 in back rent on the tabernacle, which Cook owned.[21]

The settlement of the litigation resulting from the split in the Little Rock men's and women's Klans left only the legal battle for control of the Women of the Ku Klux Klan. After examining the accounts of the women's organization, Miss Cloud filed another amended petition before Chancellor Martineau. This time she accused the Comers of fraudulent bookkeeping; of piling up a deficit of $70,000 in a seven-month period; of enjoying excessive profits from the sale of a robe factory owned by Comer in Little Rock, valued at $23,000, to the Women of the Klan for almost $73,000; and of numerous instances of petty graft relating to expenses for furniture, travel, an automobile, and other items. Chancellor Martineau, soon to become the Democratic nominee for governor, overruled the Comers' demurrers to the charges and eventually appointed a special master in chancery to hear the case. On October 8, 1926, the special master dismissed the suit because the plaintiff could not raise $250 for court costs. In February of the next year Miss Cloud dropped a suit she had filed in circuit court for the salary Mrs. Comer received after becoming Imperial Commander.[22] This action brought an end to the court fights between various factions of Klansmen and Klanswomen in Arkansas.

Mrs. Comer remained Imperial Commander of the Women of the Ku Klux Klan, while Comer carried on as Grand

[21] *Ibid.*, November 18, December 13, 17, 18, 1925, January 23, 27, February 23, March 6, 1926.

[22] *Ibid.*, January 31, February 19, August 18, 20, October 8, 1926, February 12, 1927.

Dragon of the Realm of Arkansas. Yet in Arkansas they presided over a crumbling portion of the Invisible Empire. By the early part of 1926 there were fewer than 10,000 active Klansmen in the Realm.[23] Most of the Klansmen in Little Rock had gone into the Mystic Knights of Arkansas. Klans in Stuttgart, Arkadelphia, Conway, Fort Smith, Helena, and a few other places remained active with drastically shrunken memberships. The Little Rock chapter of the Women of the Ku Klux Klan was still carrying on charity work in the city as late as the spring of 1927.[24]

The revolt among the Klansmen and Klanswomen did not connote any division along ideological lines. The Mystic Knights and their women's auxiliary on one hand and the Little Rock Klansmen and Klanswomen on the other shared the same feelings about Catholics, Jews, Negroes, foreigners, and libertines. So it was possible for Imperial Wizard Evans to return to the city in the fall of 1926 and to speak to Klansmen, Klanswomen, and "former members," including many of the secessionists, on the Klan program for the next two years. The Wizard emphasized the Klan's concern with stricter enforcement of the prohibition amendment, the upbuilding of the public school system, and, most important, a fight to the death to prevent the election of Smith to the presidency.[25] Two years later, when Smith was a presidential candidate, many Klansmen, ex-Klansmen, Mystic Knights, and ex-Mystic Knights were ready to vote against him.

No sensational episodes like the banishment of several Realm officials in Louisiana or the secession of Klansmen and Klanswomen in Little Rock punctuated the collapse of the Klan in Texas. During the last half of the twenties a few ambitious noises emanated from the Texas part of the

[23] New York *Times*, February 21, 1926, sec. viii, pp. 1, 15.
[24] Little Rock *Arkansas Gazette*, April 22, 1927.
[25] *Ibid.*, November 12, 1926.

Invisible Empire, but for the most part the order passed its last years in the Lone Star State rather quietly.

The Texas Klan suffered a crushing defeat in the summer and fall of 1924, when Mrs. Miriam A. "Ma" Ferguson won the Democratic gubernatorial nomination over Klansman Felix D. Robertson, and then triumphed over the Republican candidate, who received most of the Klan vote in the general election. The Klan never again functioned as an organization in Texas politics, at either the state or local level. The prestige of the order in Texas disappeared almost overnight. Politicians who had tagged along with the Klan for years suddenly deserted the organization, and people who had cringed in terror before the specter of the hooded fraternity now turned vengefully on it. Two mysterious explosions followed by fire destroyed the Fort Worth Klan's showplace Klavern, constructed at a cost of $50,000 and seating 4,000 people; and incendiaries made three unsuccessful attempts to burn Beethoven Hall, the rented headquarters of San Antonio Klan No. 31.[26]

In December of 1924 Z. E. Marvin, apparently yielding to growing resentment within the Realm over the disastrous events of the year, resigned from the office of Grand Dragon. He was succeeded by Marvin A. Childers of San Antonio, lawyer and high-ranking Texas Mason, who moved Realm headquarters from Dallas to San Antonio and abolished the office of Great Titan of Province No. 2, occupied in the past by such lights as Evans and Marvin.[27] Marvin's retirement and the removal of Realm offices from Dallas to San Antonio signaled the end of the dominance of Texas Klan affairs by the Dallas Klan.

The 39th Texas Legislature, showing an extraordinarily heavy turnover from the previous Klan-oriented legislature, was generally hostile to the Klan. For once trying to follow

[26] Fort Worth *Star-Telegram,* November 7, 1924; San Antonio *Express,* November 22, 1924.
[27] Fort Worth *Star-Telegram,* December 18, 1924.

the specific mandate of the state Democratic platform, the solons sought to enact laws prohibiting the wearing of masks in public and requiring the registration of secret organization membership lists. A membership registration bill died on the calendar of the state senate as the session ended. But the legislature did succeed in passing a stiff antimask bill, by votes of 84-22 in the house and 25-1 in the senate. Governor Ferguson, enjoying one of the most harmonious legislative sessions in Texas history, signed the bill into law on March 7, 1925.[28]

One estimate placed the number of Klansmen in Texas in mid-1925 at nearly 80,000, which represented a drop of perhaps one-half from the previous year.[29] But the dissolution had just begun. In October, Dallas Klan No. 66 banished Marvin after he had a bitter quarrel with the chapter leaders, evidently over his failure to be elected Exalted Cyclops of the local Klan. Marvin retired to attend to his chain of drugstores and his real estate holdings in Dallas. The next month Imperial Klan headquarters undertook an investigation of the financial affairs of Klan No. 66. The inquiry showed that the chapter accounts were in chaotic condition, with dues lagging, expenditures unitemized, and funds withheld from the Imperial treasury. To the Evans regime such circumstances were inexcusable. Atlanta demanded that the local Klans conform at all times to Imperial requirements in financial matters. National headquarters took charge of the funds of the Dallas Klan, placing a supervisor with the authority of a receiver in complete control. While the Imperial investigators were in Texas, they looked into the records of Fort Worth Klan No. 101, and they found ineptness and mismanagement similar to that in the accounts of the Dallas Klan. Once

[28] 39th Texas Legislature, *House Journal*, Regular Session, 46, 906-907; *General Laws of the State of Texas*, Regular Session, 39th Legislature, 213-14.
[29] Washington *Post*, November 2, 1930, sec. I, p. 4.

again Imperial Wizard Evans appointed a supervisor to administer the affairs of a sick chapter.[30]

Marvin, now outside the Invisible Empire, told a newspaper reporter that conditions were uniformly bad in the Realm of Texas. He said that the membership of the Dallas Klan, once the largest chapter in the Southwest and possibly the largest in the nation, had dwindled from 13,000 in 1924 to 1,200. The attendance at the weekly Konklaves once ranged from 800 to 3,500; now scarcely 150 attended. "This condition prevails over the State of Texas," observed Marvin. "At the opening of the year [1926] not a province in Texas could pay its help. In Texas there are not 18,000 members."[31]

The Texas Klan held its annual Kloreros in 1925 (at Arlington) and in 1926 (at Temple). The latter gathering combined the attendance of both Klansmen and Klanswomen, and was open to all members of the men's and women's orders in the state, whereas previous Kloreros in Texas were open only to authorized delegates from the chartered Klans. Attendance was below expectations at the outdoor meeting, held in a park owned by Temple Klan No. 33. The men and women who came watched drills and an aerial circus, listened to band concerts, and heard nativist orations by Lloyd P. Bloodworth of Fort Worth, now Grand Dragon, Imperial Klazik H. Kyle Ramsey, and Imperial Commander Robbie Gill Comer. All the speakers predicted a bright future for the Klan in America. But the Klorero of 1926, probably the last ever held in the Realm of Texas, looked more like a big picnic than a rally of determined superpatriots.[32]

The Klan no longer functioned in politics, but it could

[30] Dallas *Morning News,* October 11, November 29, 1925; New York *Times,* February 21, 1926, sec. viii, p. 1; Fort Worth *Star-Telegram,* January 31, 1926.

[31] New York *Times,* February 21, 1926, sec. viii, p. 1.

[32] Fort Worth *Star-Telegram,* September 11, 12, 13, 1925; Waco *Times-Herald,* July 29, 30, 1926.

still serve as an albatross to hang around the neck of a political enemy. In the 1926 gubernatorial campaign Ferguson and his wife, under heavy fire for their extravagant use of the pardoning power and accused of gross mishandling of state finances, resurrected the Klan issue to use against their chief opponent in the Democratic primaries, Attorney General Dan Moody. Ignoring the fact that Moody had been elected in 1924 principally on his record as an anti-Klan district attorney, the Fergusons charged that he was soliciting votes from Klansmen and ex-Klansmen, and predicted that the Klan would ride again if Moody became governor.[33] The voters of Texas paid scant attention to the fanciful charges of the husband-wife team, whose chronic misconduct in office proved to be more important than Klan and anti-Klan harangues. Moody overwhelmed the woman governor in the runoff primary. Most Klansmen and former members probably voted for Moody in the runoff, but their votes were not nearly as weighty as the ballots of the tenant farmers and anti-prohibitionists, practically all of whom voted for Mrs. Ferguson.

The state Klan hierarchy was still intact as late as 1927, when Shelby Cox, former district attorney of Dallas County, served as Grand Dragon. A few local Klans continued to hold meetings, listen to lectures, do a little charity work, and burn an occasional cross. As elsewhere, most Texas chapters had lost their more sober and substantial members, and now some local Klans were supported only by a sadistic and unruly element. Fort Worth Klansmen were probably responsible for the flogging in 1927 of Morris Strauss, a young Jewish businessman. And four years later a Com-

[33] Rice, *Ku Klux Klan in American Politics*, 72-73; Austin *American*, July 4, 1926; Dallas *Morning News*, August 14, 1926. See also Oscar B. Colquitt to J. F. McKnight, August 16, 1926, Colquitt to Dan B. Myer, same date, Colquitt to Fred C. Marth, same date, Colquitt to Paul H. Brown, same date, Oscar B. Colquitt Papers, University of Texas Archives, Austin.

munist labor organizer charged that Dallas Klansmen had abducted and beaten two of his subordinates after they were released from jail.[34] By 1928, with only 2,500 or so hooded Knights left in Texas, the Klan as an organization was incapable of fighting Al Smith in the state.[35] But the few remaining Klansmen could join forces with ex-Klansmen and other nativists and rabid prohibitionists to help swing Texas into the Republican column in the presidential election.

In Oklahoma, dissension and general loss of interest brought a steady deterioration of Klan membership. The secret order did not fare badly in the state political campaigns of 1924. It retained control of most of the county offices it had seized two years earlier, sent a strong representation of Klansmen to the state legislature, and, by concentrating both Democratic and Republican Klan votes behind one candidate in the general election, defeated the despised Jack Walton and sent W. B. Pine to the United States Senate. After the election, however, many Democratic Klansmen bitterly attacked Grand Dragon N. Clay Jewett, accusing him of intentionally frustrating the Klan's chances in the Democratic senatorial primary, conspiring to elect a Republican senator, and working for the Republican party in the presidential race in the state. The Grand Dragon's prestige was at a dismal level by late November of 1924, when Governor Martin E. Trapp called the state senate into special session to elect a new president pro tem.

Jewett had been vilifying Trapp for some time for various reasons. The governor had opposed an instructed McAdoo-for-president delegation to the Democratic national convention, and he had supported the whole Democratic

[34] Forth Worth *Star-Telegram*, July 9, 1927; New York *Times*, March 15, 1931, p. 26. See the Shreveport *Journal*, February 17, 18, 1927, for an account of the Klorero of the Realm of Louisiana held in Shreveport, attended by Texas Grand Dragon Shelby Cox and Grand Kligrapp Burt O. Snelen.

[35] Washington *Post*, November 2, 1930, sec. i, p. 4.

ticket, including Walton, in the general election. Moreover, Trapp's wife was a Catholic. Jewett did his best to organize the Klansmen in the state senate against Trapp's choice for the presidency pro tem, William J. Holloway of Hugo, who either was or had been a Klansman. Holloway was unanimously elected president pro tem, with even extreme Klansmen, like J. M. Gulager of Muskogee and Wash Hudson of Tulsa, voting for the administration candidate. As a final blow to the Oklahoma Dragon, Hudson, leader of the insurgent "Klansman's Klean-up Kommittee" of the previous September, was unanimously reelected majority leader of the Democrats in the senate. "While it is likely that both senate and house contain a majority of members who are or have been klansmen," noted the Tulsa *Tribune,* "more of them are Trapp klansmen than Jewett klansmen."[36]

Jewett's prestige continued to fall when the legislature met in regular session in January 1925. Five Klansmen were prominent in the race for speaker of the house; yet all five assailed Jewett and hoped that the Grand Dragon would eliminate one of the contenders by endorsing him. "They figure Jewett's o. k. is enough to kill any politician," commented the *Tribune.*[37] On January 5 the house members voted along straight party lines, 81 Democrats to 26 Republicans, to elect one of the Klansmen, Jess B. Harper of Talihina, speaker.[38]

It was obvious that the present Grand Dragon had become a liability to the Klan in Oklahoma. Sometime in the early part of 1925 Imperial Wizard Evans removed Jewett and appointed as Grand Dragon Claude E. Hoffman, a little-known Oklahoma City Klansman, passing over such distinguished Knights as W. Shelley Rogers of Tulsa and W. R. Sampson of Muskogee. Hoffman served for about

[36] Tulsa *Tribune,* November 9, 1924; Oklahoma City *Daily Oklahoman,* November 24, 25, 1924.

[37] Tulsa *Tribune,* December 14, 1924.

[38] Oklahoma City *Daily Oklahoman,* January 6, 1925.

two years. Zach A. Harris, a Protestant minister from Blackwell, became Grand Dragon in 1927 and held the office almost to the end of the decade.[39]

By the spring of 1926 only some 18,000 Klansmen remained active in the Realm of Oklahoma. State Klan headquarters, which once occupied the whole of a tall building in Oklahoma City, now were lodged in a single room. The Democratic State Central Committee reported Klan activity in only ten counties in the state.[40] There were still some pockets of Klan strength, such as Tulsa, Muskogee, and Okmulgee, but even in those places the membership of the order had dwindled and the remaining Klansmen were turning away from politics. General defeat awaited the few local Klans that ran candidates in the spring city elections.[41]

The Klan as an issue—but not as an organization—figured prominently in the gubernatorial campaign of 1926, when a Klansman, albeit not an active one, was elected governor. There is little doubt that at the time of his candidacy for governor Henry S. Johnston was a Klansman, although it is likely that he ceased to be active in the Klan some time before the campaign began. Johnston, from Perry, was a past Grand Master of the Oklahoma Masonic Lodge and had been chairman of the Oklahoma constitutional convention in 1907. A. E. Munrush, former secretary of the Oklahoma City Klan, and oilman Pat Henry of the capital city, one of the wealthiest Klansmen in the state, were leaders in the Johnston campaign. There were numerous rumors that Johnston held periodic conferences with high-ranking citizens of the Invisible Empire. Outgoing Governor Trapp complained that Johnston's "campaign is being conducted very much like a klan ceremonial, with all the

[39] Tulsa *Tribune*, January 18, 1925; Oklahoma City *Daily Oklahoman*, May 21, 1927.

[40] New York *Times*, February 21, 1926, sec. viii, p. 1.

[41] Tulsa *Tribune*, February 19, March 17, April 7, 15, 16, May 13, 1926.

conspicuous and known klansmen active in his behalf and in control of his state headquarters." Trapp said that Johnston's offices in the Tradesman's National Bank Building in Oklahoma City featured "a continual procession of kluds [sic], goblins, kligraphs [sic] and kleagles. It is their last, supreme stand to control Oklahoma and thwart it."[42]

In the course of the Democratic primary campaign Otto A. "Big Boy" Cargill, like Walton trying to jump from mayor of Oklahoma City to governor, was eventually forced to acknowledge that he had also belonged to the Klan. "I want to say this," added Cargill hastily. "I am not a member of the klan now." Congressman Elmer Thomas, an agrarian liberal from Medicine Park, in the process of beating down Walton's forlorn, last-minute bid for the Democratic senatorial nomination, confessed that he had joined the order and attended a few meetings back in 1922. State Senator William J. Otjen from Enid, trying for the Republican gubernatorial nomination, denied that he was presently a Klansman, but he remained silent when asked about his past affiliation with the secret organization. And Omer K. Benedict, the postmaster of Tulsa, who beat Otjen in the Republican primary, would later explain to the voters that in 1921 he, too, had joined the Klan, "having been led to believe that some such organization was necessary at that time to suppress lawlessness and vice, with which the city of Tulsa and Tulsa County were overrun." Then, however, discovering the Klan's terrorism and its political ambitions, he deserted the Invisible Empire.[43]

So it seems that two of the candidates for the Democratic gubernatorial nomination, Johnston and Cargill, were or had been Klansmen; that both Thomas and Walton, the Democratic senatorial candidates, had belonged to the Klan

[42] Edwin C. McReynolds, *Oklahoma: A History of the Sooner State* (Norman, 1954), 352-53; Oklahoma City *Daily Oklahoman*, July 18, 21, 1926; Tulsa *Tribune*, May 27, 1926.

[43] Oklahoma City *Daily Oklahoman*, June 14, July 17, 18, 20, 21, October 6, 1926.

briefly; and that the two Republican candidates for governor, Otjen and Benedict, had once put on the white robes of the order. Johnston, with the statewide backing of the Woman's Christian Temperance Union, most other dry advocates, and most of the remaining Klansmen, won the Democratic nomination and entered the general election campaign against the Republican Benedict. Thomas, polling more than twice as many votes as Walton, would go on to wrest a seat in the United States Senate from John W. Harreld, the Republican incumbent.[44]

The outstanding characteristic of the general election campaign was the rapid-fire fashion in which Republicans and Democrats tossed the Klan issue back and forth in the governor's race. The Democrats circulated photostatic copies of Tulsa Klan records to prove Benedict's connection with the order. Benedict branded the charge that he was dominated by the Klan "a contemptible, malicious falsehood," and said that in fact it was Johnston who was the Klan candidate. One newspaper referred to the Tulsa Republican as the "latest and most impressive of the recruits in this vulnerable and vociferous army of eager joiners and apologetic quitters."[45]

Even further to confuse the voters, both parties condemned the Klan by name in their state platforms, drawn up at the state conventions in August and September. The Republicans promised to keep Oklahoma free of the Klan's "pernicious" influence, while the Democrats went on record as "opposed to any attempted domination or control of the administration of any branch of the county, state or national government by the Ku Klux Klan."[46]

In Oklahoma, 1926 proved to be another Democratic year. Johnston, the dormant Klansman, defeated Benedict,

[44] *Ibid.*, August 7, 1926.

[45] *Ibid.*, August 15, 17, October 4, 24, 25, 29, 1926; New York *Times,* October 6, 1926, p. 3, October 8, p. 2.

[46] Oklahoma City *Daily Oklahoman,* August 31, September 5, 6, 1926.

the former Klansman, by a count of 213,167 votes to 170,714. More than 25,000 Democrats who had voted in the primary failed to vote in November. The Democrats won large majorities in both houses of the legislature and captured seven of eight congressional seats.[47]

The governor's race of 1926 in Oklahoma provided the anomaly of a Klansman elected governor at a time when the Klan was rapidly losing members over the state. The apparent contradiction resulted from the fact that despite the atrophy of the Oklahoma Klan, a fair number of Klansmen and ex-Klansmen retained their influence in the Democratic party. They worked ardently for Johnston, not so much because the Noble County man was a Klansman, but because his economic thinking was ultraconservative and he was willing to take care of his friends with regard to appointments, legislation, and pardons. Hence when Johnston became governor, he named several Klansmen and former members to important governmental positions, particularly in the state highway department, and pardoned two Klansmen from Altus who had been convicted on flogging charges in 1925.[48] These actions by the pliant governor alienated some of his supporters, but they formed only part of the many abuses that brought about an abortive attempt to impeach him late in 1927. Both ex-Klansmen and people who had never belonged to the order, Democrats and Republicans, helped to impeach and remove him during the 1929 legislative session.[49]

At the end of 1927 Klan membership in Oklahoma stood

---

[47] McReynolds, *Oklahoma*, 352.

[48] Oklahoma City *Daily Oklahoman*, May 3, 1927. Johnston was a good lodge man and in many ways a quite naive person. He apparently viewed the Klan as just another lodge. So when he did favors for Klansmen and ex-Klansmen, he was simply aiding his lodge friends.

[49] On the impeachment and conviction of Governor Johnston, the fifth of Oklahoma's first seven governors to be threatened with such legislative action, see McReynolds, *Oklahoma*, 353-56; Oklahoma City *Daily Oklahoman*, January 8-March 21, 1929.

at not more than 13,500.[50] This total was a long way from
the 100,000 or so Klansmen active in the state during 1924,
but it was enough to make Oklahoma one of the largest
surviving Realms in the late twenties. And while most
Americans who stayed in the Klan were, in the words of
Charles Merz, "settling down along the road to eat hot
buns and play charades," the leadership of the Oklahoma
Klan still was interested in politics.[51] Like Evans and the
other Imperial officials, Grand Dragon Harris and his
subordinates in Oklahoma were intent on heading off the
Al Smith boom within the Democratic party. In the fall
of 1927 Harris was already holding conferences with fellow-
Klansmen to plot the capture of the state delegation to
the Democratic national convention of 1928.[52]

Klansmen in the other southwestern states were no longer
as ambitious or as well-organized as their brethern in
Oklahoma. Yet the spirit of the Klan lingered—in Texas,
in Louisiana, in Arkansas, in Alabama, in Georgia, and in
many other states where the order had once commanded
respect, or still did. By combining with its allies—the
prohibitionists, the "anti-Romanists," and people who simply distrusted an Irishman from New York City—the Klan
could still fight Al Smith.

[50] This was the figure implied by Grand Dragon Zach A. Harris
when he announced that about 10,000 Klansmen, three-fourths of
the Realm membership, would attend the fifth annual Klorero.
Oklahoma City *Daily Oklahoman*, September 5, 1927.

[51] Charles Merz, "The New Ku Klux Klan," *Independent*, CXVIII
(February 12, 1927), 196.

[52] Oklahoma City *Daily Oklahoman*, September 5, October 11,
1927.

II.

The End of the Road

IN THE LAST HALF of the twenties, Hiram W. Evans and the men who ran the Klan tried in various ways to keep the order afloat. In the fall of 1925 Evans announced that the Klan was moving its main offices from Atlanta to Washington, D.C., where the organization supposedly could carry out its new "educational" program in more effective fashion. The Klan established propaganda headquarters in a building at Seventh and I streets in Washington and set to work at its new task of "Americanizing America." The character of the order now changed somewhat. Whereas earlier the Klan had operated as a political machine in most areas, during the last half of the decade it became, at least officially, a pressure group concentrating its attention on national legislation. To dramatize its power, in 1926 the Klan held its third Imperial Klonvocation in Washington. The high point of the Klonvocation was a colorful parade of some 40,000 Klansmen and Klanswomen down Pennsylvania Avenue.[1]

Attractive innovations on the fraternal side of the Klan accompanied the deemphasis of politics. The Klan turned to the hallowed fraternal device of adding new degrees to the hierarchial character of its membership. About 1925 the Imperial Klan, reactivating William J. Simmons' old idea of a "second degree of Klankraft," proclaimed that all Klansmen, or first degree Knights, could take a second degree, that of "Knights Kamelia." Probably no more than one million Klansmen paid their five dollars, the initiation fee for the second degree, and became Knights Kamelia.[2]

Early in 1928 Klan headquarters established a third degree in connection with the national unmasking of the order. By that time the mask served little purpose for the Klan. Dropping antimask bills into the hoppers of senates and houses of representatives had become something of a sport in state legislatures. Practically every northern state, as well as Texas, Oklahoma, and Louisiana in the Southwest, had passed some kind of law abolishing public mask-wearing except on specified holidays. Since there was little to lose, and perhaps something to gain in the way of public relations, Imperial Wizard Evans decreed that the Klan would lift its mask officially the night of February 23, 1928. The act of abandoning the mask, which someone called "open faces openly arrived at," coincided with the induction of all Klansmen into a third degree, the "Knights of the Great Forest." On the designated night about 85,000 Klansmen, perhaps half the surviving membership of the order, went through the mask-lifting ceremony and became Knights of the Great Forest.[3]

As the Klan lost members, it took up new issues. Claiming that the Johnson-Reed Immigration Restriction Act of 1924 adequately curbed the influx of "indigestible" immigrants from southern and eastern Europe, Evans said

[1] Fort Worth *Star-Telegram*, October 23, 1925; New York *Times*, September 14, 1926, p. 1.

[2] Washington *Post*, November 2, 1930, sec. i, p. 4.

[3] *Ibid.*; New York *Times*, February 23, 1928, p. 1; Shreveport *Journal*, February 24, 1928; "The Klan Goes In for a Face-Lifting," *Literary Digest*, XCVI (March 10, 1928), 15-16.

that the Klan would emphasize the "Americanization" of the alien elements *within* the United States.[4] Under Evans' leadership the Klan showed more concern with an isolationist foreign policy. This took form especially in highly vocal opposition to American participation in the World Court as advocated by that indisputably 100-percent-American President, Calvin Coolidge. In the late twenties rigid enforcement of the Eighteenth Amendment and the Volstead Act, the instruments of nationwide prohibition, became as important to the Imperial Klan as it had always been to the secret order in the southwestern states. Finally, the Klan trumpeted its support for a federal department of education and federal aid to the public school system as weapons for preserving the separation of church and state in America.[5]

But the one great rallying cry of Klansmen, the one prejudice that had been the ideological bulwark of the Klan since the kluxing days of Edward Y. Clarke and Mrs. Elizabeth Tyler, was anti-Catholicism. The Klan might play down racism and moral authoritarianism in favor of new goals, but hatred of "Romanists" and "Romanism" remained the prime element of its philosophy. From 1925, when the Klan went into its nosedive, through the discouraging years of the late twenties, Evans and his corps of Klan lecturers incessantly admonished patriotic Protestants to remain on guard against the "Catholic menace" and the Pope's chief agent in American politics, Al Smith.

Of all the figures in public life in the twenties, none took as much abuse at the hands of the Klan as Governor Alfred E. Smith of the state of New York. Smith, the son of Irish immigrants, represented everything the Klan, and

[4] Evans announced this alteration of policy in a speech before the Klorero of Texas, held in Arlington, reported in the Fort Worth *Star-Telegram*, September 13, 1925.

[5] Charles Merz, "The New Ku Klux Klan," *Independent*, CXVIII (February 12, 1927), 179-80; Little Rock *Arkansas Gazette*, November 12, 1926.

perhaps most rural-minded Protestant Americans, detested
—New York City, Tammany Hall, liquor, Catholicism,
foreignism. In 1924 the Klan shared credit for blocking
Smith's bid for the Democratic presidential nomination.
Four years later the hooded, but now unmasked, order was
ready to make its last stand in American politics—to rally
once more 100 percent Americans throughout the country
for the struggle against popery and Smith.

The prospect of a Catholic in the White House was as
repugnant to Klansmen in the Southwest as to Knights in
other parts of the country. Oklahoma, however, was the
only southwestern state where the Klan held on to any
political ambitions and acted with any degree of unity.
In the fall of 1927 Grand Dragon Zach A. Harris and other
Oklahoma Klan leaders held a series of conferences to
discuss their chances for capturing the state Democratic
convention, to be held the next spring, and for sending an
anti-Smith delegation to the national party convention.[6]

In the winter and early spring of 1928 the Klan failed to
control any of the county Democratic conventions, but in
several counties the delegations chosen for the upcoming
state convention contained known Klansmen. The prohibitionists, the Klansmen, and the Johnston administration
forces had a clear majority at the state Democratic convention, meeting in April at Oklahoma City. Such a coalition could easily have controlled the state convention and
sent an anti-Smith delegation to the national convention.
Instead, the followers of Governor Henry S. Johnston
united with the pro-Smith forces, overruled the ultradry
and Klan delegates, and controlled the convention. The
delegation chosen for the Democratic national convention
in Houston was officially uninstructed, but it listed a
plurality of Smith supporters. One of the anti-Klanners
gloated that "We had them [the Klansmen and drys]

[6] Oklahoma City *Daily Oklahoman*, September 23, October 11,
1927.

whipped at the start and rolled them clear out of the convention."[7]

The enthusiastic but harmonious atmosphere at the Democratic national convention in Houston contrasted remarkably with the intraparty carnage in New York four years earlier. The Al Smith boom, gaining momentum since 1927, swept through the specially constructed hall that housed the convention and gave the New Yorker the nomination on the first ballot. The Louisiana delegation voted as a unit for Smith, while seventeen of Arkansas' eighteen delegate votes went to the archenemy of the Klan. Ten Oklahomans cast their votes for Smith, eight for United States Senator James A. Reed of Missouri, and two for Cordell Hull of Tennessee. The forty votes of Texas went to its favorite son candidate, financier Jesse H. Jones of Houston.[8] To balance the ticket with the wet, eastern nominee, Senator Joseph T. Robinson of Arkansas, considered a prohibitionist, received the vice-presidential nomination. The party platform pledged support of nationwide prohibition, but in his acceptance speech Smith contradicted the pledge by advocating modification of the dry laws.[9]

Evans and his staff, who had been unobtrusive observers in Houston, went back to Washington making inflated promises that the Klan would defeat Smith in November. Oklahoma Klan leader Harris said that the Klan would bolt the Democratic party and support Herbert Hoover, the Republican presidential nominee. The state president of the Woman's Christian Temperance Union also predicted

[7] *Ibid.*, April 1, 2, 11, 1928.

[8] New York *World, World Almanac and Book of Facts* (1929), 851. Technically Smith was not nominated *on* but *after* the first ballot. At the end of the first rollcall of states Smith was ten votes short of the two-thirds majority required for the nomination. The Ohio delegation then switched its votes to the New Yorker and made him the party's candidate.

[9] Roy V. Peel and Thomas C. Donnelly, *The 1928 Campaign: An Analysis* (New York, 1931), 34-35, 165; Nevin E. Neal, "A Biography of Joseph T. Robinson" (unpublished Ph.D. dissertation, University of Oklahoma, 1958), 251-53.

a bolt of dry, Protestant Democrats. James A. Comer, the Arkansas Dragon, declared that the addition of Robinson to the Democratic ticket did not alter the opposition of the Klan and the Arkansas Anti-Saloon League to Smith. Comer then prepared questionnaires asking for a commitment on the subject of "Rum and Romanism," which he sent to state, district, and Pulaski County candidates. He encouraged local Klans in other Arkansas counties to do likewise.[10]

During the 1928 presidential campaign the Klan fought Smith openly in most states, especially in Alabama, where the order still wielded considerable power.[11] Yet its efforts as an organization to stir up sentiment against the Democratic nominee were feeble indeed. In Louisiana, for example, ex-Klansman William C. Barnette, former general counsel for the Klan in the state, said that he was personally opposed to making religion an issue in the campaign and that he would support the entire Democratic ticket "most heartily." In all the speechmaking during the campaign in Louisiana the Klan was not mentioned. Many ex-Klansmen, like Dr. E. L. Thompson, former head of the Shreveport Klan, urged Protestants, prohibitionists, and patriots in Louisiana to vote against Smith because he was a Catholic, an ally of Tammany Hall, a wet, an opponent of the 1924 immigration restriction act, and an advocate of political rights for the Negro. But in Arkansas, Lee Cazort, candidate of the Klan in its ill-fated effort to win the governorship in 1924, won the Democratic nomination for lieutenant governor and took to the hustings in behalf of the Smith-Robinson ticket in the state. And when Smith spoke to a roaring crowd in Oklahoma City, Governor Johnston, a rigid prohibitionist elected with Klan help in

[10] Arnold S. Rice, *The Ku Klux Klan in American Politics* (Washington, 1962), 86-87; Oklahoma City *Daily Oklahoman*, July 1, 1928; Little Rock *Arkansas Gazette*, July 2, 16, 1928. Several prominent Protestant ministers in Arkansas, including Robinson's own pastor at the First Methodist Church in Little Rock, spoke against the Smith-Robinson ticket. See Neal, "Robinson," 278-82.

[11] See Rice, *Ku Klux Klan in American Politics*, 87-88.

1926, sat on the platform with the Democratic nominee.[12]

Anti-Smith organizations, going under various names, were formed among Democratic voters in each of the southwestern states. As far as can be determined, the state Klan organizations had no official connection with these "Hoovercrat" groups. Yet numerous Klansmen and ex-Klansmen were active in the anti-Smith movement. In Texas, V. A. Collins and Shelby Cox of Dallas, Marvin A. Childers of San Antonio, Lloyd P. Bloodworth of Fort Worth, Edward B. Ward of Corpus Christi, and Alva Bryan of Waco were among the Knights and former Knights of the Invisible Empire who joined the "Anti-Al Smith Democrats of Texas" and worked enthusiastically for Hoover. Cox, Childers, and Bloodworth were past Grand Dragons in Texas. The leaders of the Texas opposition to the Democratic nominee, however, men like former Governor Oscar B. Colquitt and national committeeman Thomas B. Love, had been either anti-Klan or neutral during the Klan's peak years in the Lone Star State.[13] The same was true of Oklahoma, where former United States Senator Robert L. Owen served as the nominal leader of the bolting Democrats, and where the Oklahoma City *Daily Oklahoman,* long a foe of the Klan and a Democratic paper, urged drys and supporters of "clean government" to desert the party.

Despite Imperial Wizard Evans' boasts, the Klan as an organization had very little to say about which candidate carried the states of the Southwest, or any other state, in 1928. In most places the Klan was more important spiritually than physically. Religious prejudice and stern moralism, elements that had given rise to the Klan in the first

[12] Shreveport *Journal,* June 30, October 19, 1928; Little Rock *Arkansas Gazette,* October 25, 1928; Oklahoma City *Daily Oklahoman,* September 21, 1928.

[13] "State Headquarters Staff of the Anti-Al Smith Democrats of Texas with a brief summary of services performed in behalf of Mr. Hoover" and "List of those who did service in behalf of Mr. Hoover from their respective homes over the state," typescript copies, Oscar B. Colquitt Papers, University of Texas Archives, Austin.

place, were still factors in southwestern politics, and they benefited the Republican and anti-Smith cause in the region. In other parts of the country, and perhaps in the Southwest, the greatest asset the Republicans had was the unprecedented industrial and financial prosperity sweeping the nation, which many people equated with the Grand Old Party.[14]

In November, Smith, aided by Robinson's presence on the ticket, carried Arkansas by about 40,000 votes, but ran some 30,000 votes behind the state Democratic ticket. Smith and Robinson carried Pulaski County, once a hotbed of the Klan and its offshoot, the Mystic Knights, by a 2-to-1 margin. Smith polled nearly three times as many votes as Hoover in Louisiana; the Democrat's percentage of the vote was almost as great as that of John W. Davis in 1924. In Oklahoma and Texas, however, the story was different. For the second time since statehood the Republican ticket carried Oklahoma in a presidential election, Hoover polling a staggering 394,052 votes to Smith's 219,206. At the same time the Democrats retained control of the state legislature and most of the county governments. In Texas the presidential race was much closer. For the first time in history Texas, by a narrow margin, went Republican. Hoover received 372,720 votes to 347,320 for Smith. Over the nation Hoover had 21,392,190 votes and carried forty states; Smith received 15,016,443 votes and carried only eight states.[15]

The presidential campaign of 1928 demonstrated that

14 Arthur S. Link, *American Epoch; A History of the United States since the 1890's* (New York, 1956), 350-52; Peel and Donnelly, *The 1928 Campaign*, 114-16. Edmund A. Moore, *A Catholic Runs for President* (New York, 1956) emphasizes the importance of the Catholic issue in causing Smith's defeat, but also points up the critical nature of the prosperity issue.

15 Eugene H. Roseboom, *A History of Presidential Elections* (New York, 1957), 417-29; Edgar E. Robinson, *The Presidential Vote, 1896-1932* (Stanford, Calif., 1947), 24-27; Svend Petersen, *A Statistical History of the American Presidential Elections* (New York, 1963), 89-90, 120, 133, 150, 157.

while bigotry's foremost purveyor, the Klan, was almost dead, bigotry was still very much alive. The fulminations of the Klan at national and state levels represented the last political gasps of a dying organization. After that year what was left of the once-mighty secret fraternal order went to pieces. In July of 1929 the Klan, declaring that its mission in the national capital was fulfilled with the defeat of Smith, abandoned Washington and moved its headquarters back to Atlanta. Imperial Kligrapp H. Kyle Ramsey and about thirty other officials transferred their records to Atlanta, but Imperial Wizard Evans continued to live in Washington, at a home on Massachusetts Avenue. A few years later he, too, made the journey back to the birthplace of the Klan. By the end of June 1929 the nationwide membership of the order was down to about 82,000; a year later, with economic distress spreading over the country and touching all classes, there were probably fewer than 35,000 Knights left in the Invisible Empire.[16]

The figure of 7,000 Klansmen, given by one newspaper late in 1928 as the membership in Oklahoma, was probably too high. In the middle of the next year there were perhaps 2,000 Klansmen left in Oklahoma, perhaps 1,500 in 1930. The end of the decade found Klansmen numbered in the hundreds in Arkansas, Louisiana, and Texas, rather than in the thousands and tens of thousands.[17] Imperial headquarters relieved Harris of the Oklahoma Grand Dragonship in 1929 and evidently did not name a successor. Rush H. Davis of Shreveport was still Grand Dragon of the Realm of Louisiana in the fall of 1929, when Evans spoke to a sparse crowd at the Shreveport city hall on "Americanism." Two electric crosses and several robed but unmasked Klansmen, including Davis, appeared on the stage with the

[16] Washington *Post*, July 6, 1929, p. 1, November 3, 1930, sec. i, p. 4.

[17] Oklahoma City *Daily Oklahoman*, November 25, 1928; Washington *Post*, November 3, 1930, sec. i, p. 4.

Imperial Wizard.[18] The Realm organizations for Arkansas and Texas were probably disbanded after 1928, leaving the local Klan as the only organizational unit within the states. Far from the hooded crusade of the first half of the decade, but illustrative of what the few remaining Klan chapters were doing in the late twenties and early thirties, was a notice printed in an obscure corner of a Shreveport newspaper: "The Knights of the Ku Klux Klan will broadcast a program of old-time banjo and fiddle numbers over radio station KSBA Tuesday night, according to announcement by station owners. The program will be on the air for 30 minutes, beginning promptly at 8 o'clock."[19]

The Klan collapsed in the last half of the 1920s because of factors fully as varied and complex as the reasons for its rise in the first half of the decade. The conditions causing the rapid decay of the order differed from region to region, from state to state, and even from community to community. Some general developments debilitating the Klan throughout the nation, however, can be noted, as well as the more particular circumstances related to the decline of the movement in the Southwest.

One student of the white-robed fraternity has suggested that an organization like the Klan, emphasizing perpetual crisis and the divisive character of society, appealed only to a certain number of people. Sooner or later all or nearly all of these people would join the organization. When the Klan had realized its membership potential in an area, there was no place for it to go but down.[20] This thesis has much validity when applied to a state like Pennsylvania, where the Klan was very strong numerically but did not venture openly into politics. In those states where the Klan eventu-

---

[18] Shreveport *Journal*, October 11, 1929.
[19] *Ibid.*, February 26, 1929.
[20] Norman F. Weaver, "The Knights of the Ku Klux Klan in Wisconsin, Indiana, Ohio, and Michigan (unpublished Ph.D. dissertation, University of Wisconsin, 1954), 105.

ally became a political organization, however, the thesis does not quite stand. For if the Klan were successful in politics over a period of several years, it could keep growing simply because numerous people—politicians, businessmen, even criminals—would join the order to protect their own interests. Under conditions of prolonged success the membership potential of the Klan might be limited only by the size of the native-born, white, Protestant population of a community, county, state, or, perhaps ultimately, the nation.

Two observers of modern American fraternalism have shown that during the 1920s, under the impact of urbanization and industrialization, all of the adult fraternal orders, the "lodges," entered a process of decline which has continued to the present. Supplanting the fraternal orders, both in conviviality and social service, were the businessmen's clubs like Rotary, Kiwanis, and Lions.[21] The Klan, as an adult fraternal order, obviously fits into this pattern of decline; its descent was unquestionably more precipitate than that of any other established fraternal organization. Yet the Klan in the southwestern states and in other parts of the country became, in its ultimate form, a political organization. The sagging of the American institution of adult fraternalism does not adequately explain why the Klan fell apart in the Southwest.

The war-induced hysteria, which in the immediate postwar years turned into anti-Catholicism and anti-Semitism, fear of radicals and Bolsheviks, suppression of Negroes, and revulsion against foreign immigration, had gradually subsided with time. Intolerance of everything that did not square with the native white Protestant's rigid conception of "100 percent Americanism," which furnished much of the impetus behind the surge of the Klan in the early

[21] Noel P. Gist, *Secret Societies: A Cultural Study of Fraternalism in the United States* (University of Missouri Studies, XV, October 1, 1940), 43-44; Arthur M. Schlesinger, *Paths to the Present* (New York, 1949), 44.

twenties, seemed to slacken as the decade passed the halfway mark.[22] The return of prosperity, indeed the commencement of a brief era of unprecedented abundance, quieted the anxieties and diverted the energies of middle-class America. George B. Tindall has submitted that even in the South (and Southwest) "business progressivism," not prejudice and reaction, set the tone for politics and government, especially after 1925.[23]

Achievement of at least one of the Klan's objectives, the drastic curbing of immigration, probably helped to assuage the passions of some Klansmen. The stopgap immigration act of 1921 was the first to embody the national origins quota system. The 1921 measure substantially curtailed the number of immigrants eligible to enter the United States each year, and established restrictionism as permanent national policy. But because it was based on the 1910 census and thus allowed a preponderance of immigration of "inferior" and "backward" peoples from southern and eastern Europe, it did not satisfy the powerful Immigration Restriction League, the Klan, and other aggregations of racial nativists. Agitation for more discriminatory legislation brought about the more comprehensive and more severe Johnson-Reed Act of 1924, which adopted the census of 1890 as the basis for the immigrant quota to be allowed from each nation each year and prohibited Japanese immigration entirely. The act of 1924, by shifting the weight of immigration back to the supposedly superior "Nordic" or "Teutonic" peoples of northern and western Europe, satisfied the Klan and almost all the other advocates of restriction.[24]

[22] For the decline of racial and religious nativism in the late twenties, see Oscar Handlin, *Race and Nationality in American Life* (New York, 1957), ch. VII; and Thomas F. Gossett, *Race: The History of an Idea in America* (Dallas, 1963), ch. XVI.

[23] George B. Tindall, "Business Progressivism: Southern Politics in the Twenties," *South Atlantic Quarterly*, LXII (Spring 1963), 92-106.

[24] John Higham, *Strangers in the Land: Patterns of American Nativism, 1860-1925* (New Brunswick, N.J., 1955), ch. XI.

The older bedfellow of racial nativism was the concept of white supremacy. By the late twenties white people, north and south, could relax in the assurance that the demands for first-class citizenship and the stirrings of Negro nationalism appearing in the postwar years had, for the time being, subsided.[25] Two obvious signs of the recession of racial antagonism were the steady diminution of the number of lynchings reported each year and the absence of major race riots during the last eight years of the decade.

Anti-Catholic feeling apparently waned throughout the country with the enactment of the 1924 immigration legislation, aimed largely at Catholic Europeans, and with the simple passage of time and the realization that at least for the moment America was safe from the fancied ambitions of the Pope. In a sense the fact that Al Smith finally was able to nail down the Democratic presidential nomination in 1928 revealed the extent to which religious prejudice had slackened in his party. Smith's candidacy provoked only a moderate rally of the moribund Klan movement.

During the campaign of 1928, however, Smith encountered a kind of bitter, uncompromising opposition in the Southwest, especially in Oklahoma and Texas, that was immeasurably broader than the Klan was or ever had been. While anti-Catholicism may have abated somewhat throughout the nation, even in the South and Southwest, the vigor and extent of the reaction against Smith indicate that this abatement had little connection with the decline of the Klan in the overwhelmingly Protestant states.

It has been suggested and implied in this study that while nativism and racism, the ideological underpinnings of the Klan, were important to the growth of the order in the Southwest, they were secondary to moral authoritarianism—the desire to use the Klan for the radical, often violent,

[25] See Edmund David Cronon, *Black Moses: The Story of the Universal Negro Improvement Association* (Madison, Wis., 1955).

alteration of individual standards and conduct. The explanation for the disintegration of the Klan in Texas, Arkansas, Oklahoma, and Louisiana lies partly in the evil effects of its hooded vigilantism and the failure of its drive for "law and order."

Thousands of solid middle-class citizens in the four states joined the Klan because they honestly believed there was a need to bring together people who wanted adequate law enforcement and who were disturbed by the crime and vice that seemed to surround them. The Klan could, they thought, be used to promote observance of the law and moral uplift. Violence and terrorism should play no part in this campaign to establish a safer, more lawful, and more moral community. But these law-abiding citizens soon discovered that the Klan, with its secret membership rolls and its masked members, attracted all kinds of native white Protestants, including a dismayingly large number of sadists, grudge-holders, and fanatics. "In the early days of the organization," admitted Harris, the Oklahoma Klan leader, "many men joined who simply desired to take part in a whipping with some personal enemy as the victim."[26] Then, too, the Klan, like a lynch mob, seemed to bring out the worst in many timid souls, whose circumspect daytime behavior turned into vengeful vigilantism at night under the anonymity of a robe and hood. Too many of the upright Klansmen did nothing when, as frequently happened, their local chapter came under the dominance of terrorists. Nevertheless, the same extralegal activities that repelled non-Klan citizens also drove some Klansmen from the Invisible Empire.

There were, for example, the cases of Oscar F. Holcombe, the mayor of Houston, and Henry F. Tanner, the police chief of Dallas. Holcombe joined the Klan shortly after it was organized in Houston and attended a few meetings. He soon discovered that in many instances the police chief

[26] Quoted in Oklahoma City *Daily Oklahoman*, May 21, 1927.

of the southeast Texas city and most of the other law officers in town were acting in accordance with the orders of the local Exalted Cyclops, H. C. McCall. Mayor Holcombe told McCall that he was resigning from the Klan and that McCall had to stop interfering in the affairs of the police department. When McCall continued his meddling, Holcombe brought in several peace officers from West Texas counties to protect citizens from Klan vigilantes. The local chapter ran a candidate against Holcombe in one city election and fought him at every opportunity. In the spring of 1922, in the midst of an outbreak of whippings in Dallas, Police Chief Tanner publicly resigned from the Klan. He said that when he joined the organization he had the impression that it aided law enforcement, but that he quickly saw that it was more an impediment to law officers than an aid.[27] Other public figures, like United States Representative Elmer Thomas of Oklahoma and Tulsa postmaster Omer K. Benedict, became disenchanted after a short stay in the Invisible Empire and left the Klan.

When men like Holcombe, Tanner, Thomas, and Benedict dropped out, the Klan, always striving passionately for respectability, felt their absence in a loss of prestige in the community and in the state. The presence of disreputable elements inside the Klan made life in the order insufferable for men of standing. Their exit contributed to the Klan's fall.

Terrorism was by no means the only internal evil from which the Klan suffered. Probably the most important factor behind the breakup of the Klan in the Southwest was dissension. And the Klan's autocratic structure was the greatest contributor to the growth of internal conflict. The dictatorial character of the Klan hierarchy, based on the principle that all power should originate in the Imperial

[27] Testimony of Oscar F. Holcombe in *Knights of the Ku Klux Klan, Inc.* v. *George B. Kimbro, Jr.* (No. 105180) (61st District Court, Harris County, Texas), reported in Houston *Post-Dispatch,* March 25, 1925; Dallas *Morning News,* April 13, 1922.

Wizard and move downward from him, presented a ready-made opportunity for unscrupulous and power-hungry leaders. These Klan officials sometimes abused their authority in order to achieve their designs for political preferment and personal aggrandizement. Their manipulations involved the membership of the order in struggles essentially unrelated to the Klan's program of Americanism, law enforcement, and morality. In 1924, in Oklahoma, state Klan boss N. Clay Jewett switched the Klan's endorsement at the last minute, brought about the senatorial nomination of Jack Walton over two candidates who were popular with Klansmen, and set up the election of a Republican United States Senator. And in Louisiana outraged Klansmen cried betrayal when several state Klan officials struck an alliance with the tainted New Orleans machine behind gubernatorial candidate Henry L. Fuqua and then helped the Fuqua administration enact a series of laws to regulate the Klan.

Most Klansmen served the order blindly. They were supposed to obey their immediate leader, the Exalted Cyclops, and the other officials up the chain of command. They were to follow without question the decrees, commands, and instructions of the Imperial Wizard or, as in the case of Clarke during the Simmons Wizardship, the man who had the Wizard's ear. Simmons, Clarke, and later Evans rationalized that such a "military" system was necessary to protect the Klan from its enemies and to carry out the mission of the order. Many Klansmen, however, brought up in the belief that the democratic way was the best way, came to chafe under dictation from the higher-ups and to resent the fact that they had little to say about the making of policy, the endorsement of politicians, and the choice of their leaders.

Politics was the area in which the undemocratic nature of the Klan inspired the most internal disorder. Since even at the local level it was usually a minority, the Klan's only hope of success was to operate within the two established parties. The Klan worked within the Democratic party in the South and in most of the Southwest, ordinarily within the Republican party in the North, and within both parties in border states like Oklahoma and at the national level. A division of voting strength, either in the party primaries or in the general election, was fatal to the Klan's chances. Yet this necessity to concentrate the power of the order behind one candidate often led to autocratic methods on the part of its leaders and dissension among subordinates and the rank and file Klansmen.

This was the case in Texas in 1922, when Evans overrode all opposition to the naming of Earle B. Mayfield as the Klan senatorial candidate, and in 1924, when Grand Dragon Z. E. Marvin virtually dictated the endorsement of Felix D. Robertson for the governorship. In Arkansas, according to rebellious Klansman Jim G. Ferguson, Comer carefully arranged the statewide elimination primary held by the Klan so that the controversial Dragon's choice, Cazort, could become the Klan candidate for governor. Many Arkansas Klansmen refused to vote for Cazort in the August Democratic primary, and a neutral candidate got the nomination.

The heavyhanded techniques of the Klan leaders thus brought strife to the southwestern Realms. In Texas and Arkansas dissension was coupled with defeat, for the Klan failed miserably in the 1924 gubernatorial races. By the end of that year Marvin was no longer the head of the Klan in Texas, and the membership of the organization was falling off rapidly over the state. Comer kept his Realm together until the fall of 1925, when the secession of the Little Rock men's and women's Klans broke the back of the order in Arkansas. Resentment against Jewett mounted in Oklahoma until Evans removed him in 1925. In Louisiana Evans personally took charge of a Klan organization that was being torn to pieces by factionalism. He liquidated one faction, overhauled the state leadership, and had nearly every Klansman in Louisiana move his fraternal affiliation to Atlanta to escape the new state membership registration law.

The financial affairs of the Klan were beyond the knowledge or control of the rank and file. The Klan clearly took in enormous sums of money in the twenties. During 1922, according to the estimate of Simmons, the daily income of Imperial headquarters in Atlanta seldom fell below $10,000. Some 3,500 men, paying ten dollars a piece in initiation fees and most of them buying $6.50 robes, joined the Klan each day. The next year, Simmons estimated, the income of the Imperial Klan was about three million dollars. In the period from February 17 to July 14, 1923, David C. Stephenson, chief Kleagle and later Grand Dragon of Indiana, remitted $641,475 to the Imperial treasury.[28] The ascension of Evans to the Imperial Wizardship was supposed to bring a regularization of Klan finances, and in fact there was probably stricter accounting during his administration than under Simmons, Clarke, and Mrs. Tyler. On several occasions, however, the Evans regime was forced to go into court to combat suits brought by unhappy Klansmen charging corruption and Imperial theft. Not once during

[28] William G. Shepherd, "Ku Klux Koin," *Collier's,* LXXXII (July 21, 1928), 38; Marion Monteval (pseud.), *The Klan Inside Out* (Claremore, Oklahoma, 1924), 62-63. David C. Stephenson, a pudgy former coaldealer, organized the midwestern states and received almost absolute authority from Evans to govern the northern Realms. He became the most powerful individual in the state of Indiana. His henchman was elected governor in 1924, and at the next legislative session Stephenson virtually controlled the state government. In the spring of 1925 he brutally assaulted a woman who worked as a statehouse secretary and eventually went to prison for life. When Stephenson fell, he brought the mighty Indiana Klan down with him. The bibliography on the Hoosier State Klan leader is already rather large. The best scholarly treatment of his career is in Weaver, "Knights of the Ku Klux Klan in Wisconsin, Indiana, Ohio, and Michigan," ch. IV. A much more titillating account is in Isabel Leighton (ed.), *The Aspirin Age, 1919-1941* (New York, 1949), 105-29.

its long career did the Klan make a public statement of its receipts and disbursements, although Evans was proud to display the steady improvement of the Klan's assets in relation to its liabilities under his administration.[29]

Citizenship in the Invisible Empire was expensive. The initiation fee and the purchase of a robe marked only the beginning of the economic demands on the ordinary Knight. A Klansman paid an Imperial tax of $1.80 per year, plus a small additional duty, usually ten cents per month, levied by the state office. The local Klan had its own per capita tax, which customarily varied from six dollars to ten dollars annually. Klansmen had to make "voluntary" contributions when the chapter funds were low. If a member fell behind in his payments, he was automatically suspended from the Klan and could be reinstated only when he had paid his back taxes.[30]

The local Klans also required their members to pay sufficient dues for the rental of a meeting hall or the construction of the chapter's own Klavern, for the purchase of ritual equipment, for the payment of accountants' and lawyers' fees, and for the traveling expenses of the local officers. Klansmen might contribute to the campaign expenses of aspiring Klan politicians, as in Dallas; buy Klan life insurance; or subscribe to the various publications of the order. Knights were expected to give money for the maintenance of the local Klan's church work and its charity program.

All of these expenses that went with active membership in the Klan amounted to a considerable burden on the average Klansman. As long as matters went well and a Knight could feel secure in the efficacy of his movement,

[29] See *Proceedings of the Second Imperial Klonvocation, Held in Kansas City, Missouri, September 23-26, 1924* (Atlanta, 1924), 87, 90-91, 183-85, for Evans' fullest statement of the Klan's assets and liabilities under his regime.

[30] *Constitution and Laws of the Knights of the Ku Klux Klan* (Atlanta, 1921), art. xv, sec. 2, 3, art, xviii, sec. 18.

the expense was bearable. But when the Klan met defeat
and its enemies gained the advantage, or when dissension
drained the strength of the order, as happened in the
Southwest, a minion of the Imperial Wizard was apt to
doubt whether the preservation of Protestant Americanism,
white supremacy, and old-fashioned morality was really
worth the cost. Most Klansmen decided that someone else
could do the preserving; they would save their time, money,
and standing in the community.

With defeat and dissension came apathy, an even more
ravaging malady. Tens of thousands of weary Klansmen,
bored and disgusted by the continual bickering in their
chapters and state organizations, left the Invisible Empire
by the simple device of letting their dues lapse. They
remained on the membership rolls of the Klan, but they
would never again pass through the doors of the Klavern.
The meetings grew longer; the news from inside the Realm
was discouraging; there were debts to be met and people
to be helped, but less and less money with which to operate.
How many Klansmen over the Southwest and throughout
the nation were like the member of the Sour Lake, Texas,
Klan, who gave up after the close of a meeting in 1925
and burned his robe and hood by the roadside on his way
home?[31] Most Klansmen may not have cut their ties with
the Klan in such dramatic fashion. But enough of them
quit the organization to reduce the Klan, once the feared
crusader for Americanism and moral conformity, to the
status of a toothless lodge.

The Imperial Klan and a few surviving chapters carried
on into the early 1930s. Depression decimated the remaining membership of the order. Robed and masked Klansmen appeared during a Halloween celebration in Little
Rock in 1933. The next year Imperial Wizard Evans
aroused himself briefly, denounced Huey P. Long, recent

[31] This incident was related to the writer by the ex-Klansman
involved, who now lives in Jefferson County, Texas.

governor and now United States Senator, as a menace to organized society, and proclaimed that national head-quarters was organizing Louisiana Klansmen to fight Long. But the "Kingfish," as Long called himself, was not worried. He warned Evans that if he set foot in Louisiana, "he will leave both feet right here, with the toes turned up." The Wizard had no reply.[32]

In the late thirties the Klan managed to achieve a moderate revival by playing on the growing conservative reaction to the liberalism of the New Deal. The Klan vilified industrial unionism as practiced by the Congress of Industrial Organizations, sounded warnings against the new menace of communism (no longer Catholicism), and decried the destruction of the Constitution by radicals, liberals, and Communists. The Klan evidently organized some new chapters in Oklahoma, but Louisiana, Arkansas, and Texas went virtually untouched by this mild upsurge of Klanism, anti-New Deal variety.[33] In 1939 Evans finally resigned the Wizardship. Delegates to a special Klonvocation in Atlanta elected James Arnold Colescott, a veterinarian from Terre Haute, Indiana, and for two years Evans' "chief of staff," as the new national leader of the Klan.[34]

By the time he left the Wizardship, Evans had built up a thriving business as a dealer in emulsified asphalt for highway construction. In 1940 the state of Georgia brought suit under the Sherman Antitrust Act against Evans and other parties for conspiring to control the sale of asphalt

[32] John G. Fletcher, *Arkansas* (Chapel Hill, N. C., 1947), 367; New York *Times,* August 18, 1934, p. 5.

[33] New York *Times,* July 1, 1934, sec. IV, p. 7; Oklahoma City *Daily Oklahoman,* November 4, 1937. The best discussion of the Klan's posttwenties history is in Rice, *Klan in American Politics,* chs. VIII, IX. See also Edwin D. Hoffman, "The Genesis of the Movement for Equal Rights in South Carolina," *Journal of Negro History,* XLIV (October 1959), 346-69.

[34] New York *Times,* June 11, 1939, p. 47; Heywood Broun, "Up Pops the Wizard," *New Republic,* XCIX (June 21, 1939), 186-87; Rice, *Klan in American Politics,* 107.

to the state. Initially a federal district court ruled that the state was not a "person" as defined in the Sherman Act and thus could not sue in the federal courts. In 1942, however, this ruling was overturned by the United States Supreme Court.[35] The state of Georgia then prosecuted Evans and nineteen other persons in Superior Court in Atlanta on criminal charges in connection with asphalt sales, highway maintenance work, and printing jobs. Evans, claiming that he was caught in the middle of a political feud, loudly pleaded his innocence of any wrongdoing. The Georgia jury failed to reach a verdict and the Superior Court judge declared a mistrial. The state did not seek a new trial, and Evans slipped into oblivion.[36]

Under Evans' successor in the Klan, Colescott, the revival begun in the late thirties continued. Perhaps 30,000 Klansmen enrolled in the order in Florida, and by the spring of 1940 the new Imperial Wizard was boasting that the Klan operated in thirty-nine states and had 500,000 members. More sober estimates placed the membership of the Klan at about 200,000, with probably two-thirds of that total confined to the South.[37]

The coming of the Second World War destroyed whatever chance the Klan may have had for regaining its former power and prestige. On April 28, 1944, harassed by a federal suit for $685,000 in delinquent income taxes, the national officials of the Klan met in secret session and, according to Colescott, "voted to suspend the constitutional laws of the Knights of the Ku Klux Klan, Inc., to revoke all charter Klans and to order disbandment of all provisional Klans."[38] This act marked the official demise of the Invisible Empire, Knights of the Ku Klux Klan, Inc., the secret

[35] *State of Georgia* v. *Evans et al.*, 315 U. S. 482.

[36] Gustavus Myers, *A History of Bigotry in the United States* (New York, 1943), 329-31.

[37] New York *Times*, April 18, 1940, p. 48; Rice, *Klan in American Politics*, 107.

[38] New York *Times*, June 5, 1944, p. 21.

fraternal order founded by Simmons back in 1915. After the war, in 1947, Governor Ellis Arnall of Georgia had his attorney general file an ouster suit against the skeletal organization. The suit forced Colescott and the rest of the Klan officials, who had retained their titles, to surrender the charter of the order to the state under whose corporation laws the Klan had always operated.[39]

In the postwar years the Deep South experienced a renewal of Klan terrorist activities, directed primarily against Negroes. Now several more or less localized organizations, still relying on the magic of the name "Klan," sprang up in the southern states. The largest was the "Association of Georgia Klans," established under the leadership of Dr. Samuel Green, an Atlanta obstetrician who took the title Grand Dragon. The Association of Georgia Klans has since disbanded, but today scattered groups with names like "Florida Ku Klux Klan," the "Original Klan of the Confederacy," and the "Gulf Ku Klux Klan" hold meetings in the southern states. The largest present-day Klan organization appears to be the "United Klans, Knights of the Ku Klux Klan, Inc.," headed by Robert Shelton, a Birmingham auto-tire salesman. All of these Klan groups harp on one theme—that the Supreme Court desegregation decision of 1954 will "mongrelize" the South, that the "niggers" must be kept "in their place," and that the whole movement for civil rights and social equality is at base a liberal-Socialist-Communist-Jewish conspiracy.[40]

Yet today the average Southerner finds little use for these various robed and hooded societies. The southern racist

[39] *Ibid.*, June 14, 1947, p. 30.

[40] On the post-World War II career of the various Klan organizations in the South, see Rice, *Klan in American Politics,* ch. IX; Leslie Velie, "The Klan Rides the South Again," *Collier's* CXXII (October 9, 1948), 13-15, 74, 75; Carey McWilliams, "The Klan: Post War Model," *Nation,* CLXIII (December 14, 1946), 692-93; Reese Cleghorn, "The Segs," *Esquire,* LXI (January 1964), 71-76; and Ben Haas, *K.K.K.* (Chicago, 1963).

usually turns to the frankly political but more respectable White Citizens Council. The modern-day superpatriot turns to the John Birch Society or any of a host of other "antisubversive" organizations. And the moral zealot of the 1960s? There are fewer and fewer organizational outlets for his zeal, but he can probably find enough ephemeral local cleanup groups to satisfy his interests. Forty years ago the racist, the superpatriot, and the crusader for moral orthodoxy came together in a white-robed secret fraternal order that numbered its members in the millions and rode to power in every part of the nation. The Klan of the twenties has disappeared. But its spirit and its goals remain, sustenance for new crusades for 100 percent Americanism and moral conformity.

Bibliographical Notes

NOT ALL of the material cited in this study is included in the following discussion. At the same time some works of a general nature are mentioned that are not cited in the footnotes, but that have been of benefit for acquiring an understanding of national and state history during the 1920s and the Klan's place in the period.

The years from the end of the First World War to the coming of the Great Depression have offered an inescapable attraction for historians, essayists, and popular writers. There are many broad treatments of the period but comparatively few monographs. Arthur S. Link, *American Epoch: A History of the United States since the 1890's* (New York, 1955); Frederick Lewis Allen, *Only Yesterday: An Informal History of the Nineteen-Twenties* (New York, 1931; Bantam Books edition, 1946); Preston W. Slosson, *The Great Crusade and After, 1914-1928* (A History of American Life; New York, 1930); John D. Hicks, *Republican Ascendancy, 1921-1933* (New American Nation Series; New York, 1960); William E. Leuchtenberg, *The Perils of Prosperity, 1914-1932* (Chicago History of American Civilization; Chicago, 1958); and Arthur M. Schlesinger, Jr., *The Crisis of the Old Order, 1919-1933* (The Age of Roosevelt; Boston, 1957) are all helpful surveys of the twenties.

The best single volume covering the history of the southern states, including Texas, Louisiana, and Arkansas, but not Oklahoma, to the 1950's is Francis B. Simkins, *A History of the South* (2d ed., rev., New York, 1953). But a necessary starting point in understanding southern history is W. J. Cash, *The Mind of the South* (New York, 1941). A highly general treatment of the history of Texas and Oklahoma, as well as Arizona and New Mexico, is W. Eugene Hollon, *The Southwest: Old and New* (New York, 1961).

The institution of adult fraternalism in America, largely neglected by historians, receives attention in Noel P. Gist, *Secret Societies: A Cultural Study of Fraternalism in the United States* (University of Missouri Studies, XV, October 1, 1940); Arthur M. Schlesinger, *Paths to the Present* (New York, 1949), ch. II, "Biography of a Nation of Joiners"; and Charles W. Ferguson, *Fifty Million Brothers: A Panorama of American Lodges and Clubs* (New York, 1937).

The growth of racism and nativism in the United States, culminating in such developments of the twenties as the Klan and immigration restriction legislation, is treated in many places. The best survey of the subject of racism in America is Thomas F. Gossett, *Race: The History of an Idea in America* (Dallas, 1963). John Higham, *Strangers in the Land: Patterns of American Nativism, 1860-1925* (New Brunswick, N. J., 1955) is a classic in its field. Oscar Handlin, *Race and Nationality in American Life* (New York, 1957) contains a series of cogent essays on immigration and the growth of racial nativism in this country. Also helpful are Gustavus Myers, *A History of Bigotry in the United States* (New York, 1943); and David Spitz, *Patterns of Anti-Democratic Thought* (New York, 1949), which covers various aspects of totalitarian theory in the modern Western world. Early organized nativist movements in America are handled in Ray Allen Billington, *The Protestant Crusade, 1800-1860* (New York, 1938), which concentrates on the Know-Nothing movement in the northern states; William D. Overdyke, *The Know-Nothing Party in the South* (Baton Rouge, 1950); John H. Desmond, *The A.P.A. [American Protective Association] Movement* (Washington, 1912); and Donald L. Kinzer, *An Episode in Anti-Catholicism: The American Protective Association* (Seattle, 1964).

For Protestant Fundamentalism, to which the Klan was allied, ideologically if not organizationally, the standard work is Norman F. Furniss, *The Fundamentalist Controversy, 1918-1931* (New Haven, 1954). Robert M. Miller does a good job of dispelling any misconceptions about a formal connection between the Klan and Fundamentalism in "A Note on the Relationship between the Protestant Churches and the Ku Klux Klan," *Journal of Southern History*, XXII (August 1956), 257-66.

Source material for the study of the Klan, in the way of publications of the order, is of considerable magnitude. The Klan had its own press in Atlanta which printed tons of circulars, pamphlets, official documents, and speeches. Official publications of the Klan used for this study include: *Proceedings of the Second Imperial Klonvocation, Held in Kansas City, Missouri, September 23-26, 1924* (Atlanta, 1924); *Minutes of the Imperial Kloncilium, Knights of the Ku Klux Klan, Meeting of May 1 and 2, 1923, Which Ratified W. J. Simmons' Agreement with the Knights of the Ku Klux Klan Together with Certified Copies of All Litigation Instituted by W. J. Simmons against the Imperial Wizard and the Knights of the Ku Klux Klan* (Atlanta, 1923); *Papers Read at the Meeting of Grand Dragons, Knights of the Ku Klux Klan* (Asheville, N. C., 1923); *Constitution and Laws of the Knights of the Ku Klux Klan* (Atlanta, 1921); and William J. Simmons, *The Practice of Klannishness* (Atlanta, 1918).

The contemporary published matter dealing with the Klan, much of which attempts to explain the sensational growth of the organization, is also of enormous quantity. A number of books and pamphlets ostensibly exposing the Klan were published, of which the two most valuable are: Henry P. Fry, *The Modern Ku Klux Klan* (Boston, 1922), a revelation by an ex-Kleagle; and Marion Monteval (pseud.), *The Klan Inside Out* (Claremore, Oklahoma, 1924), a book by an ex-Klansman who apparently was connected with Imperial headquarters and made off with some Klan records.

Some of the best items in the interpretive literature of the Klan are: Stanley Frost, *The Challenge of the Klan* (Indianapolis, 1923, 1924); John M. Mecklin, *The Ku Klux Klan: A Study of the American Mind* (New York, 1924); Frank Tannenbaum, *Darker Phases of the South* (New York, 1924, ch. I; Frank Bohn "The Ku Klux Klan Interpreted," *American Journal of Sociology*, XXX (January 1925), 385-407; Guy B. Johnson, "A Sociological Interpretation of the New Ku Klux Movement," *Social Forces*, I (May 1923), 440-45; Rollin L. Hartt, "The New Negro," *Independent*, CV (January 15, 1921), 59-60, which does not mention the Klan but presents some interesting observations on the postwar status of the Negro; Charles Merz, "The New Ku Klux Klan," *ibid.*, CXVIII (February 12, 1927), 179-80, 196; and Robert L. Duffus, "Ancestry and End of the Ku Klux Klan," *World's Work*, XLVI (September, 1923), 527-36.

Among the most informative articles on the founding and early history of the Klan are: Robert L. Duffus, "Salesman of Hate: The Ku Klux Klan," *World's Work*, XLVI (May 1923), 31-38; William G. Shepherd, "How I Put Over the Klan," *Collier's*, LXXII (July 14, 1928), 10-11; Shepherd, "Ku Klux Koin," *ibid.* (July 21, 1928), 8-9; Shepherd, "Fiery Double Cross," *ibid.* (July 28, 1928), 8-9, all three based largely on personal interviews with William J. Simmons and Hiram W. Evans; and Walter F. White, "Reviving the Ku Klux Klan," *Forum*, LXV (April 1921), 424-34.

The later history of the Klan in the 1930s and 1940s is best covered in the New York *Times* and other newspapers. Some articles are of value, including: Stetson Kennedy and Evelyn M. Crowell, "The Ku Klux Klan," *New Republic*, CXIV (July 1, 1946), 928-30; Heywood Broun, "Up Pops the Wizard," *ibid.*, XCIX (June 21, 1939), 186-87; Leslie Velie, "The Klan Rides the South Again," *Collier's*, CXII (October 9, 1948), 13-15, 74, 75; and Carey McWilliams, "The Klan: Post War Model," *Nation*, CLXIII (December 14, 1946), 692-93.

Published material of a scholarly nature on the Klan is scarce. Benjamin H. Avin, "The Ku Klux Klan, 1915-1925: A Study in Religious Intolerance" (unpublished Ph.D. dissertation, Georgetown University, 1952) makes a good beginning toward explaining the religious bias of the movement but is marred by a concern with refuting the Klan's arguments. Four state and regional studies are presently available. Norman F. Weaver, "The Knights of the Ku Klux Klan in Wisconsin, Indiana, Ohio, and Michigan" (unpublished Ph.D. dissertation, University of Wisconsin, 1954), stresses the sociological orientation of the Klan in the Middle West. Weaver's greatest failing is a tendency to overgeneralize from the Klan experience in these four states. A fine study of a strong Klan organization in a populous eastern state is Emerson H. Loucks, *The Ku Klux Klan in Pennsylvania: A Study in Nativism* (Harrisburg, Pa., 1936). Loucks' work, based primarily on personal interviews, questionnaires, and some local Klan records, benefited from a type of material not available to later investigators of the Klan. Despite its title, Arnold S. Rice, *The Ku Klux Klan in American Politics* (Washington, 1962), is actually a regional treatment. Rice defines the Klan as mainly a southern phenomenon and then discusses the political career of the order only in the states south of the Mason-Dixon line and the Ohio River. He ignores the Klan's political activities in Louisiana almost completely and skips lightly through Arkansas, Texas, and the other states he terms southern. Rice handles the Klan in local and state politics in the South, and then he turns to national politics in 1924 and 1928 before presenting the best scholarly account yet written of the posttwenties history of the Klan. Much of the material on the career of the order in Texas included in this study also appears in Charles C. Alexander, *Crusade for Conformity: The Ku Klux Klan in Texas, 1920-1930* (Houston, 1962). A brief look at some of the doings of the Klan in Florida is David Chalmers, "The Ku Klux Klan in the Sunshine State: The 1920's," *Florida Historical Quarterly*, XLII (January 1964), 209-15.

The best single piece of source material on the Klan in the Southwest is *Senator from Texas. Hearings before a Subcommittee of the Committee on Privileges and Elections, United States Senate*, 67th Congress, 1st and 2d Sessions (1924), the widely publicized hearing on the election of Earle B. Mayfield to the United States Senate from Texas in 1922. Running to more than 1,200 pages, the publication is rich with testimony of Klansmen and ex-Klansmen relating to the Klan's role in the nomination and election of Mayfield. Of less value for the Klan in Texas and the rest of the Southwest is *The Ku Klux Klan. Hearings before the Committee on Rules, House of Representatives*, 67th Congress, 1st Session (1921), comprising testimony taken during the truncated investigation of the Klan by Congress in the fall of 1921.

One must search far and wide through manuscript materials for bits and pieces of information on the Klan in the southwestern states. In over three years of looking the writer has been unable to discover any Klan materials beyond the scarce items deposited here and there in libraries and collections. Apparently such matter as Klan records, membership rolls, and correspondence has been destroyed or safely hidden from the prying eyes of researchers. The papers of figures outside the Klan usually are not of any great value to the historian of the hooded organization. Collections examined by the writer which were not useful for this study include: Pat M. Neff Papers, Baylor University Library; Joseph W. Bailey Papers, Dallas Historical Society; Edwin DeBarr, Elmer Thomas, W. B. Pine, Thomas P. Gore, and James R. Tolbert collections, all at the University of Oklahoma Library; Charles H. Brough Papers, University of Arkansas Library; and Rene L. De-Rouen Papers, Louisiana State University Library. Former Governor Dan Moody of Austin, Texas, assured the writer that an examination of his papers would yield no information on the Texas Klan. Adjutant General Roy V. Kenny of the state of Oklahoma informed the writer that transcripts of the hearings before the military courts in Tulsa and Oklahoma City in 1923 were not in his office and that he did not know of their whereabouts.

The writer's search through manuscripts for pieces of southwestern Klan history was not entirely fruitless. The papers of Judge James R. Hamilton, in the possession of Mrs. Hamilton, Austin, Texas, contain a number of letters pertaining to Judge Hamilton's fight against the Klan from the bench of the 55th Criminal District Court in Austin. The Oscar B. Colquitt Papers, University of Texas Archives, are useful for Texas gubernatorial politics in 1924 and 1926 and the Klan's role in the governor's races. The Thomas B. Love Papers, Archives of the Dallas Historical Society, Dallas, are also of some benefit for an outside view of the Klan in Texas politics. The Campbell Russell, Jack C. Walton, and Carlton Weaver collections, Division of Manuscripts, University of Oklahoma Library, Norman, are moderately helpful. The Weaver papers contain an illuminating letter which Weaver, Cyclops and newspaper editor of Wilburton, wrote to Grand Dragon N. Clay Jewett relating to the Klan's, and specifically Jewett's, activities in the presidential and senatorial campaigns of 1924 in Oklahoma. At the General Library of the University of Arkansas, Fayetteville, the David Y. Thomas and Thomas C. McRae papers are of only slight assistance. The Harmon F. Remmel Papers, however, include a series of letters and telegrams exchanged between the Republican leader and prominent Arkansas Klansmen concerning Klan politics in Arkansas. At the Department of Archives, Louisiana State University, Baton Rouge, the James B. Aswell and Family Scrapbooks and the Huey Long Scrapbooks, together with the Jared Y. Sanders and Family Papers and the M. S. Newsom and Family Papers (Merrit M. Schlig Memorial Collection), were fairly beneficial on various aspects of Klan history in the Pelican State.

The principal source for this writer, and for anyone else who studies the Klan today, consists of daily and weekly newspapers. Klan activities were almost always newsworthy, and during the twenties dailies in every part of the nation printed thousands of dispatches and local reports on the doings of the secret order. Used with skill and discretion, newspapers can be invaluable for the history of the Klan in a particular area. The New York *Times* gave the finest coverage of national Klan affairs and reported many episodes of a state or local character in the Southwest. Most dailies in the southwestern states maintained a neutral attitude on the subject of the Klan, although at one time or another they all condemned mob violence as exemplified in the Klan's vigilante forays. In Texas the Dallas *Morning News* printed the New York *World's* syndicated expose of the Klan in 1921 and fought the order at every turn thereafter. Much less vituperative than the *News*, although anti-Klan, were the Austin *American* and *Statesman* and the Denison *Herald*. The Fort Worth *Star-Telegram*, the Houston *Post*, the Waco *Times-Herald*, and the San Antonio *Express* were noncommital on the Klan issue. In Louisiana the New Orleans *Times-Picayune*, which also printed the New York *World's* articles, was vindictively anti-Klan. The Shreveport *Journal* completely ignored the organization on its editorial pages. In the 1920s, as today, the Little Rock *Arkansas Gazette* was far and away the most important and useful daily newspaper published in the state of Arkansas. The Fort Smith *Southwest American,* like the *Gazette* neutral with regard to the Klan, is less helpful than the Little Rock daily. The Oklahoma City *Daily Oklahoman,* the Tulsa *Tribune,* and the Tulsa *Daily World* were used for coverage of Oklahoma Klan affairs. The *Daily Oklahoman,* usually Democratic, and the *Daily World,* Republican, editorialized against the Klan, while the *Tribune* was rather a friendly neutral in its relations with the organization. The *Daily Oklahoman* and the *Tribune,* but not the *Daily World,* joined forces with the Klan to fight Jack Walton during the martial law period in 1923 and when Walton ran for the United States Senate the next year.

Klan and pro-Klan weekly newspapers are invariably enlightening, not only for the policies and attitudes of the Klan in a particular area, but for coverage of specific events as well. Unfortunately libraries and newspaper collections have been generally derelict in acquiring and preserving such journals. The Newspaper Collection of the University of Texas has a nearly complete microfilm file (1921-1924) of the Houston *Colonel Mayfield's Weekly,* vigorously puritanical and blatantly pro-Klan, although not officially sanctioned by the order. The University of Texas also has scattered issues on microfilm of the Atlanta *Searchlight,* official organ of Imperial headquarters until 1923; the Forth Worth *American Citizen;* the Dallas *Texas 100 Per Cent American,* semiofficial publication of Dallas Klan No. 66; the Tyler *American;* and the Elgin *Pure Democracy.* The Newspaper Collection at Louisiana State University has random issues on microfilm of the Columbia *Caldwell* [Parish] *Watchman,* a pro-Klan newspaper published briefly in northeastern Louisiana. There are a few issues of the Oklahoma City *Fiery Cross,* the official publication of Realm headquarters, in the Campbell Russell Collection, Division of Manuscripts, University of Oklahoma Library. The writer was unable to locate copies of the Little Rock *Arkansas Traveller,* semiofficial weekly of Little Rock Klan No. 1.

Personal interviews in 1959 with two citizens of Dallas, both prominent in the Texas Klan in the 1920s, were rather productive of information on the activities of the order in the Lone Star State. The two ex-Klansmen, who asked to remain anonymous, conversed freely about general developments in the Realm of Texas but were reluctant to talk on some topics and forgetful on others. V. A. Collins, attorney-at-law now living in Livingston, Texas, was kind enough to write a long, instructive letter relating his troubles with Texas Klan officials in 1924 and the circumstances of his break with the organization and campaign for the governorship. Other attempts to secure personal interviews or exchange correspondence with important former Klan members, people in a position to throw light into the darkest corners of southwestern Klan history, proved unsuccessful. The writer talked with a number of admitted former Klansmen, suspected ex-Knights, and anti-Klanners. Such conversations, usually casual, were of little profit; for as a rule, when the writer's notebook was opened the subject was closed.

A reasonable amount of serviceable published matter dealing at least partly with the Klan in the Southwest is at hand. Most general histories of Texas, Louisiana, and Oklahoma touch on the Klan, however lightly. Of use for the political history of Texas in the twenties are: Rupert N. Richardson, *Texas, the Lone Star State* (2d ed., Englewood Cliffs, N. J., 1958), ch. xx; Seth S. McKay, *Texas Politics, 1916-1944, with Special Reference to the German Counties* (Lubbock, 1952); Ralph W. Steen, "A Political History of Texas, 1900-1930," in Frank C. Adams (ed.), *Texas Democracy* (4 vols., Austin, 1937), I, 319-464; Steen, *Twentieth*

Century Texas: An Economic and Social History (Austin, 1942); and Lee N. Allen, "The Democratic Presidential Primary Election of 1924 in Texas," *Southwestern Historical Quarterly,* LXI (April 1958), 474-93. Reinhard Luthin, *American Demagogues: Twentieth Century* (New York, 1954), contains a provocative essay on the career of James E. and Miriam A. Ferguson of Texas. But see also Charles W. Ferguson, "James E. Ferguson," *Southwest Review,* X (October 1924), 29-36; and Ouida Ferguson Nalle, *The Fergusons of Texas* (San Antonio, 1946). A concise narrative of the Klan's career in Texas politics is Charles C. Alexander, "Secrecy Bids for Power: The Ku Klux Klan in Texas Politics in the 1920's," *Mid-America,* XLVI (January 1964), 3-28. Contemporary periodical material on the Texas Klan includes: Edward T. Devine, "The Klan in Texas," *Survey,* XLVIII (April 1, 1922), 10-11; Devine, "More about the Klan," *ibid.* (April 8, 1922), 42-43; and "Klan Victories in Oregon and Texas," *Literary Digest,* LXXV (November 25, 1922), 12.

Edwin A. Davis, *Louisiana: The Pelican State* (Baton Rouge, 1959), is an able survey, but inadequate for the twentieth century. Allan P. Sindler, *Huey Long's Louisiana: State Politics, 1920-1952* (Baltimore, 1956), is useful for the general political history of the twenties, with emphasis on Long, but has little material on the Klan. Thomas E. Dabney has a chapter on the Klan in *One Hundred Great Years: The Story of the Times-Picayune from Its Founding to 1940* (Baton Rouge, 1944); while George M. Reynolds, in *Machine Politics in New Orleans, 1897-1926* (Columbia University Studies in Economics, History and Public Law; New York, 1936), covers the character of the Old Regular organization that allied with part of the Louisiana Klan in the 1924 gubernatorial campaign. T. Harry Williams provides an introduction to his forthcoming biography of Huey P. Long in "Gentleman from Louisiana: Demagogue or Democrat," *Journal of Southern History,*

XXVI (February 1960), 3-21. The Mer Rouge murder cases of 1922-1923 in Morehouse Parish, Louisiana, and the Klan's relation to the murders, received considerable contemporary periodical coverage, including: "Murders of Mer Rouge," *Literary Digest*, LXXVI (January 13, 1923), 10-12; "Mer Rouge Murders Unpunished," *ibid.* (March 31, 1923), 10-11; and Leonard L. Cline, "In Darkest Louisiana," *Nation*, CXVI (March 14, 1923), 292-93.

The best general history of Oklahoma is Edwin C. McReynolds, *Oklahoma: A History of the Sooner State* (Norman, 1954). More pedantic, but still of value, is Victor E. Harlow, *Oklahoma: Its Origins and Development* (Oklahoma City, 1949). Both McReynolds and Harlow devote more attention to the twentieth century, including the career of the Klan, than one ordinarily finds in state histories. Gilbert C. Fite looks at a portion of the anti-Klan sentiment in Oklahoma by way of describing Sooner State farm politics in "Oklahoma's Reconstruction League: An Experiment in Farmer-Labor Politics," *Journal of Southern History*, XIII (November 1947), 535-55, and "John A. Simpson: The Southwest's Militant Farm Leader," *Mississippi Valley Historical Review*, XXXV (March 1949), 563-84. For the struggle between Jack Walton and the Klan in 1923, culminating in Walton's ouster from the governorship, see: Howard A. Tucker, *Governor Walton's Ku Klux Klan War* (Oklahoma City, 1923); Ernest T. Bynum, *Personal Recollections of Ex-Governor Walton* (2d ed., Oklahoma City, 1924); W. D. McBee, *The Oklahoma Revolution* (Oklahoma City, 1955); "Masked Floggers of Tulsa," *Literary Digest*, LXXVIII (September 22, 1923), 17; "Oklahoma's Uncivil Civil War," *ibid.* (September 29, 1923), 10-11; "Constitution Week in Oklahoma," *ibid.*, LXXIX (October 13, 1923), 12-13; "Jack, the Klan-Fighter in Oklahoma," *ibid.* (October 20, 1923), 38-44; "Oklahoma Kingless, Not Klanless," *ibid.* (December 8, 1923), 9; "Martial Law in Oklahoma," *Outlook*, CXXXV (September 26,

1923), 133; Stanley Frost, "The Oklahoma Regicides Act," *ibid.* (November 7, 1923), 395-96; Frost, "Night Riding Reformers: The Regeneration of Oklahoma," *ibid.* (November 14, 1923), 438-40; Frost, "Behind the White Hoods: The Regeneration of Oklahoma," *ibid.* (November 21, 1923), 492-94; Frost, "The Klan, the King, and a Revolution: The Regeneration of Oklahoma," *ibid.* (November 28, 1923), 530-31; Aldrich Blake, "Oklahoma's Klan-Fighting Governor," *Nation,* CXVII (October 3, 1923), 353; and Bruce Bliven, "From the Oklahoma Front," *New Republic,* XXVI (October 17, 1923), 202-205.

There is no worthwhile survey of the history of Arkansas. Hazel Presson, *The Story of Arkansas* (3d ed., rev., New York, 1958) and Olin E. McKnight and Boyd W. Johnson, *The Arkansas Story* (New York, 1955) are uncritical treatments written primarily, it appears, for secondary school readers. David Y. Thomas (ed.), *Arkansas and Its People: A History, 1541-1930* (3 vols., Chicago, 1930) consists of complimentary biographical sketches and subjective writing. John Gould Fletcher, *Arkansas* (Chapel Hill, N.C., 1947) is a series of impressionistic essays on the history of the state. Henry M. Alexander has some comments on the Klan in Arkansas politics in "The Double Primary," *Arkansas Historical Quarterly,* III (Autumn 1944), 217-68. Other periodical material dealing with the history of the Klan in the Wonder State includes: Charles C. Alexander, "White-Robed Reformers: The Ku Klux Klan Comes to Arkansas, 1921-1922," *Arkansas Historical Quarterly,* XXII (Spring 1963), 8-23; Alexander, "White Robes in Politics: The Ku Klux Klan in Arkansas, 1922-1924," *ibid.* (Fall 1963), 195-214; and Alexander, "Defeat, Decline, Disintegration: The Ku Klux Klan in Arkansas, 1924 and After," *ibid.* (Winter 1963), 310-31.

Index

Duhon, Sam E., murdered, 77-78
Duncan, Carey P., 182, 213
Duncan, Okla., 164
Dunn, Byron, executed for
  murder, 77-78
Dunn, Robert: convicted of mur-
  der, 77; sentence commuted
  to life, 78

Eastern Orthodox churches, 16-17
Eaton, W. V., 39-40
Edinburgh, Tex., 24n
Edwards, Will C., 197
Elaine, Ark., 13
Elam, Richard, 156-57
El Dorado, Ark., 31, 52, 187,
  189; city election, 1923, 117;
  Klan hospital fund diverted, 92;
  "Law Enforcement League,"
  52-53
El Dorado Natural Gas and Petroleum Co., bunkhouse raided,
  64
Elections: Arkansas antievolution
  law, 1928, 86-87; Arkansas
  Democratic primary, Aug. 1922,
  114-16; Arkansas Democratic
  primary, Aug. 1924, 189-91;
  Arkansas general, 1928, 240;
  Bald Knob, Ark., school trustee,
  1923, 117-18; Baton Rouge
  city primary, summer 1922,
  119-20; Camden, Ark., school
  trustee, 1923, 117; Dallas city,
  1923, 127; El Dorado, Ark.,
  city, 1923, 117; El Paso city,
  1923, 127; Fort Smith city,
  1925, 217; Fort Smith city recall, 1923, 117, 217; Fort
  Worth city, 1923, 127; Georgia
  state, 1922, 127; influenced by
  Klan, 159; Little Rock city,
  1922, 112-14; Little Rock city,
  spring 1923, 117; Little Rock
  city primary, Dec. 1922, 116-
  17; Little Rock city primary,
  1924, 192; Little Rock Demo-

Elections (continued):
  cratic primary, 1924, 216-17;
  Little Rock special, Sept. 1922,
  116; Louisiana Democratic primary, Jan.-Feb. 1924, 182-84;
  Louisiana Fifth Judicial Dist.
  special primary, March 1923,
  120-21; Louisiana general, 1928,
  240; Oklahoma constitutional
  referendum, Oct. 1923, 149-50;
  Oklahoma Democratic primary,
  July 1922, 133; Oklahoma
  Democratic primary, Aug. 1922,
  133; Oklahoma Democratic primary, Aug. 1924, 202-203;
  Oklahoma Democratic primary,
  1926, 229-30; Oklahoma general, Nov. 1922, 135; Oklahoma general, Nov. 1924, 204-
  205, 206-207; Oklahoma general, 1926, 230-31; Oklahoma
  general, 1928, 240; Oklahoma
  state, 1922, 127; Oregon state,
  1922, 127; San Antonio city,
  1923, 127; Stuttgart, Ark., city,
  April 1925, 217; Texas Democratic primary, July 1922, 121-
  25; Texas Democratic primary,
  July-Aug. 1924, 196-99, 222;
  Texas general, Nov. 1922, 125-
  28; Texas general, Nov. 1924,
  198-99, 222; Texas general,
  Nov. 1928, 240; Texas state,
  1926, 225; Wichita Falls city,
  1923, 127
"Elimination primaries," 114,
  186, 188
Elks Theater, Baton Rouge, 120
Ellis, A. D., 90, 108
Ellis, Robert D., 120, 213
El Paso, Tex., 28; city election,
  1923, 127; Klan established, 39
El Reno, Okla., mail clerk tarred,
  46
Elrod, Milton, 167
Empire Mutual Life Insurance
  Co., 97